ADVANCED AUDITING AND ASSURANCE

Louise Kelly

Chartered
Accountants
Ireland

Published by
Chartered Accountants Ireland
Chartered Accountants House
47–49 Pearse Street
Dublin 2
www.charteredaccountants.ie

ISBN: 978-1-908199-36-2

Typeset by Compuscript
Printed by CPI Books Group UK

To all my family and friends, 'the book' is now finished!

Table of Contents

Introduction

Building on *External Auditing and Assurance: An Irish Textbook* by Martin Nolan (also published by Chartered Accountants Ireland), *Advanced Auditing and Assurance* extends this text and takes a practical, real-world approach to auditing, thereby preparing students for what they will encounter as qualified practitioners. Examples are provided to help the student understand practical application of the International Standards on Auditing (UK and Ireland) 'ISAs', together with audit documentation templates intended to bring the theory to life. To assist with the learning process, each chapter has a number of review questions which are case-study based and require extraction of audit issues. This will help students apply the technical and practical material to exam-style questions.

The text incorporates the clarified ISAs issued in October 2009, and has been updated to include the new revised ISAs 700, 705 and 706 which were published in October 2012 and are applicable to audits for years commencing on or after 1 October 2012. It also includes the new Audit Regulations (UK and Ireland) effective 1 June 2012.

Acknowledgements

In completing this textbook, I would very much like to thank Josephine Jackson, Grant Thornton UK, for her technical review and guidance.

I would also like to thank Karen Flannery for her contribution to Chapter 10.

Finally, a very special thank you to Michael Diviney and Becky McIndoe for their patience and guidance.

1

THE AUDIT ENGAGEMENT

LEARNING OBJECTIVES

In reading and studying this chapter, your objectives will be to:
- demonstrate detailed knowledge of the statutory and regulatory frameworks which set criteria by which the audit is conducted, including the auditor's and directors' responsibilities;
- demonstrate an understanding of the case law which has impacted upon the legal liability of auditors;
- demonstrate a practical understanding of the Ethical Framework within which auditors perform their duties;
- understand the principal steps of the audit process and how they relate to International Standards on Auditing (UK and Ireland).

1.1 WHAT IS AN AUDIT?

An audit can be defined generally as an evaluation of a person, organisation, system, process, enterprise, project or product. An evaluation is the systematic collection and analysis of data needed to make decisions. Whilst this is a very basic definition, it suitably summarises that it is the auditor's role to *evaluate*.

An audit of financial statements is, more specifically, a search for evidence through carrying out certain procedures, then an 'evaluation' of that evidence in such a manner that enables the auditor to deliver an opinion on the truth and fairness of the financial statements of an entity. It is the issuance of that opinion, more commonly known as '*the auditor's report*', which increases the credibility and therefore usefulness of the financial statements.

Ultimately, though there are many definitions of an audit, it is the professional, regulatory and legislative environment that shapes the way auditors carry out their work. Auditing standards in particular serve as requirements and guidelines to ensure that financial statement audits are conducted in a consistent manner, across businesses and jurisdictions.

The overall aim of a financial statement audit prepared under International Standards on Auditing ('auditing standards' or 'ISAs' – see also the note below in **Section 1.3**) is to enhance the degree of confidence of intended users in the financial statements. This is achieved by the expression of an opinion by the auditor on whether the financial statements are prepared, in all material respects, in accordance with an applicable financial reporting framework.

ISA 200 (UK and Ireland) *Overall Objectives of the Independent Auditor and the Conduct of an Audit in Accordance with International Standards on Auditing* (ISA 200), at paragraph 11 states that the objectives of the auditor when conducting an audit of the financial statements are as follows:

"(a) To obtain reasonable assurance about whether the financial statements as a whole are free from material misstatement, whether due to fraud or error, thereby enabling the auditor to express an opinion on whether the financial statements are prepared, in all material respects, in accordance with an applicable financial reporting framework; and

(b) To report on the financial statements, and communicate as required by the ISAs (UK and Ireland), in accordance with the auditor's findings."

In achieving these objectives the auditor plans, executes and completes an audit using guidance from the auditing standards. (The audit process is discussed in more detail below in **Section 1.6**.)

As noted above, in conducting an audit, there are various frameworks, including professional auditing standards, such as legislation and regulation, which set criteria by which the audit is conducted and, indeed, who should be allowed to perform an audit.

1.2 THE LEGISLATIVE FRAMEWORK

1.2.1 Audit Requirements

Companies legislation in both the Republic of Ireland (ROI) and Northern Ireland (NI) requires companies to have their financial statements audited on an annual basis, with some exceptions.

1.2.1.1 Northern Ireland

Section 485 of the Companies Act 2006 (CA 2006) requires all private companies to appoint an auditor, unless the company does not fall within audit requirements as dictated by section 75 CA 2006 noted below.

Section 475 CA 2006 requires all companies to have their annual accounts audited; however, they are exempt from audit if the company meets certain size requirements. Specifically, a company is exempt from audit if it meets **all** of the following criteria:

1. the company qualifies as small under section 382 CA 2006 where at least two out of the following three criteria are met:
   - the company has annual turnover of £6.5 million or less,
   - the company has a balance sheet total of £3.26 million or less, and
   - the company has an average number of employees during the year of 50 or fewer;
2. the company has turnover of not more that £6.5 million; and
3. the company's balance sheet total is not more than £3.26 million.

Section 480 CA 2006 also exempts companies from audit requirements if the company is dormant.

This can be illustrated in the following examples:

EXAMPLE 1.1: COMPANY INCORPORATED IN NORTHERN IRELAND

Company A

Turnover	£4.5 million
Balance sheet total	£2.25 million
Employee numbers	5

Company A is audit exempt as it meets all three criteria.

Company B

Turnover	£5.5 million
Balance sheet total	£3.1 million
Employees	51

Company B is not audit exempt as it does not meet the definition of a small company due to employee numbers being greater than 50.

1.2.1.2 Republic of Ireland

Section 160 of the Companies Act 1963 (CA 1963) requires all companies to appoint an auditor. However, the Companies (Amendment) (No. 2) Act 1999 (C(A)(No.2)A 1999) allows exemption from the audit requirement if the company meets **all** of the following criteria:
1. the company's turnover does not exceed €8.8 million;
2. the company's balance sheet total does not exceed €4.4 million; and
3. the company's average number of employees does not exceed 50.

These audit exemption thresholds were raised by European Union (Accounts) Regulation 2012 (S.I. No. 304 of 2012).

EXAMPLE 1.2: COMPANY INCORPORATED IN REPUBLIC OF IRELAND

Company A

Turnover	€6.5 million
Balance sheet total	€2.25 million
Employee numbers	5

Company A is audit exempt as it meets all three criteria.

Company B

Turnover	€8.9 million
Balance sheet total	€3.1 million
Employees	20

Company B is not audit exempt as it does not meet all three criteria.

This audit exemption does not apply to:
• parent or subsidiary undertakings incorporated in the Republic of Ireland;
• public companies; and
• companies limited by guarantee.

Furthermore, in order to avail of the exemption, the directors must be of the opinion that the company satisfies the conditions in respect of the current **and** previous financial years.

1.2.2 Auditor's and Directors' Responsibilities

Companies legislation in both jurisdictions sets out a number of requirements regarding directors' and auditor's responsibilities in relation to the preparation of the financial statements and audit of the financial statements respectively.

1.2.2.1 Directors' Responsibilities

In producing the annual financial statements, directors acknowledge their responsibilities by including a directors' responsibility statement in the financial statements summarising their responsibilities in relation to the preparation of the financial statements. In a set of financial statements, this statement will be found either within the Directors' Report or alongside the Directors' Report. Examples of directors' responsibility statements have been included below.

EXAMPLE 1.3: DIRECTORS' RESPONSIBILITIES: NORTHERN IRELAND[1]

The directors are responsible for preparing the Directors' Report and the financial statements in accordance with applicable law and regulations.

Company law requires the directors to prepare financial statements for each financial year. Under that law the directors have elected to prepare the financial statements in accordance with United Kingdom Generally Accepted Accounting Practice (United Kingdom Accounting Standards and applicable law). Under company law the directors must not approve the financial statements unless they are satisfied that they give a true and fair view of the state of affairs of the company and of the profit or loss of the company for that period.

In preparing those financial statements, the directors are required to:
• select suitable accounting policies and then apply them consistently;
• make judgements and estimates that are reasonable and prudent;
• state whether applicable UK Accounting Standards have been followed, subject to any material departures disclosed and explained in the financial statements; and
• prepare the financial statements on the going concern basis unless it is inappropriate to presume that the company will continue in business.

The directors are responsible for keeping adequate accounting records that are sufficient to show and explain the company's transactions and disclose with reasonable accuracy at any time the financial position of the company and enable them to ensure that the financial statements comply with the Companies Act 2006. They are also responsible for safeguarding the assets of the company and hence for taking reasonable steps for the prevention and detection of fraud and other irregularities.

---

[1] Source: APB Bulletin 2010/2 (Revised) *Compendium of Illustrative Auditor's Reports on United Kingdom Private Sector Financial Statements for periods ended on or after 15 December 2010 (Revised).*

EXAMPLE 1.4: DIRECTORS' RESPONSIBILITIES: REPUBLIC OF IRELAND[2]

The directors are responsible for preparing the Annual Report and the financial statements in accordance with applicable Irish law and Generally Accepted Accounting Practice in Ireland including the accounting standards issued by the Accounting Standards Board and published by the Institute of Chartered Accountants in Ireland.

Company law requires the directors to prepare financial statements for each financial year which give a true and fair view of the state of affairs of the company and of the profit or loss of the company for that year. In preparing those financial statements, the directors are required to:

- select suitable accounting policies and then apply them consistently;
- make judgements and estimates that are reasonable and prudent; and
- prepare the financial statements on the going concern basis unless it is inappropriate to presume that the company will continue in business.

The directors are responsible for keeping proper books of account that disclose with reasonable accuracy at any time the financial position of the company and enable them to ensure that the financial statements are prepared in accordance with accounting standards generally accepted in Ireland and comply with the Companies Acts, 1963 to 2012. The directors are also responsible for safeguarding the assets of the company and hence for taking reasonable steps for the prevention and detection of fraud and other irregularities.

1.2.2.2 *Auditor's Responsibilities*

Companies legislation, in both Northern Ireland and Republic of Ireland, sets out a number of requirements for auditors. For example, the UK Companies Act 2006 and the Irish Companies Acts 1963–2012 have a number of reporting requirements which expand the scope of the audit beyond that set out in professional standards. Furthermore, case law also dictates additional responsibilities of which auditors need to be aware. Auditor's responsibilities are considered in more detail in **Chapter 8**, Audit Reports.

1.3 THE REGULATORY FRAMEWORK AND PROFESSIONAL STANDARDS

1.3.1 The Regulatory Framework

The regulatory framework includes guidance on how an audit is conducted, who should be allowed to perform an audit, and who should develop auditing standards. It also includes rules and regulations around monitoring of audit firms.

---

[2] Source: APB Bulletin 2006/1 *Auditor's Reports on Financial Statements in the Republic of Ireland.*

The regulatory framework relevant to the UK and Republic of Ireland is summarised below in **Figure 1.1**.

The Financial Reporting Council (FRC) has overall responsibility for the regulation of auditing, accounting and the actuarial profession. The Irish Auditing and Accounting Supervisory Authority (IAASA) provides an independent oversight of the regulation in the Republic of Ireland. The Chartered Accountants Regulatory Board (CARB) was established by Chartered Accountants Ireland to provide, among other things, monitoring of the quality of the audit function.

All audit firms based in ROI or the UK that wish to conduct statutory audits in ROI must be authorised to do so by one of the accountancy bodies recognised under the Companies (Auditing & Accounting) Act 2003. The Institute of Chartered Accountants

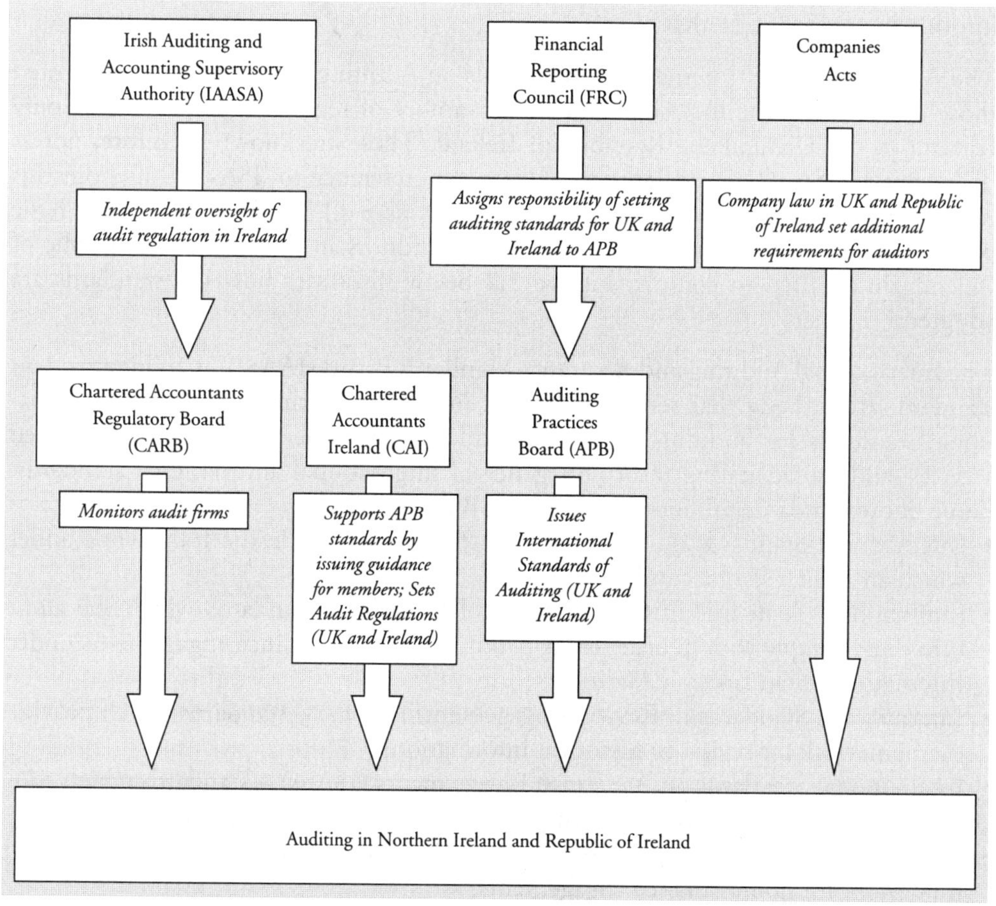

FIGURE 1.1: SUMMARY OF REGULATORY FRAMEWORK IN THE UK AND IRELAND

in Ireland is one such 'recognised accountancy body'. Further information relating to the registration and regulation of audit firms may be obtained from the website of IAASA at www.iaasa.ie. Similar provisions exist in the UK where authorisation must be obtained from one of the Recognised Professional Bodies (certain accountancy bodies) in accordance with the provisions of the Companies Act 2006. The Professional Oversight Board in the UK is ultimately responsible for regulation of statutory auditors. Chartered Accountants Ireland established CARB to regulate its members, in accordance with the provisions of the Institute's bye-laws, independently, openly and in the public interest. CARB is responsible for developing standards of professional conduct and supervising the compliance of members, member firms and affiliates and this is done by regular reviews of member firms.

As shown above in **Figure 1.1**, the Auditing Practices Board (APB) is overseen by the FRC and is responsible for the development of auditing practice in the UK and Ireland. This includes, among other things, setting auditing standards and issuing guidance on the application of auditing standards in particular circumstances and industries. These can all be accessed on Chartered Accountants Ireland's online technical reference and information service (CHARIOT).

The APB has adopted International Standards on Auditing standards and augmented those standards by the inclusion of a small number of regulatory requirements only relevant to the UK and the Republic of Ireland. These are known therefore, not as 'ISAs' but as 'ISAs (UK and Ireland)'. (**Note**: any reference to 'ISAs' throughout this text refers to ISAs (UK and Ireland), if not already stated.) The ISAs set out the basic principles and essential procedures with which auditors in the UK and Republic of Ireland are required to comply. **Figure 1.2** below illustrates how the standards are adopted:

The International Auditing and Assurance Standards Board (IAASB) is an independent standard-setting body that serves the public interest by setting high-quality international standards for auditing, quality control, review, other assurance, and related services, and by facilitating the convergence of international and national standards. Some of the standards produced by the IAASB are as follows:

- International Standards on Auditing (ISAs) – these provide the framework under which an audit must be conducted;
- International Standards in Quality Control (ISQCs) – standards which the audit firm must comply with in order to carry out audit and assurance engagements under International Standards on Auditing;
- International Standards in Review Engagements (ISREs) – standards which provide the framework for review of historical information;
- International Standards on Assurance Engagements (ISAEs) – standards which provide the framework for assurance engagements that are not audits; and
- International Standards on Related Services (ISRSs) – standards which provide the framework for non-assurance engagements.

FIGURE 1.2: SUMMARY OF AUDITING AND ASSURANCE STANDARDS
ADOPTED IN NORTHERN IRELAND AND REPUBLIC OF IRELAND

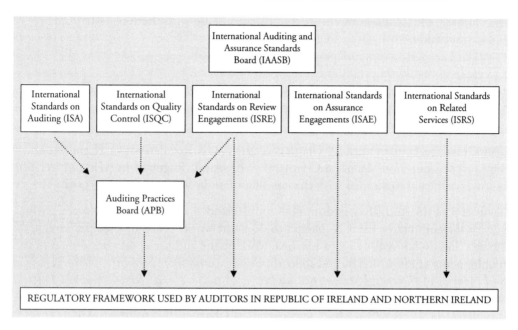

As can be seen from **Figure 1.2** above, the APB has not adopted all of the IAASB assurance standards. This is because the APB's focus is on audit practice. However, other standards, e.g. ISAEs and ISRSs, are still applicable for use in the UK and the Republic of Ireland in appropriate circumstances.

1.3.2 Audit Regulations

Chartered Accountants Ireland also issue, along with the UK and Scottish institutes, Audit Regulations (UK and Ireland). These regulations set-out standards and requirements which a registered audit firm must comply with in order to carry out audit work as governed by Chartered Accountants Ireland. The regulations can be accessed on Chartered Accountants Ireland's online technical reference and information service (CHARIOT). These regulations are referred to as Audit Regulations & Guidance (UK and Ireland) and are effective from 1 June 2012. The regulations also have a guidance booklet referred to as Audit Guidance (UK and Ireland) which sets out guidance for firms in implementing the Audit Regulations (UK and Ireland).

The objectives of the Institutes in issuing these audit regulations are to make sure:
• auditors registered with the Institutes maintain high standards of work;
• the reputation of registered auditors with the public is maintained;
• the application of the Regulations is fair but firm;

- the Regulations are clear; and
- the Regulations apply to all sizes of firm.

In summary, the Regulations ensure that by complying with them registered auditors:
- carry out audit work with integrity;
- are, and are seen to be, independent;
- comply with auditing standards;
- make sure that all principals and employees are fit and proper persons; and
- make sure that all principals and employees are competent and continue to be competent to carry out audit work

You should be familiar with all chapters of the Audit Regulations (UK and Ireland). This text sets out more detail on Chapter 3 of the Audit Regulations (UK and Ireland) as it is specifically concerned with the conduct of audit work by an audit firm.

Chapter 3 of the Audit Regulations (UK and Ireland) includes rules and practices that govern the conduct of firms registered to do audit work. None of these requirements are new and do not require any additional work by the auditor as they are similar to the requirements of ISQC 1 (UK and Ireland) *Quality Control for Firms that Perform Audits and Reviews of Financial Statements, and other Assurance and Related Services Engagements* ('ISQC 1') and ISA 220 (UK and Ireland) *Quality Control for an Audit of Financial Statements* ('ISA 220'), which are covered in **Chapter 2** of this textbook.

The requirements of Chapter 3 of the Audit Regulations (UK and Ireland) are summarised below.

Independence and Integrity   No registered auditor may accept an appointment or continue as auditor if there is a potential conflict that may impair the auditor's independence. The auditor is required to adhere to ethical standards in this regard. The regulations give some examples of when independence may be impaired, e.g. the auditor is a shareholder in the audited entity, personal or family relationships exist between the auditor and the audited entity, and acting as auditor for a prolonged period of time.

The auditor is also required to conduct audit work with integrity, which means honesty, fair dealing, truthfulness and the desire to follow and maintain high standards of professional practice.

The auditor must consider his or her independence and ability to perform the audit before he or she accepts appointment or reappointment as auditor. These are similar requirements to those of ISA 220 *Quality Control for an Audit of Financial Statements* (which is covered in **Chapter 2**).

The Regulations also note that the audit firm must ensure that all principals and employees of the audit firm are, and continue to be, fit and proper persons. This means, e.g. that they have no criminal convictions and are of good reputation and character. In practice, this is confirmed each year by way of a questionnaire issued to all principals and employees; an example of questions that may be included in an annual declaration is included below in **Figure 1.3**.

FIGURE 1.3: EXAMPLE OF 'FIT AND PROPER' STATUS QUESTIONS
THAT WOULD BE INCLUDED IN AN ANNUAL DECLARATION

Financial integrity and reliability

1. In the last 10 years has a court, in the United Kingdom, Republic of Ireland or elsewhere, given any judgment against you about a debt?
    If yes, give particulars.

2. In the last 10 years have you made any compromise arrangement with your creditors?
    If yes, give particulars.

3. Have you ever been declared bankrupt or been the subject of a bankruptcy court order in the United Kingdom, Republic of Ireland or elsewhere, or has a bankruptcy petition ever been served on you?
    If yes, give particulars.

4. Have you ever signed a trust deed for a creditor, made an assignment for the benefit of creditors, or made any arrangements for the payment of a composition to creditors?
    If yes, give particulars.

5. Have you at any time been found guilty of any offence? If so, give details of the court which convicted you, the offence, the penalty imposed and date of conviction.
    If yes, give particulars.

6. In the last five years have you, in the United Kingdom, the Republic of Ireland or elsewhere, been the subject of any civil action relating to your professional or business activities which has resulted in a finding against you by a court or a settlement being agreed?
    If yes, give particulars.

7. Have you ever been disqualified by a court from being a director, or from acting in the management or conduct of the affairs of any company?
    If yes, give particulars.

8. Have you, in the United Kingdom, the Republic of Ireland or elsewhere, ever been:

    (a) Refused the right or been restricted in the right to carry on any trade, business or profession for which a specific licence, registration or other authority is required?
    If yes, give particulars.

11

(b) Investigated about allegations of misconduct or malpractice in connection with your professional activities which resulted in a formal complaint being proved but no disciplinary order being made?
If yes, give particulars.

(c) The subject of disciplinary procedures by a professional body or employer resulting in a finding against you?
If yes, give particulars.

(d) Reprimanded, excluded, disciplined or publicly criticised by any professional body to which you belong or have belonged?
If yes, give particulars.

(e) Refused entry to or excluded from membership of any profession or vocation?
If yes, give particulars.

(f) Dismissed from any office (other than as auditor) or employment or requested to resign from any office, employment or partnership?
If yes, give particulars.

(g) Reprimanded, warned about future conduct, disciplined, or publicly criticised by any regulatory body, or any officially appointed enquiry concerned with the regulation of a financial, professional or other business activity?
If yes, give particulars.

(h) The subject of a court order at the instigation of any regulatory body, or any officially appointed enquiry concerned with the regulation of a financial, professional or other business activity?
If yes, give particulars.

9. Are you currently undergoing any investigation or disciplinary procedure as described in 8 above?
If yes, give particulars.

Technical Standards   The auditor must comply with company law requirements, and any other relevant legislation in relation to appointment, ceasing to hold appointment, and the responsibilities of the auditor to make sure that financial statements on which a report is given are in accordance with the legislation.

The auditor must also comply with auditing standards and the quality control standards. These quality control standards are ISQC 1 and ISA 220 as noted above, and are covered in **Chapter 2** of this textbook.

The Audit Regulations (UK and Ireland) also require audit firms to keep audit working papers for a period of at least six years after the last accounting period.

Consultation   As is also required by ISQC 1 and ISA 220, an audit firm must have procedures in place whereby all principals and employees can consult on ethical and technical issues with appropriate individuals. For example, if there is an ethical issue, the employee should know to revert to the designated ethics partner; or if there is a difficult technical issue on the audit engagement, there should be someone within the firm, or external to the firm, who can be consulted on such issues. All these consultations should be documented on the audit file.

Audit Reports   The Regulations require that audit reports in the UK, Northern Ireland and the Republic of Ireland include the engagement partner signing on behalf of the firm, the firm's name and the firm's address. (Audit reports are covered in detail in **Chapter 8** of this text.)

Maintaining Competence   The Regulations require audit firms to make arrangements to ensure that all principals and employees carrying out audit work are, and continue to be, competent. This involves audit firms recruiting appropriately skilled people, developing adequate performance management processes to monitor competence and developing regular training to maintain competence of all partners and staff.

Furthermore, in maintaining the competence of those conducting audits, firms should also produce audit manuals, programmes and checklists to ensure consistency of approach on audits and assist in skilling the team.

Monitoring   The audit firm must also monitor, at least once a year, how effectively it is complying with these regulations. As ISQC 1 also requires monitoring, these reviews are carried out as one review as the requirements are the same. The annual review will cover the firm's obligations under the regulations such as independence, fit and proper status, competence and so on. Furthermore, the audit firm is also required to review completed audit work to ensure the firm's procedures are being followed. These are often referred to as 'cold file reviews'.

An audit firm appoints an audit compliance partner to ensure that the firm complies with these regulations.

1.3.3 Professional Standards

The professional standards (ISAs) contain requirements with which, at a minimum, auditors must comply when performing their audit work. In addition, the ISAs include guidance which is intended to help them interpret and apply the requirements. As the focus of this textbook is on the audit process, we will discuss the relevant ISAs throughout.

1.3.3.1 Quality Control

Professional standards also require the audit firm to implement and maintain a system of quality control for audits, including internal monitoring controls. International Standard on Quality Control (UK and Ireland) 1 *Quality Control for Firms that Perform Audits and Review of Financial Statements, and other Assurance and Related Services Engagements* (ISQC 1) includes the requirements and guidance for quality control in audit firms. In addition, the audit engagement team is also responsible for maintaining a system of quality control on all audit engagements. The requirements and guidance for quality control at engagement level are set out in ISA 220 (UK and Ireland) *Quality Control for an Audit of Financial Statements* ('ISA 220'). These standards are discussed further in **Chapter 2**.

1.4 LEGAL LIABILITY OF AUDITORS

Audited financial statements may be relied upon by third parties and, as a result, auditors may find themselves in a position whereby they are sued by a third party who relied on the financial statements which contained an error, or resulted in the third party making an incorrect decision. Many such cases over the years have resulted in auditors ensuring that it is very clear who their 'contract' is with, i.e. the shareholders and therefore they are not responsible for any other party who relies on the audited financial statements.

You are referred to Chapter 6, Sections 6.14 and 6.15 of *External Auditing and Assurance* by Martin Nolan,[3] which summarises a number of legal cases that have highlighted the risk that an auditor faces in signing an audit report. It is advised that you read these sections of *Nolan* and understand the case history that has shaped the audit report over the years.

These cases have resulted in Chartered Accountants Ireland issuing guidance to its members regarding wording in the financial statements. Thus, in all Northern Ireland and Republic of Ireland audit reports, Chartered Accountants Ireland recommend including a clarification paragraph in auditor's reports which has become known as the 'Bannerman' paragraph (after the Scottish firm that was successfully sued for negligence in the absence of such a paragraph in their audit report). The Bannerman paragraph attempts to protect the auditor against exposure to third party claims as it states that the audit report is made solely to the company's shareholders and therefore should not be relied upon by any other party. Examples of Bannerman paragraphs that are included in UK and Irish audit reports are provided below.

---

[3] Martin Nolan, *External Auditing and Assurance: An Irish Textbook* (1st Edition, Chartered Accountants Ireland, 2010), hereinafter referred to as *Nolan*.

1.4.1 Bannerman Paragraph – Northern Ireland

The suggested wording issued by Chartered Accountants Ireland for insertion in a Northern Ireland audit report is set out below.

"This report is made solely to the company's shareholders, as a body, in accordance with Chapter 3 of part 16 of the Companies Act 2006. Our audit work has been undertaken so that we might state to the company's shareholders those matters we are required to state to them in an auditor's report and for no other purpose. To the fullest extent permitted by law, we do not accept or assume responsibility to anyone other than the company and the company's shareholders as a body, for our audit work, for this report, or for the opinions we have formed."

1.4.2 Bannerman Paragraph – Republic of Ireland

The suggested wording issued by Chartered Accountants Ireland for insertion in a Republic of Ireland audit report is set out below.

"This report is made solely to the company's members, as a body, in accordance with section 193 of the Companies Act, 1990. Our audit work has been undertaken so that we might state to the company's members those matters we are required to state to them in an auditor's report and for no other purpose. To the fullest extent permitted by law, we do not accept or assume responsibility to anyone other than the company and the company's members as a body, for our audit work, for this report, or for the opinions we have formed."

1.5 THE ETHICAL FRAMEWORK

The APB has also set Ethical Standards.[4] In carrying out an audit, all auditors must comply with the Ethical Standards (ESs), the main objective of which is to ensure that the audit of financial statements is conducted with integrity, objectivity and independence. Auditors' adherence to ethical standards is vital to maintain the credibility of their audit report.

There are five ethical standards, and one for smaller entities. These are set out below.

1.5.1 Integrity, Objectivity and Independence

ES 1 (Revised) *Integrity, Objectivity and Independence* focuses on the importance of auditors acting with integrity, objectivity and independence, and the requirement for audit firms to ensure they have adequate structures in place to monitor this.

---

[4] See http://www.frc.org.uk/apb/publications/ethical.cfm

ES 1 states that all those involved in the audit engagement are in a 'position to influence' the outcome and conduct of the audit and therefore should all act with integrity and objectivity to ensure that a timely, independent audit is executed at all times. These are discussed further below.

- **Integrity** – it is a prerequisite that anyone acting in the public interest should be seen to act with integrity, which means honesty, fairness, candour and confidentiality;
- **Objectivity** – this is also a fundamental ethical principle and requires that an auditor's judgement is not affected by conflicts of interest. Auditors need to adopt a rigorous and robust approach and should be prepared to disagree, where necessary, with the directors' judgements; and
- **Independence** – this underpins objectivity and ensures that circumstances surrounding the audit, including any financial, employment, business and personal relationships between the auditor and the audited entity do not impact on the objectivity of the audit. Where such relationships do exist, and threats may exist or be perceived to exist, the auditor must implement safeguards. (This is discussed further in **Section 1.5.1.2.**)

An audit firm must establish policies and procedures to ensure that requirements of ES 1 are adhered to. Examples of procedures adopted by firms to ensure compliance with ES 1 are detailed below.

1.5.1.1 Examples of Procedures Adopted by Firms to Ensure Compliance with ES 1

Appointment of an ethics partner to monitor independence issues and address them suitably   The ethics partner will act as the partner to consult if there is a suspected independence issue or breach. An ethics partner is a partner designated in the firm as having responsibility for:

1. The adequacy of the firm's policies and procedures relating to integrity, objectivity and independence, its compliance with APB Ethical Standards, and the effectiveness of its communication to partners and staff on these matters within the firm; and
2. Providing related guidance to individual partners with a view to achieving a consistent approach to the application of the APB Ethical Standards.

Annual declaration by all staff within the firm of any relationships with audit clients, either personal or financial   This may be an online declaration or in written format whereby, at the same time each year, e.g. at the commencement of the firm's financial year, all partners and staff declare any relationships they may have with audit clients, or sign-off that they have no such relationships. Any relationships identified on these declarations would be reviewed by the ethics partner who would then determine a course of action, e.g. ensuring that anyone with relationships with audit clients is not involved in the engagement.

An example of questions contained in such a declaration are included below in **Figure 1.4**.

FIGURE 1.4: EXAMPLE OF INDEPENDENCE QUESTIONS INCLUDED
IN AN ANNUAL DECLARATION

1. Have you received a significant benefit by way of goods or services on favourable terms or hospitality from any audit client?
   If yes, give particulars.

2. Have you been an employee of any audit client within the last two years?
   If yes, give particulars.

3. Are you intending to join or currently negotiating joining an audit client?
   If yes, give particulars.

4. Do you have any family or personal relationships with a director, officer or employee of a client?
   If yes, give particulars, and confirm whether you have any involvement in work carried out for this client.

5. Do you have any mutual business interests with an audit client or with an officer or employee of that client?
   If yes, give particulars.

6. Do you, or does anyone closely connected with you, have any beneficial or trustee investments in an audit client?
   If yes, give particulars.

7. Do you, or does anyone closely connected with you, have a beneficial interest in a trust having a shareholding in an audit-client company?
   If yes, give particulars.

8. Are you, or is anyone closely connected with you, the trustee of a trust which holds shares in an audit-client company?
   If yes, give particulars.

9. Do you hold any voting rights in any other Registered Auditor?
   If yes, give particulars.

10. Do you hold any directorships or shares in any registered Irish companies?
    If yes, give details of the company name, the number of shares held and the companies in which directorships are held. Please provide details of the principal activities of the company involved and please indicate whether this is a client.

Regular training on ethics and independence to allow staff to identify potential breaches or concerns and alert the ethics partner Firms need to ensure that partners and staff can identify independence breaches should they occur, and therefore may provide annual training to ensure that all potential breaches and concerns will be identified and reported to the ethics partner. This training may be, e.g. a face-to-face session, or online.

Monitoring of compliance by carrying out periodic review of audit engagement partner's portfolios The ethics partner will regularly review audit partner's portfolios to address any issues that may impair their independence. Examples of some such issues are noted below:

- if they have a financial interest in an audit entity;
- they have an economic dependence on certain audited entities that may impair independence, e.g. one audit client fees are a large percentage of total portfolio fees;
- they perform extensive non-audit services that may result in the auditor reviewing his own work; and
- the audit partner has been involved in this audit for more than 10 years which could thus impair independence.

The presence of the above policies and procedures will allow the audit firm to identify threats to independence on a timely basis and apply suitable safeguards.

Principal threats to independence that should be considered by an audit firm are detailed below.

1.5.1.2 Principal Threats to the Auditor's Objectivity and Independence

The principal threats to an auditor's objectivity and independence are:

Self-interest Threat Where the auditor has financial or other interests that may cause a reluctance to challenge the directors of the company at the risk of negatively impacting upon the relationship. For example, if an auditor had an investment in, or was still owed fees by, an audited entity, the auditor might be reluctant to disagree with management's choice of accounting treatment.

Self-review Threat Where the auditor, or others within the audit firm, perform non-audit work on financial information which is included in the financial statements that are being audited. The auditor may find it difficult (or may be perceived to find it difficult) to carry out a fully independent review and challenge any potential deficiencies in work that was carried out by their own audit firm.

Management Threat Where the auditor is perceived to be involved in management decisions. For example, if the auditor makes decisions on impairment calculations and management uses those calculations in preparing the financial statements, or management are required to make judgements and take decisions based on the auditor's work, such as design, selection and implementation of a financial information technology system. In such situations, the audit firm may become (or may be perceived to become) too closely aligned with the views and interests of management and, therefore, the auditor's objectivity and independence may be impaired.

Advocacy Threat   Where the audit firm undertakes work that involves working on behalf of the audited entity, e.g. acting as legal advisors in a litigation or regulatory investigation. As the audit firm is adopting a position closely aligned with management, this may pose a threat to the auditor's objectivity and independence.

Familiarity Threat   Where there are close personal relationships between auditor and audited entity due to, e.g. longevity, which may result in the auditor's reluctance to sufficiently question and challenge the audited entity's point of view.

Intimidation Threat   Where the auditor's conduct is influenced by fear and threats from an aggressive individual in the audited entity.

In evaluating these threats, the audit firm should assess the significance of threats to the auditor's objectivity and independence at various stages throughout the audit. These stages are detailed below.

1.5.1.3 Stages of the Audit where Threats to the Auditor's Objectivity and Independence should be Assessed

Threats to the auditor's independence should be considered at the following stages during the audit:

At the Client Acceptance or Re-Acceptance   Prior to commencing the engagement, as discussed in **Chapter 2**, the audit firm must consider if there are any threats to independence or objectivity. If there are threats that cannot be safeguarded, the auditor will not accept the engagement.

During the Planning of the Audit   More information may come to light during the planning procedures that may indicate a threat to objectivity or independence. The auditor should always be looking out for potential threats.

At the completion stage when forming an opinion   Prior to signing the audit report, the auditor assesses if any further information obtained during the audit fieldwork indicates a threat to the auditor's independence or objectivity.

When considering whether to accept an engagement to provide non-audit services to an audited entity Prior to accepting an engagement to provide non-audit services, the auditor must determine if such an engagement will result in a threat to objectivity and independence of the audit. This may occur, e.g. if the non-audit fees were very substantial and therefore the auditor may be compromised if issues are discovered during the audit.

When Potential Threats are Reported Once any potential threats are reported, the ethics partner should be consulted and appropriate action must be taken. This may involve changes in team personnel, or in resignation from the engagement, depending on the significance of the threat.

Once identified, the audit firm must assess the threat and apply safeguards which limit the threat or, if no safeguard can limit the threat to an appropriate level, the audit firm must not accept the assignment or withdraws from the engagement. Examples of safeguards will be examined further in this section in discussing Ethical Standards 2–5.

It should be noted that audit firms must also consider threats to independence and objectivity if there are other audit firms, either within or outside the network, involved in the audit. This is relevant, e.g. for the auditor of a group engagement where some of the subsidiaries are audited by other firms.

All considerations of threats to independence and objectivity are required to be documented in audit files and communicated to those charged with governance on a timely basis.

1.5.2 Financial, Business, Employment and Personal Relationships

ES 2 (Revised) *Financial, Business, Employment and Personal Relationships* provides requirements and guidance on specific circumstances arising out of financial, business, employment and personal relationships with the audited entity, which may create threats to the auditor's objectivity or perceived loss of independence.

1.5.2.1 Financial Relationships

ES 2 defines two types of financial interests:
1. direct financial interests – owned directly e.g. shares in an audited entity owned directly by an individual; and
2. indirect financial interests – owned through intermediaries, e.g. a pension scheme has financial interests in an audited entity and the individual is a member of that pension scheme; or the individual owns shares in an open-ended investment company which has a financial interest in an audited entity.

The impact of various financial relationships are summarised in **Table 1.1** below:

TABLE 1.1: EXAMPLES OF FINANCIAL RELATIONSHIPS AND RECOMMENDED ACTION

Relationship	Threat?	Action
A member of the engagement team, or immediate family member, has direct financial interest in the audited entity or an affiliate of the audited entity	Yes	No safeguard can eliminate or reduce this threat to an acceptable level – the holding is disposed of or the firm withdraws from the engagement. Alternatively, if the financial interest is held by a member of the engagement team who is not a partner, that person can be removed from the engagement team.
A member of the engagement team, or immediate family member, has indirect financial interest in audited entity or affiliate of audited entity but investment is material to audit firm or individual	Yes	No safeguard can eliminate or reduce this threat to an acceptable level – the holding is disposed of or the firm withdraws from the engagement. Alternatively, if the indirect financial interest is held by a member of the engagement team who is not a partner, that person can be removed from the engagement team.
A member of the engagement team, or immediate family member, has an indirect financial interest in the audited entity or an affiliate of the audited entity and (a) is aware of the investment; and (b) has the ability to influence the investment decisions of the intermediary	Yes	No safeguard can eliminate this threat or reduce it to an acceptable level – the holding is disposed of or the firm withdraws from engagement. Alternatively, if the indirect financial interest is held by a member of the engagement team who is not a partner, that person can be removed from the engagement team.
An immediate family member of a partner not involved in the audit holds a financial interest in the audited entity or an affiliate of the audited entity	No	The ethics partner ensures that adequate safeguards are in place, i.e. that the partner has no involvement in the audit.

Relationship	Threat?	Action
A member of the engagement team, or immediate family member, has an indirect financial interest in the audited entity or an affiliate of the audited entity and (a) is not aware of the investment; and (b) has no ability to influence investment decisions of the intermediary	No	The ethics partner ensures that the person holding the indirect interest is not involved in the audit of the intermediary and is not in a position to influence investment decisions.
A member of the audit team, or an immediate family member, holds direct or indirect financial interests in a trustee capacity	Yes	The ethics partner ensures that trustee interest is only held when: • the relevant person is not a beneficiary of the trust; • the financial interest held by the trust in the audited entity is not material to the trust; • the trust is not able to exercise significant influence over the audited entity; and • the relevant person does not have significant influence over the investment decisions of the trust.
An audit firm's pension scheme has a financial interest in the audited entity or its affiliates	Yes	If the firm has an influence over the trustees' investment decisions, no safeguards can reduce the threat to an appropriate level – the holding is disposed of or the audit firm withdraws from the engagement. If there is no influence over investment decisions, the ethics partner considers the issue with regard to the materiality of the financial interest to the pension scheme.
A member of an audit team, or an immediate family member, accepts or makes a loan to or from the audited entity	Yes	Not allowed unless the audited entity is a financial institution and the loan is made in the ordinary course of business on normal business terms.

1.5.2.2 Business Relationships

ES 2 defines a '**business relationship**' as that between the audit firm or a member of the audit team, or immediate family of such a person and the audited entity, its affiliates or management, which involves the two parties having a common interest. Such relationships may create self-interest, advocacy or intimidation threats to the auditor's objectivity.

Examples of such relationships are as follows:
- joint ventures with the audited entity or the directors/management of that audited entity;
- an arrangement between an audited entity and an audit firm to market products together;
- distribution or marketing arrangements whereby the audit firm would act as a distributor or marketer of any products or services of the audited entity, and vice versa; and
- an audit firm leasing office space to an audited entity.

Such relationships are not permitted unless the transactions involve the purchase of goods and services in the ordinary course of business in transactions that are at arm's length and are not material to either party, e.g. leasing of office space is permitted if it is at arm's length and not material to either party. For reference purposes, an arm's-length transaction is one in which the buyer and the seller have no significant, prior relationship and neither party has an incentive to act against his or her own interest.

If such relationships, as outlined above, are entered into, then the relationship should be terminated or the firm does not accept the engagement. If it is a member of the audit team that is involved in the transaction rather than the audit firm, a safeguard could be implemented whereby that member is removed from the audit team.

1.5.2.3 Employment Relationships

The standard (ES 2) provides guidance on three types of employment relationships:
1. **Loan Staff Assignments** Loan staff assignments are where an audit firm provides an employee to work in an audited entity. For example, the audit firm may have lost an accountant in their finance team and the auditor provides a qualified accountant to fill the role until the entity recruits a replacement. Audit firms are permitted to provide an employee to work in an audited entity if:
   - it is for a short period of time;
   - it does not involve staff or partners performing non-audit services not permitted under ES 5 (see **Section 1.5.5**);

- the individual is not holding a management position in the audited entity; and
- on return to the audit firm, that individual will not be involved in the audit team.

2. **Audit Staff Joining an Audit Client** Where a member of the audit team leaves the firm and joins an audit client, the audit firm must consider the significance of the self-interest, familiarity and intimidation threats. These will be assessed on the following factors:
   - positions that the individual holds in the engagement team or firm, e.g. a partner joining a client will have more severe consequences than a more junior member of staff;
   - the position the individual has taken at the audited entity, e.g. if the position was that of Finance Director, more safeguards would have to be implemented than if the individual took on a more junior role, such as an accounts clerk;
   - the amount of involvement the individual will have with the engagement team, e.g. if the individual was not involved in the audit process, fewer safeguards would need to be put in place than if the individual was responsible for the financial statements being audited; and
   - the length of time that the individual was a member of the engagement team or employed by the audit firm, e.g. an individual who was with the firm for a short time is less of a risk than an individual who was a member of the audit engagement team for a number of years.

   Following assessment of any such threats, appropriate safeguards are applied as necessary.

   However, it is important to note that safeguards cannot be applied when the individual who is leaving the audit firm is a partner and they are appointed as a director of the audited entity. In this case, the audit firm must resign as auditors and not re-accept the engagement for a period of two years.

3. **Family Members Employed by Audited Entity** ES 2 defines 'family members' as 'immediate family members', being an individual's spouse and dependents, and 'close family members', being parents, non-dependents and siblings.

   If an individual employed by the audited entity is in a position to exercise influence over the financial statements (e.g. the financial controller) and the engagement team includes an immediate or close family member of that individual (e.g. wife of the financial controller) the following rules apply:
   - *immediate family member* – the partner or member of the audit team must not be involved in the audit; and
   - *close family member* – this should be reported to the audit engagement partner who will discuss with the ethics partner and decide on an appropriate safeguard.

The standard also has some general guidance regarding relationships between the audit firm and the audited entity. The standard notes that partners or staff in an audit firm shall not accept board appointments to an audited entity, and if immediate family or close family of a member of the audit team takes such board appointments, the individual should be removed from the audit team. Furthermore, if a former employee of an audited entity who had influence over the preparation of the financial statements joins the audit firm, they shall not be a member of the audit team for a period of two years.

Firms should have procedures in place so that all relationships are reported to engagement partners and ethics partners to ensure that any safeguards necessary are adopted. Furthermore, procedures adopted for partners and staff should also be applied to external consultants involved in an audit to ensure that they are independent as required by ES 1.

1.5.3 Long Association with the Audit Engagement

ES 3 (Revised) *Long Association with the Audit Engagement* provides requirements and guidance on specific circumstances arising out of long association with the audit engagement, which may create threats to the auditor's objectivity or perceived loss of independence.

In general, the standard states that, where audit engagement partners, key partners involved in the audit, and partners and staff in senior positions are involved in the audit for a long period of time, self-interest, self-review and familiarity threats to the auditor's independence may arise. Therefore, audit firms must address these threats. Examples of safeguards are detailed in **Figure 1.5** below.

FIGURE 1.5: EXAMPLES OF SAFEGUARDS ADDRESSING LONGEVITY IN AUDIT ASSIGNMENTS

In addressing longevity in audit assignments, an audit firm may implement the following safeguards:
- rotating partners from audits after a specified period of time (10 years is assumed to be a reasonable benchmark);
- involving independent review partner to review the audit file; and
- involving an independent quality reviewer to review the audit file.

In relation to listed companies, however, ES 3 has additional and more stringent provisions. Due to the higher stakeholder group interested in the audited financial statements of listed companies, it is even more important to ensure that there are no threats to independence as a result of long association with the audit engagement. The standard includes specific provisions regarding personnel involved in the audit. These are detailed in **Table 1.2** below.

TABLE 1.2: ES 3 PROVISIONS FOR LISTED COMPANIES

Engagement Team Members	ES 3 Provisions
Audit engagement partner	Only act for five years as audit engagement partner on the listed client, and must wait for a period of five years before acting as engagement partner again.
Key partners and engagement quality control reviewers	Only act on the engagement for a period of seven years. The engagement quality control reviewers shall not be involved in the audit again for a period of seven years. Key partners shall not be involved in the audit again for a period of two years. Where a key partner becomes an audit partner, the combined period of service in these positions shall not exceed seven years.
Staff in senior positions	Staff in senior positions on a listed audit for a period of seven years should be discussed with the engagement quality control reviewer and ethics partner. Safeguards, such as changes in roles and additional reviews, can be implemented to reduce this threat to an acceptable level.

1.5.4 Fees, Remuneration and Evaluation Policies, Litigation, Gifts and Hospitality

ES 4 (Revised) *Fees, Remuneration and Evaluation Policies, Litigation, Gifts and Hospitality* is mainly focused on guidance surrounding audit fees to prevent threats to an auditor's objectivity or independence. All elements are discussed below.

1.5.4.1 Fees

The ultimate objective of the guidance provided by ES 4 is to ensure that an audit firm is not economically dependent on the fees of one client. Auditors should always be in a position to disagree with management, and economic dependence may inhibit this.

Contingent audit fees Audit fees should not be on a contingent-fee basis, e.g. a pre-determined amount based on an expected outcome. These create a self-interest threat to the auditor's objectivity and independence.

Non-audit fees It is the engagement partner's responsibility to ensure that audit fees are not influenced by the level of non-audit services provided to the audited entity. All non-audit fees must be communicated to the audit engagement partner and ethics part-ner. Furthermore, non-audit fees in relation to listed companies must be communi-cated to the audit committee.

Over-due fees If audit fees from the previous period remain unpaid at the commence-ment of the audit, the audit engagement partner and ethics partner should consider if this causes a self-interest threat. If the outstanding fees are significant, the audit firm may have to consider withdrawing from the engagement. Alternatively, if the outstanding fees are not considered to be significant, safeguards such as a review partner may be applied.

$resign \longrightarrow x > 15\% \ (NL), \ x > 10\% \ (L)$

Fee income of client If total fees for audit and non-audit services for one client regu-larly exceed 10% of annual fee income if client is listed, or 15% of annual fee income if client is not listed, the audit firm should resign from the engagement.

If total fees for audit and non-audit services for one client regularly exceed 5%, but do not regularly exceed 10% of annual fee income if client is listed on a recognised stock exchange, or exceed 10%, but do not regularly exceed 15% of annual fee income if cli-ent is not listed, the audit engagement partner shall:

$10\% > x > 5\% \ (L)$
$15\% > x > 10\% \ (NL)$

- disclose the fact to the ethics partner;
- disclose the fact to those charged with governance; and
- apply safeguards such as independent quality reviewer or reduce non-audit work to reduce total fees.

1.5.4.2 Remuneration and Evaluation Policies

ES 4 provides that audit teams should not be remunerated based on the value of non-audit services sold to audit clients as this may pose a threat to objectivity and indepen-dence. While audit teams may identify an area that requires improvement which would involve provision of a non-audit service, any potential threat should be considered before the firm accepts this engagement.

1.5.4.3 Threatened and Actual Litigation

Where there is threatened or actual litigation between an audit firm and an audited entity in relation to either audit or non-audit services, the audit firm should withdraw from the engagement. Since the audit firm's interest will be the favourable outcome of such litigation, this would create self-interest, advocacy and intimidation threats to the auditor's objectivity and independence.

1.5.4.4 Gifts and Hospitality

An audit firm, members of the audit team and their immediate family should not accept gifts from an audited entity unless they are clearly insignificant as these create self-interest and familiarity threats. In relation to hospitality, the standards recognise that it is a very important component in business relationships and, therefore, while not prohibited, firms should consider its frequency and cost. Regular hospitality, which would have a material value, would also create a self-interest and familiarity threat.

Therefore, firms should ensure that they have established policies and procedures to ensure that gifts and hospitality are measured and kept to an acceptable amount.

1.5.5 Non-audit Services Provided to Audited Entities

ES 5 (Revised) *Non-audit Services Provided to Audited Entities* requires audit firms to establish policies and procedures that will ensure that, when acceptance of non-audit services is under consideration, e.g. valuation services or tax services, this is communicated to the audit engagement partner.

The firm should only accept engagements to provide non-audit services when the objectives of the proposed engagement are consistent with the audit of the financial statements. Furthermore, the firm should have assessed any potential threat to the auditor's independence and they should be satisfied that suitable safeguards can be applied.

Provision of non-audit services creates the potential for all the threats illustrated in ES 1 (see **Section 1.5.1**):
- **self-interest threat:** where substantial fees are generated from non-audit services, it may compromise an auditor's willingness to challenge management;
- **self-review threat:** where the auditor is reviewing work as part of the audit which has been prepared by the audit firm through provision of non-audit services, they may be reluctant to fully challenge it;
- **management threat:** where non-audit services involve making judgements to assist management this could result in the audit firm's intentions being more akin to management's than an independent approach; and

- **advocacy threat:** where the non-audit services involve working on behalf of the client and therefore are closely aligned with management, which could hinder the fully independent and objective nature of the auditor's work.

Where no appropriate safeguards can reduce these threats to an appropriate level, the firm must not accept the non-audit engagement or withdraw from the engagement.

ES 5 provides some guidance in relation to specific non-audit services such as internal audit services, information technology services and tax-related services. In general, non-audit services can only be accepted if:
- the service is provided by partners and staff with no involvement in the audit;
- an independent quality reviewer is involved in the audit;
- the provision of services will not result in the auditor placing reliance on the work carried out by the audit firm; and
- the provision of services does not result in the audit firm taking a management role.

1.5.6 Provisions Available for Small Entities

The standards acknowledge that, while compliance with ES 1–5 is integral in providing an objective and independent audit, full compliance with these standards may not be practical when auditing small entities. Therefore, the APB Ethical Standard – Provisions Available for Small Entities (Revised) ('PASE') can be applied to audits of small entities (defined as small under UK and Irish companies legislation) and, if so, should be referenced as such in the audit report.

The PASE allows the following alternative provisions:
- Where audit fees of a small entity regularly exceed 10% of total fee income for the firm but do not regularly exceed 15% of total fee income, there is no requirement to assign an independent quality control reviewer to the audit.
- When undertaking non-audit services for a small entity, an audit firm is not required to apply safeguards required by ES 5. Instead, they should:
  o inform management;
  o ensure that the assignment is included in the audit firm's cyclical quality review process as required by ISQC 1.
- Where the non-audit services result in the audit firm undertaking part of the role of management, the audit firm is allowed to carry out those services as long as it:
  o discusses the objectivity and independence issues with those charged with governance confirming that management accept responsibility for decisions taken;
  o discloses the application of the PASE in the audit report.
- The audit firm is allowed to accept tax-related services where they would be acting as an advocate, e.g. before a court on resolution of an issue, as long as they have disclosed the application of the PASE in the audit report.

- If an audit partner of the audit firm joins an audited entity, the audit firm does not have to resign for a period of two years as long as they take appropriate steps to determine there has been no significant threat to the audit team's integrity, objectivity and independence; and discloses the application of the PASE in the audit report.

1.5.7 Practical Application – Examples of Ethical Threats

Table 1.3 below illustrates examples of threats and what, if any, safeguards should be implemented in line with the requirements of the ethical standards.

TABLE 1.3: EXAMPLES OF ETHICAL THREATS AND SAFEGUARDS

Situation	Threat	Safeguard
A member of the audit team holds shares in an audit client	Self-interest	Remove the individual from the audit team or resign from the audit. If the shareholder is a partner, they must sell the shares or the firm must resign.
The audit firm is commencing an audit and there are substantial fees outstanding from the prior year's audit	Self-interest	Agree a payment plan with the client prior to the commencement of the audit, or request full payment. If the fees remain outstanding, appoint the review partner to ensure independence is not compromised.
The audit firm prepares the payroll for the audit client	Self-review	The audit team does not contain individuals who are responsible for preparing the payroll.
The financial controller of an audit client joins the audit firm	Self-review	The new staff member must not be involved in the audit for at least two years.

The forensics department of the audit firm is acting on behalf of the client in a legal dispute	Advocacy	The audit team does not contain individuals who are involved in the advice. An independent review partner is appointed to the audit.
A staff member of the audit firm is a daughter of an audit client	Familiarity	The staff member does not form part of the audit team.
A recently appointed partner is engagement partner on an audit assignment and he/she previously spent 12 years as audit director on the audit assignment	Familiarity	The client should be rotated to another audit partner or an independent reviewer should be appointed to the engagement team.
The financial director is insisting that the audit is done for 50% lower fees than the prior year	Intimidation	The audit firm should not accept the engagement if the level of work carried out for the fee would compromise quality.

1.6 THE AUDIT PROCESS

This chapter has discussed the context of the audit and how it fits into the larger regulatory and legal framework. The remainder of this text examines the audit in much more detail, including a chapter which covers other assurance reports which an auditor can provide.

Aligned to the logical flow of this textbook, the audit process can be divided into four key stages:
1. Pre-engagement,
2. Planning,
3. Fieldwork, and
4. Audit Completion and Reporting.

Table 1.4 below summarises the key activities at each stage and where they can be found in this text.

TABLE 1.4: SUMMARY OF AUDIT PROCESS AND RELATED CHAPTERS

Stage in Audit Process	Activities	Key ISAs	Relevant Chapter
Pre-engagement	• Firm compliance procedures • Client acceptance procedures • Agreeing terms of engagement	ISQC 1 ISA 210 ISA 220	Chapter 2
Planning the audit	• Understanding the business • Risk assessment • Setting materiality • Responding to risks – developing audit tests to address the risks	ISA 240 ISA 250 ISA 260 ISA 265 ISA 300 ISA 315 ISA 320 ISA 330	Chapter 3 Chapter 4
Fieldwork	• Execution of audit plan • Conducting substantive or controls testing • Gathering audit evidence • Documenting audit tests and conclusions • Determining if there is a material misstatement caused by fraud or error	ISA 500 ISA 501 ISA 505 ISA 510 ISA 520 ISA 530 ISA 540 ISA 550 ISA 402 ISA 610 ISA 620	Chapter 5 Chapter 6
Audit Completion and Reporting	• Concluding if financial statements are free from material misstatement • Review of errors • Communication to those charged with governance • Forming an opinion on the financial statements	ISA 450 ISA 560 ISA 570 ISA 580 ISA 700 ISA 705 (NI) ISA 706 (NI) ISA 710 ISA 720	Chapter 7 Chapter 8

1.7 CONCLUSION

In conclusion, this chapter has covered the framework under which an audit is conducted, highlighting the responsibilities of auditors and directors in this process. The chapters following this will cover the auditor's responsibilities when conducting an audit under International Standards on Auditing (UK and Ireland).

SUMMARY OF LEARNING OBJECTIVES

Learning Objective 1 Demonstrate detailed knowledge of the statutory and regulatory frameworks which set criteria by which the audit is conducted, including the auditor's and directors' responsibilities

An audit is conducted due to a statutory requirement under company law. The regulatory framework which underpins the conduct of this audit is monitored in an oversight capacity by the Financial Reporting Council in the UK and the Irish Auditing and Accounting Supervisory Authority in Ireland. The issue of auditing standards and related guidance is governed by Chartered Accountants Ireland.

Learning Objective 2 Demonstrate an understanding of the case law which has impacted upon the legal liability of auditors

Historical cases have dictated that auditors are very aware of risks associated with issuing an audit report. This case law has shaped the audit report and, more recently, resulted in the inclusion of a Bannerman paragraph to protect the auditor against exposure to third party reliance on the report.

Learning Objective 3 Demonstrate a practical understanding of the Ethical Framework within which auditors perform their duties

The main objective of ethical standards is to ensure that the audit of the financial statements is conducted with integrity, objectivity and independence by auditors. In carrying out an audit, all auditors must comply with the ethical standards. Where circumstances exist that may threaten the integrity, objectivity or independence of an auditor, the auditor will either resign from the engagement or develop adequate safeguards to mitigate the threat.

Learning Objective 4 Understand the principal steps of the audit process and how they relate to International Standards on Auditing (UK and Ireland)

The audit process can be split into four logical steps: pre-engagement, planning, fieldwork, and audit completion and reporting. At each stage of the audit, International Standards on Auditing contain requirements which the auditor must adhere to.

QUESTIONS

In the scenario presented in the question below, there is an issue/(s) which needs to be addressed by the auditor (an indicator) in relation to ethical considerations. You should read the question and attempt to address the issue/(s) relating to ethical considerations.

(See **Appendix One** for Suggested Solutions to the Review Questions.)

Review Questions

Question 1.1 (Based on Chartered Accountants Ireland, FAE 2011 Mock Paper, Simulation 1)

Raps Limited

Your firm is a medium-sized firm of chartered accountants with an office located in (ROI) Cork/(NI) Belfast. One of your firm's largest clients is Raps Limited (RAPS), which has been a client of your firm for 15–20 years. Your client operates five large supermarkets, each of which is located within a radius of 30 miles from (ROI) Cork/ (NI) Belfast.

You have recently joined the firm, having finished your training contract with one of the Big 4 Firms, and having completed your Final Admitting Examinations. You have just been informed that the audit of RAPS is scheduled to commence in a fortnight and that you have been appointed as Senior-in-charge of the audit assignment reporting to the Audit Manager, Tom Dunne and the Audit Engagement Partner, Paul Reynolds.

At a meeting this morning attended by yourself, Tom Dunne and Paul Reynolds, you discussed a number of matters relating to the impending audit at which you took copious notes which you subsequently noted in a file note of the meeting and which is attached as Appendix 1. You are further provided with information in relation to summary details of the Balance Sheet and preliminary draft results for the year ending on 31 December 2010 which is set out in Appendix 2.

On your arrival to commence the audit of RAPS in March 2011 for the year ending 31 December 2010, in view of the significance of the stock figure, you have decided to deal personally with the audit of stock and to allocate other audit areas to your two audit assistants. Stock, as might be expected in an entity of this nature, is a material figure in the financial statements and is stated in the current year end draft accounts in the amount of €/£419,200.

Having satisfied yourself that your colleagues are embarked upon the audit work you have assigned to them, you arrange a short meeting with Kevin Cronin during which you elicited the following information:

- After he was appointed Financial Controller in October 2010, he examined carefully the company's previous stock taking/stock recording system with a view to eliminating any obvious inefficiencies.

  The system operated by his predecessor involved extensive staff commitment with consequent disruption to the activities of the business. The previous system involved staff recording descriptions and quantities of each stock line which subsequently had to be identified in the purchasing records and were then priced-out from these records on a FIFO basis. Kevin Cronin suggested to the MD, Chris O'Connor, that the costs involved could be significantly reduced if an alternative method was utilised.

  The alternative method he suggested, which the MD found acceptable, involves recording, by individual department, the quantities on hand for each stock line together with the retail selling prices marked thereon. He estimated this work was capable of being completed in each department by staff in that department in "a couple of hours" on the stocktaking date. The resulting listings would then be extended, totted and summarised by Kevin Cronin's two clerical assistants to present a total overall stock figure to him. He explained that he reduced this total stock figure by the theoretical overall gross profit margin produced by the management reporting system and the resultant amount is the stock figure of €/£419,200, details of which he has presented to you in his summarised priced-out stock sheets.

- You have examined the information presented to you and have established that the cost of sales figure of €/£4,025,600 has been arrived at as follows:

	€/£
Opening stock at beginning of period	320,000
Purchases during the period	4,124,800
	4,444,800
Less: Closing stock at end of period	(419,200)
	4,025,600

You have verified that the opening stock figure as quoted is in accordance with your prior year working papers and is as shown in the 2009 audited financial statements.

- Having returned to the office allocated to you and your assistants for the purpose of carrying out the audit on the client's premises, you have started to examine the lever-arch file containing the priced-out stock listings. The first page therein contains a summary of all subsequent pages and sets out the following information:

	€/£
Total retail selling price for all stock (i.e. 'sales-ticket') prices	502,036
× 83.50%	419,200

The summary working paper contains a note explaining that the figure of 83.5% is the company's overall theoretical percentage for cost of goods sold.

- Staff from your firm attended the client's annual physical stock count on 31 December 2010. You have examined the 'stock attendance report' contained in your working papers and are satisfied that the stock quantities appear to have been accurately recorded although there were some instances of double counting and some queries noted as to the saleable condition of some of the perishable stock.
- RAPS has a computerised management reporting system which, inter alia, involves regular reporting to management of performance across the relevant departments of the five supermarkets. You recollect your discussions with Tom Dunne/Paul Reynolds a fortnight previously whereby you are informed that the system produces a theoretical gross profit margin. Such theoretical gross profit margin shows that the cost of goods sold should be, on an overall basis, 83.5% of the net sales revenue. From an examination of last year's working papers, you have noted that RAPS did not yield a gross margin close to the theoretical overall gross margin of 16.5%. Your audit testing on a departmental basis shows that the overall average gross margin (weighted on a departmental basis by turnover) is coming in around 12.5% to 13.5% which is broadly consistent with last year's reported margin.

Arising from your assimilation of the above information, the following considerations strike you:
- Whether the introduction of the new system introduced by Kevin Cronin for determining the value of closing stock for financial statement purposes represents a change in accounting policy?
- At your brief meeting this morning with Kevin Cronin, when you asked him about the cost of sales formula utilising 83.5% of net sales revenue, he reminded you that the 'Retail Method' of valuing stocks (i.e. sales value less percentage gross margin) is commonly used in the retail industry for valuing inventories of large numbers of rapidly changing items with similar margins, where other costing methods would be impractical. You are pondering whether the manner of calculation of cost of closing stock is acceptable, and whether any changes are necessary in the calculation process used.
- What further considerations, if any, arise from the reported gross margin appearing to be different from the expected gross margin.

APPENDIX 1

Before you seek advice from Tom Dunne, as this is your first audit assignment for your new firm, you propose setting out your views on the issues arising in a memo which you intend to circulate to him and Paul Reynolds.

File Note of Meeting on 14 March 2011
Re: RAPS

Present: Paul Reynolds (AEP)
Tom Dunne (AM)
Gerry Byrne (Senior-in-charge)

1. RAPS has been a client of the office for a period of between 15–20 years. It ranks as one of the firm's largest audit clients. Paul Reynolds has been Audit Partner on this audit since his admission to the partnership 12 years previously. Paul asked, in response to a query from Gerry Byrne if his ongoing involvement might be an issue and to revert to him on it.

2. Kevin Cronin was recently appointed Financial Controller of the company. He was externally recruited to this position during 2010 with a specific brief of introducing efficiencies in the finance/accounting/administration areas.

3. RAPS' supermarket business is, like most such businesses operating in Ireland, divided into a number of departments which include grocery, household goods, meat and fish, fruit and vegetables, a delicatessen counter, toy section and it also operates an off-licence.

4. Chris O'Connor is a well-known, local businessman, holding numerous other directorships in other companies and is also the principal shareholder in RAPS. Chris O'Connor has already reported the draft results of the company to the company's bankers and to the Board and has informed Paul Reynolds that he does not want any changes made to the draft figures as a result of the current audit.

5. The firm carried out an assignment for RAPS two years ago to update the company's departmental and overall management reporting system. This system has now undergone two audits and is seen to be reliable and accurate.

Gerry Byrne
Senior-in-charge
14 March 2011

APPENDIX 2

Raps Limited

SUMMARY DETAILS OF THE BALANCE SHEET
as at 31 December 2010 (and earlier years)
(extracted from management accounts)

	2008	2009	2010
	€/£000	€/£000	€/£000
Tangible assets	425	410	350
Current assets (including stocks)	200	410	700
Creditors payable in less than one year	(125)	(155)	(99)
Net assets	500	665	951
Representing:			
Share capital	200	200	200
Prior year retained earnings	240	300	465
Current year profit	60	165	286
	500	665	951

The draft results for the year ended 31 December 2010 as presented by Kevin Cronin are set out below:

	€/£
Sales	4,800,000
Less: Cost of sales	(4,025,600)
Gross profit	774,400
Distribution/selling/other expenses (including depreciation)	(488,400)
Draft profit (before taxation)	286,000

2

PRE-AUDIT ACTIVITIES

LEARNING OBJECTIVES

In reading and studying this chapter, your objectives will be to:
- explain the concept of pre-audit activities;
- demonstrate an integrated knowledge of the quality control requirements at firm-wide level and engagement level; and
- demonstrate detailed integrated knowledge in order to evaluate and apply pre-engagement procedures.

2.1 INTRODUCTION

Prior to commencing an audit engagement, there are certain activities that should be completed by the audit team to comply with auditing standards. These procedures include the following:
- performing client acceptance procedures for initial audits;
- performing client re-acceptance procedures for continuing audits;
- determining whether the firm and the audit team (including the engagement quality control reviewer) are compliant with relevant ethical requirements, including independence; and
- establishing and understanding the terms of engagement.

These procedures are called '*pre-audit activities*'. Pre-audit activities impact on how the audit firm will approach the current period audit and, in some cases, may affect whether the firm chooses to accept an engagement, whether it is a new engagement or a recurring engagement. Accordingly, the timing of pre-audit activities will vary, but should always be performed before other significant audit activities (e.g. risk assessment procedures, fieldwork, etc.) are performed.

Pre-audit activities should not be confused with risk assessment procedures because pre-audit activities are performed before the audit work begins, whereas risk assessment procedures are completed at the planning stage of an audit. However, information obtained when performing pre-audit activities will be utilised when performing risk assessment procedures. For example, when performing client acceptance procedures, the audit team learns that the predecessor auditor communicated to the client some internal control deficiencies relating to the financial reporting process. In this situation, the audit team should consider the impact of those control deficiencies when determining their overall audit strategy.

Many pre-audit activities can be performed by the audit team and others in the firm without the direct involvement of client personnel, especially for continuing engagements. However, the audit team may need to conduct preliminary discussions with client personnel to effectively perform certain other pre-audit procedures. These discussions would take place prior to acceptance of the engagement and may include:
• understanding matters impacting upon independence and client continuance, e.g. if there are any ethical breaches that may impact upon independence and the subsequent acceptance of the engagement;
• establishing an understanding of the terms of the engagement, including fees;
• determining the tentative timetable; and
• maximising use of client personnel.

While assessments of independence, ethics and management integrity are completed at the beginning of the audit, these must also be re-evaluated throughout the audit as circumstances change.

Pre-audit activities are covered by the following standards:
• ISA 300 (UK and Ireland) *Planning an Audit of Financial Statements* ('ISA 300');
• ISQC 1 (UK and Ireland) *Quality Control for Firms that Perform Audits and Reviews of Financial Statements, and other Assurance and Related Services Engagements* ('ISQC 1');
• ISA 220 (UK and Ireland) *Quality Control for an Audit of Financial Statements* ('ISA 220'); and
• ISA 210 (UK and Ireland) *Agreeing the Terms of Audit Engagements* (ISA 210).

2.2 PRELIMINARY ENGAGEMENT ACTIVITIES

ISA 300 deals with the auditor's responsibilities when planning an audit (which are discussed in **Chapter 3**), but also includes requirements relating to activities the auditor must undertake in the pre-audit stage. These are described in the standard as 'preliminary engagement activities'. However, the preliminary engagement activities in ISA 300 are merely to direct the audit engagement team to undertake the requirements in ISA 220 regarding continuance of the client relationship and evaluating compliance with relevant ethical requirements, including independence (see **Section 2.3**). The preliminary engagement activities also direct the engagement team to undertake the requirements in ISA 210 (see **Section 2.4**).

2.3 QUALITY CONTROL

All firms that carry out statutory audit work must ensure they implement and maintain a robust system of internal control both at firm level (ISQC 1) and engagement level (ISA 220).

2.3.1 Quality Control at Firm Level

ISQC 1, paragraph 11, sets out that:

> "The objective of the firm is to establish and maintain a system of quality control to provide it with reasonable assurance that:
> (a) the firm and its personnel comply with professional standards and applicable legal and regulatory requirements; and
> (b) reports issued by the firm or engagement partners are appropriate in the circumstances."

ISQC 1 is applicable to firms who issue assurance reports, i.e. audit reports and other assurance reports. (Other assurance reports are discussed in **Chapter 10**.)

A quality control system required by ISQC 1, paragraph 16, has six elements:
> "(a) Leadership responsibilities for quality within the firm.
> (b) Relevant ethical requirements.
> (c) Acceptance and continuance of client relationships and specific engagements.
> (d) Human resources.
> (e) Engagement performance.
> (f) Monitoring."

Every audit firm must comply with all these elements.

2.3.1.1 Leadership Responsibilities for Quality within the Firm

The leadership of the audit firm should set the 'tone at the top' as one that believes quality is imperative to providing any service. If the leadership of the firm instils a culture of quality, this should filter through to the whole organisation. The firm's leadership should create a culture of quality which is communicated regularly to staff, e.g. through training seminars, meetings or newsletters.

In difficult economic times, when fees are constantly being reduced, a firm must ensure that it has robust quality policies and procedures to ensure that the quality of the work is not compromised because of cost-saving activities required to compensate for reduced fees. This responsibility is usually given to an individual within the firm who will then ensure that the firm's policies and procedures comply with the requirements of ISQC 1.

2.3.1.2 Relevant Ethical Requirements

ISQC 1 requires the audit firm to establish policies and procedures designed to provide reasonable assurance that it and its personnel comply with relevant ethical requirements (see **Chapter 1**). This can be achieved by training, strong communication and monitoring of compliance with policies and procedures. Examples of policies and procedures adopted by firms to comply with this ISQC 1 requirement are detailed below:
- training all firm personnel about the ethical standards and the necessity for compliance;
- establishing and communicating policies and procedures in relation to ethical requirements, e.g. all audit engagement partners must rotate from listed company audits every five years;
- monitoring compliance with the firm's policies and procedures by carrying out regular checks, e.g. checking that non-listed audit clients do not remain with the same engagement partner for longer than 10 years. This would form part of the monitoring checks discussed in **Section 2.3.1.6**; and
- establishing a process to deal with matters of non-compliance, e.g. immediately rotating a partner off an audit engagement because he or she has breached the five-year rotation policy, and communicating to all partners that such a breach is not acceptable.

ISQC 1 also specifically refers to independence, and the importance of establishing policies and procedures to provide reasonable assurance that a firm, its personnel and its network firm personnel are independent. It is therefore imperative that audit firms adopt procedures specifically targeting compliance with independence requirements.

Procedures adopted by an audit firm to comply with independence requirements may include the following four key steps:
1. Prior to commencing a new assignment, all engagement partners should communicate to the firm, including any network firms, details of the potential client and proposed services. This is usually done electronically, e.g. via e-mail, or a shared intranet site.
2. Any independence threats or potential independence threats should then be communicated to the engagement partner. For example, an entity registered as a

company in Ireland invites a partner in a firm to perform an audit engagement, but the partner is personally related to the finance director of that entity.

3. The firm can then assess information received and determine whether any threats to independence exist.
4. The relevant person(s) in the firm assesses the information received and determines whether any threats to independence exist and whether they can be sufficiently mitigated by appropriate safeguards.

Finally, all firms are required to obtain annual confirmation from all staff that they have complied with all policies and procedures in relation to independence requirements.

2.3.1.3 Acceptance and Continuance of Client Relationships and Specific Engagements

ISQC 1 requires an audit firm to establish policies and procedures for the acceptance and continuance of engagements to ensure that it only accepts engagements where it:
1. is competent to perform, and has the capabilities and resources to do so;
2. has considered the integrity of the client; and
3. can comply with all ethical requirements.

Competence, Capabilities and Resources Before accepting an engagement, an audit firm should consider if it has sufficient knowledge, experience and resources to carry out the engagement. Detailed considerations that should be undertaken by the firm in this regard are given below.

- *Do firm personnel have knowledge of industries or subject matters relevant to the client?*
  For example, if the client operates in a specific industry in which the audit firm has no other clients (e.g. the client has single-industry expertise in retail companies) and a financial services client approaches the firm, consideration needs to be given to the ability of the audit firm to perform the engagement.
- *Do firm personnel have experience with the relevant regulatory or reporting requirements, or the ability to gain the necessary skills and knowledge effectively?*
  For example, if the potential engagement was an audit of an insurance broker entity, consideration needs to be given to whether the firm has experience of the relevant regulatory body's additional reporting requirements sufficient to undertake the audit.
- *Does the firm have sufficient personnel with the necessary competence and capabilities?*
  For example, the firm should have an adequate number of staff who are fully qualified accountants and have the necessary technical skills to perform audit engagements.
- *Are experts available, if needed?*
  For example, a client may have a pension fund and the engagement team need an actuary to assist them in obtaining audit evidence on the valuation of that pension fund.[1]

---

[1] ISA 620 *Using the Work of an Auditor's Expert* deals with the auditor's responsibilities relating to the work of an expert engaged by the auditor when that expert is not already engaged by the firm. See **Chapter 6** of this book on auditor's experts.

- *Does the firm have individuals to act as engagement quality control reviewers, if applicable?*
  For example, ES 3 (Revised) *Long Association with the Audit Engagement* requires an engagement quality control reviewer to be appointed to a listed entity audit.
- *Is the firm able to complete the engagement within the reporting deadline?*
  For example, the firm should not accept an assignment if there are unrealistic reporting deadlines that will put pressure on the engagement team and may have a negative impact on quality.

If there are any doubts over the considerations above, the audit firm may not be in a position to accept the engagement.

Integrity of Client Before accepting an engagement, a firm should consider if the client has the type of reputation that the firm would like to be associated with. Points for consideration and practical considerations regarding how auditors would obtain this information are summarised below in **Table 2.1**:

TABLE 2.1: AUDIT FIRM CONSIDERATION OF INTEGRITY OF CLIENT

Consideration	Practical Implication	Practical Application
The identity and business reputation of the client's principal owners, key management, and those charged with governance	Is the client known for taking risks in the industry, e.g. illegal dumping of waste? Has is a strong reputation – if not, does the audit firm want to be associated with the client? Is there a risk of unfavourable media in the future?	• Google search for any articles about the client • Discuss with banking and legal contacts • More advanced firms may have systems which include adverse media reports that highlight any negative media about the company or any of its directors/shareholders
The attitude of the client's principal owners, key management and those charged with governance regarding aggressive interpretation of accounting standards and the internal control environment	Does the client adopt an aggressive interpretation of accounting standards which may result in conflict with the engagement team, and perhaps a qualified audit report?	• Review financial statements for accounting policies • Discuss with outgoing auditors, if possible

If the client is aggressively concerned with maintaining fees as low as possible	Will the level of fees allow the firm to carry out assurance work without compromising/negative impact on audit quality? The audit firm should not accept an audit client where there is a risk quality will be impacted by the level of fees	• Discuss fee arrangements with client • Review audit fees on financial statements and compare to similar client size/fee ratio
Indications of limitation in the scope of work	If it is a group audit, can we get access to the components as is required by ISA 600? If the client has adopted a revaluation policy, have they obtained a report from a qualified valuer? If there are limitations identified prior to acceptance, the auditor should consider the materiality of the impact, and not accept the engagement if it would result in a limitation of scope qualification; disclaimed opinion	• Discuss with the client • Discuss with previous auditors, if possible • Review financial statements and information on investments in other entities
Indications that the client might be involved in money laundering or other criminal activities	The firm has a legal obligation to report such activities. Furthermore, would the firm want to be associated with such a client?	Carry out anti-money laundering procedures as detailed in M42 (Revised) *Anti-Money Laundering Guidance – Republic of Ireland*[2] and M40 (Revised) *Anti-Money Laundering Guidance for the Accountancy Sector in the UK*[3]

---

[2] Chartered Accountants Ireland, September 2010. See the CHARIOT service.
[3] Chartered Accountants Ireland, August 2008. See the CHARIOT service.

The reasons for the appointment and non-reappointment of the previous audit firm	What are the reasons for the client changing auditors? Do they pay their fees? Do they consistently disagree with auditors? Are there continually qualified audit reports?	• Review financial statements for last few years • Send letter of professional clearance to outgoing auditors and discuss with outgoing auditor, if possible
The identity and business reputation of related parties	Does the potential client carry out business with related parties who have a poor reputation? How does this reflect on our client? Do we want this client to be associated with our firm?	• Online search (e.g. Google) • Background searches using specific systems • Discussion with banking and legal contacts • Discussion with outgoing auditors, if possible • Review of financial statements and disclosure notes on related parties and related party transactions

The points listed in **Table 2.1** above must be considered both at acceptance of a new client, and re-acceptance of an existing client. If, as a result of these checks, a conflict of interest is identified where safeguards can be implemented, and the firm decides to accept or continue with the engagement, then it should document how the issues were resolved. However, if a conflict of interest is identified that cannot be resolved by implementing appropriate safeguards, then the firm should either not accept the engagement or consider withdrawing if it is an existing client.

2.3.1.4 Human Resources

The audit firm should establish policies and procedures to ensure that all personnel have sufficient competence, capabilities and commitment to ethical principles necessary to:

1. perform engagements in accordance with professional standards and applicable legal and regulatory requirements; and
2. enable the firm or engagement partners to issue reports that are appropriate to the circumstances.

Examples of such policies and procedures that would be expected in an audit firm are detailed below:
• robust recruitment policies and procedures which ensure that all personnel who commence employment with the firm have the correct qualifications and

are competent to carry out their job, e.g. screening of candidates and required interview competencies;

- regular performance evaluations of personnel to ensure that they maintain competence and capabilities necessary to perform the firm's work, and that they are awarded appropriately and, if not, that this is addressed, e.g. this would take the form of annual or bi-annual performance appraisals;
- the development of the competence of staff through professional exams, internal and external training pre- and post-qualification, and through a programme of coaching and mentoring; and
- promotion and career development structures that are communicated to all personnel and which are achievable.

Within the human resources requirements of ISQC 1, every engagement must be assigned an engagement partner whereby:
- the responsibilities of the engagement are clearly defined and communicated to that partner;
- the engagement partner has the appropriate competence, capabilities and authority to perform the role; and
- the role of the engagement partner is communicated clearly to the client.

Furthermore, the audit firm should implement policies for assigning the engagement team to ensure that the engagement is performed in accordance with professional standards and applicable law. That is, the engagement team should be appropriately qualified, have sufficient and relevant practical experience and have a range of technical knowledge and expertise.

In order to comply with these requirements, examples of a firm's considerations when assigning engagement teams are detailed below:
- The audit team's understanding and practical experience of similar engagements, e.g. if a member of the engagement team has little experience of the industry in which the client operates, the firm should ensure that there is a more senior person reviewing that individual's work.
- The audit team's understanding of professional standards and legal and regulatory requirements, e.g. does the team have the required technical knowledge to interpret the legal and regulatory reporting requirements for, say, a financial institution?
- Technical knowledge and expertise, e.g. does the engagement team comprise an appropriate mix of qualified and non-qualified staff?
- Knowledge of relevant industries in which the clients operate, e.g. the firm may establish a policy that requires at least one member of the engagement team to be qualified and have previous audit engagement experience in the industry in which the client operates.
- Understanding of the firm's quality control policies and procedures, e.g. the engagement team should understand the importance of quality and adhering to the requirements of ISQC 1.

2.3.1.5 Engagement Performance

ISQC 1 requires firms to implement policies and procedures to ensure that assurance engagements are performed in accordance with professional standards and applicable legal and regulatory requirements so that the firm or engagement partner can issue appropriate reports. In relation to assurance engagements, ISQC 1 is very specific about the policies and procedures that should be implemented. These policies and procedures can be summarised as follows, and are then discussed below:

1. consistency in the quality of engagement performance;
2. supervision;
3. review;
4. consultation;
5. engagement quality control review;
6. differences of opinion; and
7. engagement documentation.

Consistency in the Quality of Engagement Performance In order to ensure that the firm maintains consistency throughout all engagements it should communicate policies and procedures to all assurance personnel. This may be achieved through, for example:

- regular training;
- an audit manual;
- audit programmes;
- standard documentation; and
- technical factsheets.

Supervision All engagements should have a level of supervision whereby:

- the progress of the engagement is tracked;
- the competence and capabilities of engagement team members is considered, i.e. the members of the engagement team understand their instructions and can carry out the work to an appropriate standard;
- significant matters are addressed as they arise during the engagement and the audit approach can be modified if appropriate; and
- matters are identified that require further consultation with more experienced members of the engagement team or others with expertise within the firm.

Depending on the size and complexity of the client, supervision responsibilities may sit with the most senior team member on the assignment or the manager.

Review All elements of the audit engagement should be reviewed by a more senior member of the team than those who prepared the work. For example, the audit senior may review the work of a team member; the manager may review the senior's work, and the audit partner will carry out an overall review of the engagement. All reviews consist of the following considerations:

- if the work has been performed in accordance with professional standards and applicable legal and regulatory requirements;
- if significant matters have been raised for consideration;
- whether appropriate consultations have taken place on technical or contentious issues and the resulting conclusions have been documented and implemented;
- whether there is a need to revise the nature, timing and extent of work performed;
- whether the work performed supports the conclusions reached and is appropriately documented; and
- if the evidence obtained is sufficient and appropriate to support the report, i.e. the objectives of the engagement procedures have been achieved.

Depending on the size and complexity of the client, review responsibilities may sit with the engagement manager or engagement partner.

Consultation If a difficult or contentious matter(s) arises during an engagement, the audit firm should have the necessary procedures in place for engagement teams to consult at an appropriate level. This may be an internal resource, e.g. the audit technical group on an auditing matter or the ethics partner on an ethical issue; or it may be an external expert in a particular area, e.g. consulting a solicitor on a legal issue.

Consultation helps to promote quality and improves the application of professional judgement. All consultations should be appropriately documented and recommendations implemented.

Engagement Quality Control Review An engagement quality control review is a review of the engagement by a partner within the firm who is independent of the engagement. The client need not be made aware of the presence of an engagement quality control reviewer, as this role is primarily used as an additional layer of quality control, i.e. checking of the quality of work and compliance with regulatory and ethical principles.

All firms should have policies and procedures in place for the appointment of engagement quality control reviewers. While an engagement quality control reviewer is required for all listed entity audit clients, the firm should develop other criteria which dictate when an engagement quality control reviewer is appointed. Examples of these criteria are as follows:

- when clients are over a particular size or fee bracket, it may be reflective of more complexity in the audit and therefore would be regarded as higher risk requiring an additional level of review when clients are of public interest and may be of interest to the media, e.g. a political party or public body, an additional level of review may be introduced to further reduce audit risk since the audit report may receive increased attention in the media; and
- when clients are regulated entities such as financial institutions they would be regarded as having more complex accounting and additional reporting requirements to the financial regulator, therefore requiring an additional level of review.

An engagement quality control reviewer is appointed at the planning stage of the engagement and reviews the work on a timely basis, usually at the planning stage of the audit and then at completion, after the audit file has been reviewed by the engagement partner.

In carrying out a quality control review the reviewer discusses significant matters with the engagement partner, reviews the financial statements, reviews judgements, and evaluates conclusions. Furthermore, for audits of listed entities, the reviewer must also consider the team independence and whether significant judgements have been consulted on, documented and concluded on appropriately.

In selecting an engagement quality control reviewer, the audit firm must have suitable procedures so that the most suitable reviewer is selected. The reviewer should be selected and assigned to an engagement on the following basis:

- *Technical expertise, experience and authority required to perform the role* For example, if it is a reviewer for a listed entity audit, the individual should have sufficient experience in reporting requirements for listed entities, e.g. technical knowledge in International Financial Reporting Standards and compliance requirements of the UK Corporate Governance Code;
- *Ability of the engagement partner to consult with the engagement quality control reviewer, without compromising the reviewer's objectivity* If the level of consultation throughout the engagement is regarded as so significant that it begins to impair the reviewer's objectivity, another individual should be appointed as engagement quality control reviewer; and
- *Objectivity of the reviewer* For example, reviewers are not selected by the engagement partner, they do not participate in the engagement other than as the reviewer, and they do not make decisions for the engagement team.

An example of an audit programme for a quality control review is included in **Figure 2.1**.

FIGURE 2.1: EXAMPLE OF AUDIT PROGRAMME
FOR QUALITY CONTROL REVIEWER

	Procedure	Schedule/ Comments	Done By
1.	Determine that you have the background and experience to accomplish the objectives of this review.		
2.	Affirm that you have neither assumed any of the responsibilities of the engagement partner nor have responsibility for the audit of any significant divisions, benefit plans, or affiliated or related entities.		

	Procedure	Schedule/ Comments	Done By
3.	Read the Summary of Significant Matters		
4.	Discuss significant accounting, auditing, and financial reporting matters with the engagement partner.		
5.	Review documentation of the resolution of significant accounting, auditing, and financial reporting matters, including documentation of consultations with Firm personnel outside the audit team.		
6.	Review the Summary of Unrecorded Misstatements.		
7.	Review the Summary of Control Deficiencies.		
8.	Review the audit partner's consideration of the firm's objectivity and independence, including non-audit services provided by the firm and other group auditors during the year, together with other factors identified by the audit partner as possibly impacting on the firm's objectivity and independence. Affirm that, where necessary, appropriate safeguards were identified and implemented and, as a result, the firm's objectivity and independence in relation to the audit opinion has not been impaired in practice.		
9.	Review the need for the application of rotation or alternative safeguards and affirm that appropriate measures are to be taken in this respect to safeguard the firm's independence and therefore to enable the firm to continue to act.		
10.	Read the financial statements and report.		
11.	Confirm with the engagement partner that there are no significant unresolved matters.		
12.	Determine that significant matters identified by you have been satisfactorily resolved by the audit team.		
13.	Based on the results of the procedures evidenced above, I am satisfied that the engagement was performed in accordance with professional standards and Firm policies and agree with the issuance of the Firm's report.		
14.	I have reviewed the post audit review section of the continuance form (Acceptance of Assignment database) and agree with the action proposed.		

The firm should ensure that, in performing a quality control review, it is in line with its own requirements and that it is completed before the date of the report.

Differences of Opinion As with consultation, the audit firm should implement procedures whereby differences of opinion within and outside the engagement team are consulted, documented and resolved. For example, this may be done by consulting with the ethics partner and including a memo documenting the reasons for the conclusion.

Engagement Documentation An audit firm should ensure that they have adequate policies and procedures surrounding engagement documentation to ensure that it is appropriately assembled, stored and retained. Such procedures would include:

- *Archiving Policies* Setting time limits whereby engagement files are to be completed and closed. Some laws and regulations dictate this time period, e.g. audits of SEC-listed entities are required to have engagement files completed no more than 45 days after the report date. The application material of ISQC 1 notes that, in the absence of a required time frame, a recommended time limit for audit files is 60 days after the report date.[4]
- *Confidentiality* Respecting the confidentiality of the information in the engagement file is very important, particularly taking account of data protection laws.
- *Authorised Access* Only allow authorised access to the engagement information, e.g. using passwords on an electronic audit package.
- *Post-archiving Amendments* Prohibition of changes to evidence on the engagement file after the final file assembly date – this is easier to implement with an electronic file than a paper file.
- *Data Retention* Retain the engagement file in line with laws and regulations. For example, for audit engagements, the retention period would be no shorter than five years from the date of the audit report.
- *Accessibility* In retaining the documentation, it should be accessible should it be required for reference or investigation.

2.3.1.6 Monitoring

As discussed thus far in this chapter, ISQC 1 requires firms to implement policies and procedures to develop and maintain good quality control within a firm. The standard also requires the firm to monitor and document results of this monitoring on a regular basis. This is to ensure that the firm's quality control practices are maintained to a standard which provides reasonable assurance that reports that are issued by the firm or engagement partners are appropriate in the circumstances.

---

[4] ISQC 1, paragraph A54 sets the time limit for engagement files to be completed and closed as 60 days after the report date.

The inspection that is carried out by specified personnel in the firm is split into two levels:
- **firm quality monitoring**, e.g. all items covered in **Section 2.3.1** above such as human resource policies and consultation policies; and
- **engagement quality monitoring**, whereby an engagement will be selected from each audit engagement partner over a cyclical period, e.g. three years, and reviewed for compliance with quality control procedures such as, among other things, client acceptance procedures, allocation of a competent engagement team and quality of audit documentation. This is specifically discussed in **Section 2.3.2** below.

The results of the monitoring inspections should be documented and communicated to all engagement partners, and any deficiencies dealt with in an appropriate manner.

2.3.2 Quality Control at Engagement Level

ISQC 1 must be applied by all firms undertaking assurance assignments, which includes both audit and non-audit engagements. However, ISA 220 specifically refers to quality control for an audit engagement. The requirements in ISA 220 for audit engagements are identical to those in ISQC 1 for assurance engagements, as discussed above.

In summary, for all audit engagements, ISA 220 requires that:
- the engagement partner shall take responsibility for the overall quality of the audit engagement, e.g. complying with the firm's quality control procedures and issuing an appropriate audit report;
- the engagement partner should be alert to ethical requirements throughout the engagement and consult with others in the firm if members of the engagement team have not complied with ethical standards;
- independence requirements are complied with, as detailed in ISQC 1, and the engagement partner shall form a conclusion on compliance with independence requirements;
- client acceptance and continuance procedures are complied with, as detailed in ISQC 1;
- an appropriate engagement team is assigned to the audit engagement (in terms of competence and capabilities, as detailed in ISQC 1);
- the engagement partner should take responsibility for the direction, supervision and performance of the engagement team, as detailed in ISQC 1;
- the engagement partner should take responsibility for reviews being performed, as detailed in ISQC 1;
- the engagement partner shall ensure that consultation is carried out where appropriate, and be satisfied with the nature and scope of conclusions (ISQC 1);
- the engagement partner shall ensure that an engagement quality control reviewer is appointed where appropriate (ISQC 1); and
- the engagement partner shall consider the results of monitoring processes as circulated by the firm and whether deficiencies noted in that information might affect the audit engagement.

In summary, the requirements in ISQC 1 and ISA 220 must be complied with by any firm carrying out audit engagements. Furthermore, ISQC 1 and ISA 220 contain the client re-acceptance requirements that must be met before continuing with the assurance assignment.

The final pre-audit activity involves agreeing the terms of engagement and this is discussed in **Section 2.4** below.

2.4 AGREEING THE TERMS OF AN AUDIT ENGAGEMENT

2.4.1 Introduction

ISA 210 *Agreeing the Terms of Audit Engagements* deals with the auditor's responsibilities when agreeing the terms of engagement with the client. These include requirements, or 'preconditions', that must be achieved before the engagement letter can be issued. The majority of the preconditions are there to ensure that the client's management understands that an audit engagement is conducted on the basis that management accept and acknowledge their fiduciary responsibilities, including their regulatory and reporting responsibilities. Once management has accepted those responsibilities, the auditor has a reasonable expectation of obtaining the information necessary to conduct the audit.

Preconditions of an audit include that management acknowledge and understand its responsibility to:
- prepare financial statements in accordance with the applicable financial reporting framework;
- ensure adequate internal control to enable the preparation of the financial statements that are free from material misstatement; and
- provide the auditor with access to all information necessary to complete the audit.

Furthermore there are two additional preconditions that the auditor must determine:
- That there are no known limitations on the scope of the auditor's work imposed by management prior to engagement that might result in a qualification which would be so pervasive as to necessitate a disclaimer of opinion. For example, if the auditor knew in advance of an audit engagement that management of the entity was not willing to give the auditor access to records management holds (i.e. evidence) which relate to a very significant matter that impacts upon the preparation and presentation of the financial statements as a whole, then the auditor faces an imposed scope limitation. (Qualified audit reports are further discussed in **Chapter 8**.); and

- That the financial statements will be prepared using an acceptable financial reporting framework. For example, for a statutory audit in Ireland, this would be UK/Irish GAAP or IFRS, along with relevant company law requirements.

If any of the above are not met, the auditor must consider whether or not they can accept the engagement.

Once the pre-conditions for an audit are met, the auditor must agree the terms of engagement, which is usually achieved through a written engagement letter.[5]

An engagement letter will always contain:
- the objective and scope of the audit;
- the responsibilities of the auditor and of management;
- identification of the applicable financial reporting framework; and
- reference to the form and content of reports to be issued by the auditor.

The auditor may also wish to include in the engagement letter:
- the fact that, due to inherent limitations and unavoidable risk, there may be some material misstatements undetected;
- a description of arrangements regarding the planning of the audit;
- an expectation that management will provide written representations, where required;
- the basis of fees and billing arrangements;
- a request for management to acknowledge receipt of the letter, that is, send back a signed copy;
- the fact that other auditors and experts may be involved, where necessary;
- the fact that internal auditors and client staff may also be involved;
- a description of arrangements to be made with any previous auditor, if relevant;
- the restriction of the auditor's liability, where possible; and
- any obligations to provide audit working papers to other parties.

2.4.2 Group Engagement Letters

If the audit is of a group entity, then there are some additional considerations that need to be taken into account as to whether or not separate engagement letters should be issued to the component(s) as follows:
- Who appoints the component auditors – if those charged with governance of the group are different individuals to those of the component(s) then a separate engagement letter should be issued.
- Whether the component(s) requires a statutory or regulatory audit, e.g. if the component(s) does not require an audit to be performed for legal or regulatory

---

[5] Paragraphs 9, 10, A23-A25 of ISA 210 detail the form and content of an engagement letter.

purposes, and only a group audit report is required, then one group engagement letter would usually suffice.

- Legal requirements in relation to audit appointments – there may be specific requirements in different jurisdictions regarding engagement letters.
- Degree of ownership by the parent – if the majority shareholder is not the immediate group entity, it would be more fitting to issue separate engagement letters to the immediate group entity and the component(s).

Group audits are discussed in more detail in **Chapter 9**.

2.4.3 Recurring Engagements

The auditor is not required to issue a new engagement letter every year; however, there are some factors which may trigger the requirement to issue a new engagement letter:
- an indication that the entity misunderstands the scope of an audit;
- revised or special terms of the audit engagement;
- a change in senior management;
- a significant change in ownership;
- a significant change in the nature or size of the entity's business;
- a change in legal or regulatory requirements; and
- the adoption of a different financial reporting framework for the preparation of financial statements, e.g. a change from Irish GAAP to IFRS.

2.4.4 Changing Engagement Terms

Once the terms of the audit engagement have been agreed and notification of the agreement conveyed via a signed engagement letter, the auditor should not agree to change the terms of engagement unless there is a valid justification for doing so. Any changes should be in the form of a written agreement. If the auditor is unable to agree to any changes to the audit engagement, and management will not permit them to continue with the original terms, the auditor should withdraw from the engagement.

An example of an audit engagement letter, from ISA 210 *Agreeing the Terms of Audit Engagements*, Appendix 1, is reproduced below. This is an example of an audit engagement letter for an audit of general purpose financial statements prepared in accordance with International Financial Reporting Standards. This letter is not authoritative but is intended only to be a guide that could be used in conjunction with the considerations outlined in this ISA. It will need to be varied according to individual requirements and circumstances. It is drafted to refer to the audit of financial statements for a single reporting period and would require adaptation if intended or expected to apply to recurring audits (see paragraph 13 of this ISA). It may be appropriate to seek legal advice that any proposed letter is suitable.

EXAMPLE 2.1: AUDIT ENGAGEMENT LETTER

To the appropriate representative of management or those charged with governance of ABC Company:

The objective and scope of the audit

You have requested that we audit the financial statements of ABC Company, which comprise the balance sheet as at December 31, 20X1, and the income statement, statement of changes in equity and cash flow statement for the year then ended, and a summary of significant accounting policies and other explanatory information. We are pleased to confirm our acceptance and our understanding of this audit engagement by means of this letter. Our audit will be conducted with the objective of our expressing an opinion on the financial statements.

The responsibilities of the auditor

We will conduct our audit in accordance with International Standards on Auditing (ISAs). Those standards require that we comply with ethical requirements and plan and perform the audit to obtain reasonable assurance about whether the financial statements are free from material misstatement. An audit involves performing procedures to obtain audit evidence about the amounts and disclosures in the financial statements. The procedures selected depend on the auditor's judgment, including the assessment of the risks of material misstatement of the financial statements, whether due to fraud or error. An audit also includes evaluating the appropriateness of accounting policies used and the reasonableness of accounting estimates made by management, as well as evaluating the overall presentation of the financial statements.

Because of the inherent limitations of an audit, together with the inherent limitations of internal control, there is an unavoidable risk that some material misstatements may not be detected, even though the audit is properly planned and performed in accordance with ISAs.

In making our risk assessments, we consider internal control relevant to the entity's preparation of the financial statements in order to design audit procedures that are appropriate in the circumstances, but not for the purpose of expressing an opinion on the effectiveness of the entity's internal control. However, we will communicate to you in writing concerning any significant deficiencies in internal control relevant to the audit of the financial statements that we have identified during the audit.

…

Our audit will be conducted on the basis that management acknowledge and understand that they have responsibility:
(a) For the preparation and fair presentation of the financial statements in accordance with International Financial Reporting Standards;
(b) For such internal control as management determines is necessary to enable the preparation of financial statements that are free from material misstatement, whether due to fraud or error; and

(c) To provide us with:

    (i)   access to all information of which [management] is aware that is relevant to the preparation of the financial statements such as records, documentation and other matters;

    (ii) additional information that we may request from [management] for the purpose of the audit; and

    (iii) unrestricted access to persons within the entity from whom we determine it necessary to obtain audit evidence.

As part of our audit process, we will request from management written confirmation concerning representations made to us in connection with the audit.

We look forward to full cooperation from your staff during our audit.

Other relevant information

[Insert other information, such as fee arrangements, billings and other specific terms, as appropriate.]

Reporting

[Insert appropriate reference to the expected form and content of the auditor's report.]

The form and content of our report may need to be amended in light of our audit findings.

Please sign and return the attached copy of this letter to indicate your acknowledgement of, and agreement with, the arrangements for our audit of the financial statements, including our respective responsibilities.

XYZ & Co.
Acknowledged and agreed on behalf of ABC Company by
(signed)

....

Name and Title
Date

2.5 CONCLUSION

The audit firm has significant obligations to develop adequate policies and procedures which ensure that all assurance engagements are adequately considered prior to accepting the assignment. Once the audit firm has agreed to accept the assignment, the auditor must agree the terms of the engagement prior to carrying out any planning procedures as discussed in **Chapter 3**.

SUMMARY OF LEARNING OBJECTIVES

Learning Objective 1 To explain the concept of pre-audit activities

Pre-audit activities are performed by the audit team prior to accepting an engagement. These activities are a prerequisite to any engagement acceptance as they consider the ability of the audit firm to accept the assignment from an independence, reputational and competence perspective.

Learning Objective 2 To demonstrate an integrated knowledge of the quality control requirements at firm-wide level and engagement level

All audit firms carrying out assurance assignments must ensure they implement and maintain a robust system of internal control both at firm level (ISQC 1) and engagement level (ISA 220). An integral part of this internal control system specifically deals with the procedures an audit firm must demonstrate in relation to client acceptance.

Learning Objective 3 To demonstrate detailed integrated knowledge in order to evaluate and apply pre-engagement procedures

In applying client acceptance procedures, the audit firm considers if they are competent to perform the engagement, the integrity of the client and whether they can comply with all ethical requirements. Non-compliance with these requirements will result in the audit firm not accepting the engagement.

QUESTIONS

In each of the scenarios presented in the questions below, there is an issue/(s) which needs to be addressed by the auditor (an indicator) in relation to pre-audit activities. You should read the questions and attempt to address the issues relating to pre-audit activities.

(See **Appendix One** for Suggested Solutions to the Review Questions.)

Review Questions

Question 2.1 (Based on Chartered Accountants Ireland, FAE Autumn 2010, Simulation 1)

Daniels Stores

It is January 2010. You are an audit manager with O'Sullivan & Co, a small firm of chartered accountants. The senior partner, Ronan O'Sullivan, has asked you to get involved with a prospective new client – Daniels Stores Ltd, a family owned supermarket business with a December year end. Originally established by Mr and Mrs James Daniels, the company has operated in your local town for the past 30 years. Mr and Mrs Daniels have recently retired and have been succeeded as owners by their son, Simon, and daughter, Caroline. Simon and Caroline have exciting plans for the business and approached your firm to act as auditors and business advisors as they feel that your firm provides a good fit with their fresh approach and plans to develop the business. The partner that their parents dealt with at their existing audit firm, Mulligan and Aherne, recently also indicated his intention to retire and this prompted Simon and Caroline to contact your firm. The partner has asked that you identify and document all relevant matters that the firm must consider before accepting appointment as auditors.

The partner has provided you with some notes of a meeting with Simon and Caroline (Appendix A), together with an extract from their most recent set of management accounts (Appendix B), to enable you to understand their business, document the related business risks for the audit file and to help you research under what circumstances the firm could undertake work for the potential investors. He also asks you to draft an example report (with details of the work required) to address the requirements of the potential investors.

Appendix A

Notes of a Meeting
with Simon *and* Caroline Daniels, Proprietors of

Daniels Stores Ltd

Date: 12 December 2009
In attendance: Ronan O'Sullivan (ROS); Simon Daniels (SD); Caroline Daniels (CD)

SD set out the background to their business – Daniels Stores has been operating successfully for the last 30 years as an independent owner-operated neighbourhood supermarket surrounded by a number of residential developments. Simon and his sister Caroline recently assumed ownership of the business following the retirement of their parents. Their parents managed and worked in the supermarket on a regular basis and had built up an excellent relationship with many of their regular customers who valued the personal service. Mr and Mrs Daniels also offered credit to certain customers they knew well which was particularly welcome over the past year when unemployment in the area increased due to the general economic downturn.

ROS commented that, in their preliminary telephone conversation, SD had mentioned that they had plans for developing the business over the next couple of years and asked if they would like to expand on their plans.

CD replied that in the medium term they would like to acquire or open other similar outlets in neighbouring towns and villages to increase their buying power, thereby reducing their cost base. Margins have been eroded over recent months as the company has been unable to pass on increased costs from suppliers in full. Simon and Caroline are seeking investors to help finance their plans. SD commented that in preliminary discussions some of these potential investors have sought a report from independent accountants setting out the average revenue per customer transaction over the past year. He asked ROS whether he could prepare a suitable report to satisfy their needs. ROS replied that he would consider this and get back to SD or CD within a few days.

SD added that in the short term they have been in discussion with a premium coffee shop chain about opening a franchise in the corner of the existing supermarket. This would require significant upfront investment but they hope to recoup this via their share of the profits plus an increased footfall in the supermarket. They recently secured a loan from a local bank to finance this investment – whilst the interest rate is favourable they must comply with two banking covenants – providing monthly management accounts and maintaining an interest cover of two-times profit before interest and tax.

SD indicated that they are keen to progress with their improvement and expansion plans as soon as possible as they are aware that the local petrol station, with a convenience store, is undergoing refurbishment and has also secured a post office franchise. Currently the nearest post office is about three miles away.

ROS enquired as to year-to-date trading performance and CD passed him the management accounts for the 11 months year-to-date. SD commented that in the past year Simon and Caroline had assisted their parents in selecting and implementing a new EPOS system which automatically monitors stock levels and reorders directly from suppliers. Whilst the system is now working properly it did suffer a few teething problems which resulted in certain grocery stock lines being over-ordered. They have attempted to manage this through special offers on the affected lines but still have higher than normal stock levels on certain lines. All other aspects of the EPOS system including the recording and reporting of customer transactions have been operating successfully since it was implemented on 1 January 2009.

ROS replied that we would bear the stock reorder issue in mind should we accept appointment as auditors. He thanked SD and CD for their time and indicated that he would get back to them within a few days to indicate whether the firm would be able to accept appointment as auditors and whether he would be able to prepare the report they requested for the potential investors.

APPENDIX B

Daniels Stores Ltd

EXTRACT FROM MANAGEMENT ACCOUNTS
for the 11 months to November 2009

INCOME STATEMENT

	November 2009	November 2008	YTD 2009	YTD 2008
	€/£	€/£	€/£	€/£
Turnover	216,579	234,897	2,168,907	2,345,742
Cost of sales	191,060	201,643	1,978,868	2,111,780
Gross profit	25,519	33,254	190,039	233,962
Administrative expenses	17,813	17,684	174,867	193,874
Operating profit	7,706	15,570	15,172	40,088
Interest payable	1,425	648	10,618	7,689
Profit before tax	6,281	14,922	4,554	32,399
Tax	816	2,104	592	4,212
Profit after tax	5,465	12,818	3,962	28,187

BALANCE SHEET

	November 2009	November 2008
	€/£	€/£
Tangible fixed assets	227,623	211,965
Current assets		
Stock...	219,673	184,872
Trade debtors...	44,589	10,785
Cash...	3,984	38,847
	268,246	234,504
Current liabilities		
Bank overdraft..	14,876	-
Bank loan..	100,000	-
Trade creditors.......................................	68,844	119,773
Accruals..	4,894	28,732
	188,614	148,505

Net current assets	**79,632**	85,999
Net assets	**307,255**	297,964
Share capital..	**100,000**	100,000
Profit and loss account	**<u>207,255</u>**	<u>197,964</u>
	307,255	297,964

Question 2.2 (Based on Chartered Accountants Ireland, FAE 2011 Mock Paper, Simulation 3)

Pybex Limited

Your firm, Alan & Burke, Chartered Accountants & Registered Auditors was recently approached by the senior management team of a non-client, Pybex Limited, a large computer software company, who wishes to appoint a new firm of Chartered Accountants to act as the company's auditors. The approach is regarded as an important opportunity for your firm because Pybex would be a substantial new audit client and also because the firm has no other clients in the computer software business and is anxious to develop a presence in this area.

During its most recently completed financial year ended on 31 May 2011, the company's sales were €/£22 million, profit before taxation €/£2.8 million and shareholders' funds at the year end amounted to €/£3.75 million.

Some days ago you (Joe Dowling), as Audit Manager, along with one of your firm's Audit and Assurance partners, John Brennan, attended a preliminary meeting with the Chief Executive (Tom Murray) and Finance Director (Fiona Healy) of Pybex Limited. The preliminary meeting had been arranged to enable management to introduce you to their company and to provide a forum to allow you to request any information or documentation which you feel you need in the context of your proposed appointment.

During the course of the meeting, you established that the company has wholly owned subsidiaries operating in Italy, in France and just recently commenced in Bulgaria. In answer to your query, Fiona Healy confirmed to you that the Bulgarian company was quite small though they were anticipating reasonable growth in the short to medium term. Overall, she indicated that the combined net assets of the subsidiaries located abroad was in the region of 20%/25% of the group's net assets and generated approximately one-third of the group's profits. Tom Murray said that they are very satisfied with the work of the local auditors located in each of the countries concerned and do not propose that there should be any changes arising from your proposed appointment as group auditor. Fiona Healy commented: "I know from my own days in practice, there are some client acceptance procedures you need to deal with for a new client. Perhaps you would get back to me on these together with your views on how you will deal with the local auditors in the Italy France, etc."

You asked who the outgoing auditors are and are informed that they are a Dublin/Belfast based firm, SRFI. You know SRFI to be a very reputable firm of Chartered Accountants and Registered Auditors. In response to your query as to how long they had been the company's auditors, you were told for two years i.e. they audited the 2009 and 2010 financial statements. When you raised the issue as to why they were considering replacing SRFI with Alan & Burke, the response from Tom Murray was: "Best not to go there!"

During a wide ranging discussion at the meeting, Tom Murray informed you that the next possible market in which they were considering establishing a subsidiary is in Spain/Portugal where they currently have a one third interest in a joint venture which was successful commercially. However, in view of relationship difficulties arising in dealing with the other joint venture parties, they are now looking at the possibility of doing 'their own thing' in that area. You elicited additional information from them with respect to the joint venture investment which confirmed to you that there were significant transactions entered into between all of the group companies and the joint venture entity, including the provision of significant management services, for which no charge was made. However, because of "certain sensitivities" arising, according to Fiona Healy, it is their joint wish that there should be no reference to these transactions in the audited financial statements.

They further confirmed they propose exiting the joint venture which is currently shown as a financial asset in the balance sheet in the amount of €/£650,000.

Not surprisingly there was a discussion with respect to the likely proposed fees that your firm will charge in relation to the new audit assignment. John Brennan indicated that he will, of course, get back to them in due course with respect to your firm's fee proposals. You received the not-unexpected 'rider', from Tom Murray, that it is anticipated that your fee proposal will be very conscious of the current difficult economic environment.

As the meeting was drawing to a close, your colleague, John Brennan, mentioned the fact that on a few occasions he had met socially with the former Chief Executive (Jack O'Brien) who left Pybex a few months ago. This prompted Fiona Healy to inform you that, at the time of the resignation of the former Chief Executive, there were 15 months to run on his service contract and, accordingly, compensation of €/£350,000 was paid to him. She indicated that she had recently spoken to some of the executive directors of Pybex and asked you to appreciate they were sensitive in relation to the potential reaction of shareholders and others to the compensation payment made to the outgoing Chief Executive. She said that, she, at the request of some of the directors, drafted a proposed note for their consideration for subsequent inclusion in the 2011 audited financial statements on this issue and said she would forward it to you subsequent to the meeting. John Brennan received an e-mail from Fiona Healy the following day which is attached.

John Brennan has forwarded her e-mail to you with some additional comments of his own; his e-mail is attached in Appendix 2.

APPENDIX 1

From: Fiona Healy (Finance Director)   Sent: 12/06/2011 11:30

To: John Brennan

Re: Pybex Limited – Former Chief Executive

I refer to our discussions at your offices yesterday afternoon which Tom Murray and I found particularly helpful and encouraging. We were both impressed with the input from your colleague Joe Dowling.

I understand you will revert to us with respect to the matters we discussed at the meeting.

I attach our proposed note for incorporation in the audited accounts with respect to directors' remuneration and would like you to have a look at it and come back to me with your views.

Note 14 – Directors' remuneration and transactions (extract)

	2011	2010
	€/£	€/£
Directors' remuneration	540,000	480,000
For services as director	3,400,000	2,700,000
Other remuneration including pension contributions	650,000	230,000
	4,590,000	3,410,000

The above note contains all relevant information with respect to directors' remuneration. Jack O'Brien's compensation payment of €/£350,000 is included under the caption "Other remuneration including pension contributions" in the proposed note.

As I want to 'put this matter to bed' as soon as possible, would you confirm to me that the proposed note is acceptable to you. If, for any reason, you have any problem with it, would you outline the implications of same?

You might also let me have your preliminary views on the other issues we discussed and, when we have had a chance to consider them, we can at that later stage deal with the fee issues.

Regards

Fiona

Appendix 2

From: John Brennan   Sent: 12/06/2011 11:50

To: Joe Dowling

Re: Pybex Limited

I attach an e-mail just received this morning from Fiona Healy (Pybex). *(Note to student: this is the email attached at Appendix 1.)*

I thought yesterday's meeting went well and I hope we succeed in 'landing' them as they would be a very reputable new client in an area where we do not have strong presence at the moment.

Would you come back to me as soon as possible with your views on her query on the proposed note and on the other matters from our meeting yesterday to enable me to do a formal response? From memory, the other matters from the meeting we need to consider are:
- Client acceptance procedures.
- Issues surrounding joint venture in Spain/Portugal.
- Any other issues you consider relevant.

I know you are up to your eyes at the moment with FloorStyle but we need to appear efficient so your early response would be appreciated.

Regards

John

3

PLANNING AN AUDIT

LEARNING OBJECTIVES

In reading and studying this chapter, your objectives will be to:
- gain a detailed understanding of the concept of developing an audit strategy and audit plan in line with ISA 300 (UK and Ireland) *Planning an Audit of Financial Statements*;
- be able to calculate materiality and understand its purpose in line with ISA 320 (UK and Ireland) *Materiality in Planning and Performing an Audit*;
- be able to execute the risk assessment stage of an audit as required under ISA 315 (UK and Ireland) *Identifying and Assessing the Risks of Material Misstatement Through Understanding the Entity and Its Environment*;
- develop appropriate responses to assessed risks in line with ISA 330 (UK and Ireland) *The Auditor's Responses to Assessed Risks*; and
- understand the auditor's responsibilities to communicate with those charged with governance at the planning stage as required by ISA 260 (UK and Ireland) *Communication With Those Charged With Governance*.

3.1 INTRODUCTION

The planning of an audit can be simplified into four steps:

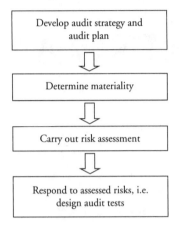

We will cover each of these steps in detail throughout the chapter.

3.2 AUDIT STRATEGY AND PLAN

ISA 300 (UK and Ireland) *Planning an Audit of Financial Statements* ('ISA 300') states: "The objective of the auditor is to plan the audit so that it will be performed in an effective manner."

Planning the audit is vitally important in order to carry out an efficient and effective engagement. An effectively planned audit will allow the auditor to assign appropriate team members and time to various areas of the audit. For example, at the planning stage the auditor may conclude that, because revenue is a high-risk area, more experienced members of the team need to perform the fieldwork.

Establishing the audit strategy and detailed audit plan are not necessarily distinct tasks, and are often performed together and combined into one **audit planning memorandum**. This document, and the work carried out in order to prepare it, gives the auditor the opportunity to consider the business and its environment, to ascertain reporting deadlines and consider factors that are significant in directing the audit team's efforts. In basic terms:

- the **audit strategy** is where the auditor ascertains the nature, timing and extent of **resources** necessary to perform the engagement; and
- the **audit plan** is where the auditor sets out the **detailed procedures** required.

This is further explained below.

The Appendix to ISA 300 outlines a number of matters auditors should consider in developing audit strategies. **Table 3.1** provides examples of some of these matters, along with explanations as to why they might be considered and how they would impact upon the audit plan. These considerations would be carried out through combining: team discussions; discussions with management/those charged with governance; and analytical review of the preliminary financial statements.

TABLE 3.1: AUDIT STRATEGY CONSIDERATIONS AND IMPACT ON AUDIT PLAN

Matter	Consideration	Impact
Characteristics of the engagement	Under which reporting framework are the financial statements prepared e.g. UK and Irish GAAP, US GAAP or IFRS?	If the financial reporting framework applied has complex requirements, the audit team may need more specialised knowledge.
	Is it a group audit and, if so, are the components audited by another auditor?	The audit team needs to consider the level of access to components and component auditors.
	How automated is the client's accounting system?	This will impact upon the availability of data to the auditor and expected use of computer-assisted audit techniques.
	Are there any industry-specific reports required (e.g. insurance entities regulated by IFSRA require the auditor to report annually)?	If additional reports are required, the timing for these must be documented in the audit strategy.

Matter	Consideration	Impact
Reporting objectives, timing of the audit and nature of communication	Does the entity have reporting deadlines that need to be met?	If the client is a listed entity which always makes a preliminary announcement, then the auditor must ensure that the timing of the preliminary announcement is documented in the audit strategy.
	What type of output is required by the client's management, and when?	Are management expecting a written report summarising the audit and significant matters to be presented at a meeting? These expectations and timings must be included.
	What are the reporting obligations of the components and component auditors?	The auditor must incorporate deadlines for component auditors which are required to be met for timeous completion of the group audit.
Significant factors, preliminary engagement activities and knowledge gained on other engagements	Determination of materiality (materiality is discussed in **Section 3.3** below)	Consideration of the most appropriate benchmark(s) to apply in the circumstances of the entity.
	Experience from previous audits in relation to the internal control environment and any deficiencies	Knowledge the auditor has gained from previous audits will impact upon the audit strategy and the audit plan. For example, if rebates were materially misstated in a prior year due to weak controls, the auditor may assign more experienced team members to that work and then adjust the nature, timing and extent of audit procedures set out in the audit plan accordingly.

	What is the volume of transactions? Is it high volume of low value?	A high volume of transactions may lead the auditor to determine that there should be more focus on using tests of control.
Nature, timing and extent of resources	What competencies are required for the audit?	Does the auditor need to assign experienced members to the team as the audit will be complex? Is an expert required?
	What review resources are required?	If there are complex areas, should a schedule of reviews be planned, rather than only one at the end of the fieldwork? When will team briefings take place? Will the engagement partner perform their review onsite? Is an engagement quality control reviewer required?

Once the auditor has considered these matters, they then develop a detailed audit plan which sets out the nature, timing and extent of planned risk assessment, and audit procedures. The audit plan will include other audit procedures that are required to ensure the engagement complies with the auditing standards. It must be documented on the audit file, and based on the considerations outlined above as well as other considerations, which may include items such as:

- *Background of the business*, e.g. if the business is a start-up, the auditor may not be in a position to rely on the controls as they have not operated effectively in the past; or if a business has any history of non-compliance with tax regulations, the auditor may decide that taxation is a significant risk.
- *Accounting and business risks*, e.g. the company has subsidiaries in a number of foreign countries and therefore has a high volume of foreign exchange transactions in the financial statements. This may lead to additional testing required on foreign exchange balances.
- *Significant risks*, e.g. the auditor may have considered revenue as a significant risk if the company has aggressive revenue recognition policies and revenue is a material figure in the financial statements.
- Details of the *client's accounting system and internal reporting structures*, e.g. a basic accounting system may result in the auditor carrying out all substantive testing, and no controls testing.

- *Materiality*, setting materiality and documenting the basis of the materiality calculation, e.g. documenting the percentage and benchmark utilised. The materiality set will determine the level of audit risk and testing.
- Details of the *audit team* will be documented in the audit plan, including reasons why the individuals are considered to be competent to perform the engagement;
- *Timing and logistics* of fieldwork, review and reporting to the client.
- *Audit approach*, e.g. the level of testing on significant risks and the use of sampling techniques.

It should be noted that, while the risk assessment procedures always take place at the commencement of an audit, the planning of audit procedures takes place **at all stages**. That is, the audit plan will be updated so that it includes details of any further audit procedures required following conclusions the team makes about the risk assessment. In addition, as the audit team gathers evidence, they may need to modify either the audit strategy or audit plan or both as a result of unexpected events or conclusions. Any such changes should be documented.

To put an audit strategy and plan output into context, an example of an audit planning memorandum template is provided in **Appendix 3.1** to this chapter.

3.3 DETERMINING MATERIALITY

3.3.1 Introduction

As noted above, a key element to the audit strategy and plan is to determine materiality.

ISA 320 (UK and Ireland) *Materiality in Planning and Performing an Audit* ('ISA 320') states that, as part of establishing the overall audit strategy, the auditor shall determine materiality as a basis for:
- identifying and assessing the risks of material misstatement;
- determining the nature, timing and extent of further audit procedures; and
- evaluating the effect of uncorrected misstatements, if any, on the financial statements.

Therefore, getting materiality right has a significant impact on the audit. For example, if materiality is set too low, there is the potential for performing unnecessary audit procedures leading to an inefficient audit ('over-auditing'). Setting materiality too high may result in not obtaining sufficient, appropriate audit evidence to form an opinion on whether the financial statements are free from material misstatement.

There are three different levels of materiality an auditor will determine:
1. materiality for the financial statements as a whole (for the purpose of this text '**overall materiality**');
2. **performance materiality** – this is the materiality utilised for the purposes of assessing the risk of material misstatement and determining the nature, timing and extent of further audit procedures;

3. **materiality for specific classes of transaction**, account balance or disclosure, e.g. for transactions or balances where misstatements of a lower amount than performance materiality may influence the economic decisions of users of the financial statements, such as directors' remuneration or research and development costs for a pharmaceutical company

These are explained below.

3.3.2 Overall Materiality

Overall materiality is the basis for the other materiality levels that are calculated, as well as the basis for testing and accumulation of errors. It is the first materiality calculation that the auditor should undertake. As noted in **Table 3.3** below, it is largely used when reviewing errors in the financial statements.

When setting overall materiality, ISA 320 suggests that the auditor use a percentage of a suitable benchmark. While this will depend on the nature of the entity's activities, the most common benchmarks used are:
• Revenue,
• Profit before tax,
• Total assets, or
• Net assets.

As noted above, when choosing a suitable benchmark, the auditor should consider the nature of the entity's activities. For example, if the client is a manufacturing company, the most suitable benchmark might be profit before tax as the most significant transactions in the business would be revenue and related costs resulting in profit. Similarly, if the client is a property development company, the most suitable benchmark might be total assets as assets would be the most significant balance in the financial statements. While it is more common to choose one overall level of materiality, in certain circumstances two may be appropriate. For example, if the client is a property investment company with large property balances on its balance sheet, and rental income and property management costs in its income statement, it might be more appropriate to have two levels of materiality: one for the balance sheet (e.g. based on total assets) and one for the income statement (e.g. based on profit).

Once the benchmark is chosen, the auditor must calculate materiality based on a percentage of that benchmark. The auditing standards do not specifically state what these percentages should be and, therefore, this requires judgement on the part of the auditor.

Nevertheless, the ranges given in **Table 3.2** are useful as a guide:

TABLE 3.2: MATERIALITY BENCHMARK GUIDES

Benchmark	Measurement Percentage
Earnings before tax	5% to 10%
Total revenues	½% to 1%
Total assets	½% to 1%
Equity	1% to 2%
Net assets	½% to 1%

3.3.3 Performance Materiality

Following the calculation of overall materiality, ISA 320 requires the auditor to calculate a lower level of materiality known as '**performance materiality**'.

Performance materiality is important because it is there to reduce the probability that the aggregate of uncorrected and undetected misstatements in the financial statements does not exceed materiality for the financial statements as a whole, i.e. it allows auditors to have a margin for errors that they will not be able to find. It is therefore utilised at the planning stage to determine the level of audit testing.

While there is no guidance in the standard as to what the performance materiality level should be, it will be significantly lower than overall materiality, e.g. 60% of overall materiality might be used.

As mentioned, this lower materiality is utilised to provide a 'cushion' for errors that may exist but which will remain undetected or underestimated. This can be illustrated using a simple example:

EXAMPLE 3.1: ILLUSTRATION OF PERFORMANCE MATERIALITY

Overall materiality: €100,000

Performance materiality: €60,000

Total creditor balance: €75,000. Within this total creditor balance there is an error – a purchase invoice of €80,000 has been omitted.

If the auditor only used overall materiality when assessing risk, they might choose not to perform any procedures on the total creditor balance because it is €75,000, which is below the overall materiality level of €100,000. As a result of not performing audit work on creditors, the error of €80,000 would not be detected. Therefore, if there were any more errors in the financial statements amounting to €20,000 or over, the financial statements would be materially misstated without the auditor being aware of this.

However, because the auditor is required to use performance materiality, they will perform audit procedures on creditors and detect the misstatement. Therefore, by using performance materiality in the risk assessment process, the auditor is minimising audit risk in that the financial statements are less likely to be materially misstated.

It should be noted that while overall materiality and performance materiality are used throughout the audit, performance materiality is used primarily during planning and fieldwork in assessing the level of audit risk and determining transactions and balances that should be tested. A table illustrating materiality used at various stages of the audit is provided below:

TABLE 3.3: MATERIALITY UTILISED DURING THE AUDIT

Stage of Audit	Materiality	Reason
Planning	Performance materiality	To determine when audit work is necessary, e.g. only transaction balances over performance materiality will be considered for testing.
Planning	Performance materiality	To determine what items to test within a transaction balance. For example, if creditors were material, the auditor would then choose a sample to substantiate. This sample would always include balances over the performance materiality level.
Fieldwork	Performance materiality	To evaluate the results of sample tests. For example, if on a particular test the extrapolated difference of potential adjustments is greater than performance materiality, the auditor would carry out further testing to determine that the potential error is less than performance materiality.

| Fieldwork | Overall materiality | To determine errors that are accumulated on the audit adjustment schedule as per ISA 402, all errors above the clearly trivial should be documented. (As discussed in **Chapter 7**, best practice would calculate 'clearly trivial' as 2% of planning materiality.) |
| Completion | Overall materiality | To assess the accumulated misstatements. If the accumulated unadjusted misstatements are greater than materiality, further adjustments need to be made or it may result in qualification of the audit report. |

Using materiality to evaluate the impact of misstatements at completion is discussed further in **Chapter 7** when we cover ISA 450 (UK and Ireland) *Evaluation of Misstatements Identified during the Audit.*

It is important also to note that materiality should be re-assessed as the audit progresses. For example, materiality may have been calculated at the planning stage on draft figures; if these change significantly, materiality may need to be recalculated.

3.3.4 Materiality for Specific Classes of Transactions

In carrying out a risk assessment, the auditor may conclude that there are particular classes of transactions, account balances or disclosures for which misstatements of **lesser** amounts than materiality for the financial statements as a whole could reasonably be expected to influence the economic decisions of users of the financial statements. Therefore, for these particular balances or transactions, the auditor may calculate a lower level of materiality and use that for the testing and review of uncorrected errors.

Factors that may influence the auditor to calculate a lower materiality level for particular balances or transactions include:
- Whether law, regulation or the applicable financial reporting framework affect users' expectations regarding the measurement or disclosure of certain items, e.g. related party transactions, or directors' transactions required under Irish company law.
- Key disclosures in relation to the industry in which the entity operates, e.g. research and development costs for a pharmaceutical company.
- Whether attention is focused on a particular aspect of the entity's business that is separately disclosed in the financial statements, e.g. a newly acquired business.

In considering whether, in the specific circumstances of the entity, such classes of transactions, account balances, or disclosures exist, the auditor may find it useful to obtain an understanding of the views and expectations of those charged with governance and management.

3.4 RISK ASSESSMENT

Risk assessment means identifying the risks that could cause the financial statements to be materially misstated. Risk assessment **procedures** are performed to understand the entity, its environment and its internal control. It is important to note that, when an auditor is performing risk assessment procedures, they are looking at risks that could impact upon the financial statements.

This understanding is essential in identifying risks of material misstatements, whether due to error or fraud, relating them to the financial statement assertions and assessing the likelihood that they could cause a material misstatement. This assessment will then dictate what audit testing should be performed on the financial statements. Understanding the entity is also important in determining if the levels of materiality chosen are appropriate, identifying areas where special audit consideration may be necessary (e.g. the going concern assumption), developing expectations when performing analytical procedures, **responding** to the risk assessment by designing further audit procedures and also evaluating whether you have sufficient appropriate audit evidence.

The auditing standard that addresses the risk assessment process is ISA 315 (UK and Ireland) *Identifying and Assessing the Risks of Material Misstatement Through Understanding of the Entity and Its Environment* ('ISA 315'). However, there are a number of other auditing standards that set out additional considerations for the auditor at the risk assessment stage, including:

- ISA 240 (UK and Ireland) *The Auditor's Responsibilities Relating to Fraud in an Audit of Financial Statements* ('ISA 240');
- ISA 250 Section A (UK and Ireland) *Consideration of Laws and Regulations in an Audit of Financial Statements* ('ISA 250 Section A');
- ISA 402 (UK and Ireland) *Audit Considerations Relating to an Entity Using a Service Organisation* ('ISA 402');
- ISA 500 (UK and Ireland) *Audit Evidence* ('ISA 500');
- ISA 510 (UK and Ireland) *Initial Engagements – Opening Balances* ('ISA 510');
- ISA 540 (UK and Ireland) *Auditing Accounting Estimates, Including Fair Value Accounting Estimates, and Related Disclosures* ('ISA 540');
- ISA 550 (UK and Ireland) *Related Parties* (ISA 550);
- ISA 570 (UK and Ireland) *Going Concern* ('ISA 570');
- ISA 610 (UK and Ireland) *Using the Work of Internal Auditors* ('ISA 610'); and
- ISA 620 (UK and Ireland) *Using the Work of an Auditor's Expert* ('ISA 620').

During the process of the risk assessment the auditor will consider all of these standards. This is illustrated in **Sections 3.4.1–3.4.5** below.

In summary, the risk assessment process can be split into the following steps:
1. understanding the entity and its environment;
2. understanding internal control;
3. relating the identified risks to assertion level or financial statement level; and
4. considering whether the risks could result in a material misstatement.

We will now go through each of these steps.

3.4.1 Understanding the Entity and its Environment

Understanding the entity and its environment should encompass the events, transactions and other practices that may have a significant effect on the financial statements. This understanding will help the auditor to:
- identify areas that may need special attention;
- assess how accounting data is produced, recorded, processed, reviewed and stored;
- evaluate the reasonableness of estimates, such as valuation of inventories, bad debt provisions and percentage completion of long-term contracts;
- make judgements on the valuation of assets;
- evaluate the reasonableness of management representations; and
- make judgements about the appropriateness of the accounting policies applied and the adequacy of presentation and disclosures in the financial statements.

As stated in ISA 315, and **Nolan**,[1] in gaining an understanding of the entity and its environment, the auditor should focus on five specific areas which are discussed below.

Nature of the Entity The auditor should gain an understanding of the nature of the entity's business, structure and accounting principles in order to assess if the structure and operations may indicate areas of audit risk that may lead to potential misstatement. In gaining this understanding, the auditor should consider the following points:
- the entity's business operations, including location, products and/or services, sources of revenue, markets, major customers and suppliers, competition, related parties, outsourced activities, employment;
- the entity's ownership and governance, i.e. who owns the business and is responsible for governance;
- the types of the entity's investments (planned or recent acquisitions, securities, loans, fixed assets, special-purpose entities), including related matters such as debt covenants, leasing activities, off-balance sheet arrangements and the use of derivatives;

---

[1] Martin Nolan, *External Auditing and Assurance: An Irish Textbook* (1st Edition, Chartered Accountants Ireland, 2010), Chapter 3, Section 3.7.

- the way the entity is structured and how it is financed (including how the business obtains funds to operate); and
- the accounting principles and industry practices adopted by the entity such as revenue recognition policies, the method of accounting for complex or unusual transactions and financial statement presentation and disclosure.

All these factors enhance the auditor's understanding of the structure and operations of the entity. This knowledge allows the auditor to identify areas that may lead to a risk of material misstatement. For example, if the entity had a very complex group structure, the auditor may consider the completion of intercompany transactions to be a significant risk; or if the entity had significant borrowings, this may lead the auditor to conclude that going concern is a risk area. All these factors are considered by the auditor and may impact upon the audit procedures.

Industry, Regulatory and Other External Factors, including the Applicable Accounting Framework The auditor should gain an understanding of the industry and regulatory environment in which the entity operates in order to assess the risk of material misstatement as a result of external factors. The areas which the auditor should consider are as follows:

- industry conditions affecting the entity, such as the competitive environment, supplier and customer relationships, technological considerations related to its products, and energy supply and cost;
- the entity's regulatory environment including the applicable accounting principles and industry-specific practices, the type and extent of regulatory oversight, the legal and political environment, including taxation and trade issues and government policies, and environmental requirements; and
- general economic conditions, interest rates, availability of financing, inflation rates, etc.

These factors will enable the auditor to identify external risks that may have an impact on the financial statements. For example, knowledge of the regulatory environment will allow the auditor to understand if the company is complying with applicable laws and regulations as non-compliance may result in a material misstatement, i.e. provisions required as a result of a legal claim against the entity for non-compliance or the company's ability to continue as a going concern as a result of this non-compliance.

Objectives, Strategies, and Related Business Risks The auditor should gain an understanding of the business strategies and risks to enable evaluation of whether the future plans and strategy may result in potential misstatement and therefore be regarded as an audit risk. In gaining this understanding, the auditor should consider:

- the objectives or overall plans for the entity (defined by those charged with governance) to address business risks;
- strategies (operational approaches set by management to achieve these objectives);
- the related business risks (events, conditions, circumstances or actions that could adversely affect the entity's ability to achieve its objectives and execute its strategies, including the risk of a material financial statement misstatement).

These risks may be related to industry developments; new products and services (e.g. increased product liability risks); business expansion; new accounting requirements; financing requirements (current or future); and use of information technology.

In gaining an understanding of the business strategies and risks, the auditor is able to determine if such risks will impact the financial statements. For example, if the company has an aggressive growth strategy to enter into new markets, the auditor will consider if this may lead to a risk of material misstatement. This may result in additional audit work to ensure that all relevant laws and regulations in the new markets have been complied with.

Measurement and Review of Financial Performance The auditor should gain an understanding of the performance of the business in order to assess audit risks. This is particularly relevant in relation to going concern considerations at the planning stage. Key considerations by the auditor should include:
- key ratios, operating statistics and performance indicators (financial and non-financial);
- budgets, variance analysis, segment information and divisional, departmental, and other level performance reports;
- comparison of performance with peers; and
- employee performance measures.

Review of financial performance is a key method to understand the entity and identify any potential risks of material misstatement. For example, if the auditor compares revenue year on year in an entity and there is an unexpected variance, this may indicate that there is an error in the revenue calculation and therefore potential misstatement. This will then result in audit procedures specifically designed to address this potential risk. Furthermore, if the auditor identifies at the planning stage that there may be a going concern risk, they will carry out additional testing on forecasts and budgets to determine if the going concern concept is acceptable.

The Five Components of Internal Control Finally, the auditor must also understand the internal control system within the entity to determine the risk of material misstatement. By understanding how effective the controls are operating, the auditor can determine both the level of testing and the type of testing required, i.e. tests of control or tests of detail. This is further discussed in **Section 3.4.2.**

In obtaining this understanding of the entity and its environment as discussed in the above five points, the auditor will use a variety of audit procedures as follows:
- discussion with management and others within the entity;
- analytical procedures;
- observation and inspection; and
- discussions among the audit team.

Each of these audit procedures is discussed below.

3.4.1.1 *Discussion with Management and Others within the Entity*

At the planning stage, the audit team should engage in discussions with management and/or those charged with governance in order to obtain an understanding of the entity. During the course of these discussions, the audit team often learns about plans and policies that might affect the financial statements, items which relate to the business and the industry in which it operates, and about important legal and regulatory matters. Through these interviews and discussions, the audit team can quickly obtain an understanding of the entity, its organisation and operating characteristics to assess risk.

However, to obtain additional information in order to identify risks of material misstatements, it is often appropriate to interview others who are knowledgeable about the client's operations, its internal controls, and the manner in which such functions and controls are carried out. Personnel to interview in this context may include internal audit personnel, finance department personnel and in-house legal personnel, each of which is now discussed.

Internal Audit Personnel These personnel may provide information about internal audit procedures performed during the year relating to the design and effectiveness of the entity's internal control and whether management has satisfactorily responded to findings from those procedures. This information will assist the auditor in assessing the operating effectiveness of the internal control system; if they can potentially rely on the work carried out by internal audit; or if they have to carry out additional testing.

Finance Department Personnel Employees involved in initiating, processing or recording complex or unusual transactions, may help the auditor to evaluate the appropriateness of the selection and application of certain accounting policies. Discussion with these individuals will enhance the auditor's understanding of the basis of transactions before concluding if they have been accounted for correctly, or may indicate a risk of material misstatement.

In-house Legal Personnel In-house legal personnel may provide information about litigation, compliance with laws and regulations, knowledge of fraud or suspected fraud affecting the entity, and so forth. This will assist the auditor in determining the risk of fraud and undisclosed liabilities in relation to legal provisions. For example, these discussions may result in greater emphasis on review of compliance with laws and regulations if the legal personnel have indicated that the entity is often non-compliant.

In these planning discussions with management and/or those charged with governance and others within the entity, the possibility of misstatement due to fraud will form a large part of the discussions. As noted in ISA 240 (UK and Ireland) *The Auditor's Responsibilities Relating to Fraud in an Audit of Financial Statements*:

> "When performing risk assessment procedures and related activities to obtain an understanding of the entity and its environment, including the entity's internal control ... the auditor shall perform ... procedures ... to obtain information for use in identifying the risks of material misstatement due to fraud" (ISA 240, para. 16).

Therefore, in the planning discussions with management, the auditor should also obtain the following information:

- Management's assessment of the risk that the financial statements may be materially misstated due to fraud, and the frequency of these assessments. For example, do they adopt a highly structured approach, or are they very weak in assessing the risk of fraud. The latter will result in the auditor applying a higher level of professional scepticism while carrying out the procedures.
- Management's process for identifying and responding to the risks of fraud in the entity. For example, a robust system for responding to fraud risk will reduce audit risk in this area.
- Management's communication, if any, to those charged with governance regarding policies and procedures surrounding fraud assessment.
- Management's communication, if any, to employees regarding its views on business practices and ethical behaviour. An auditor will get a strong sense from interviews with others within the entity as to how the tone from the top has permeated throughout the organisation.
- Whether internal audit personnel, if any, have knowledge of any actual, suspected or alleged fraud affecting the entity.

3.4.1.2 Analytical Procedures

Analytical procedures performed during the planning phase of the audit are used to identify unusual changes in the financial statements, absence of expected changes, and specific risks. They are required on all audits. During the planning stage, analytical procedures are usually focused on account balances aggregated at the financial statement level and relationships between account balances. Because the analytical procedures at this stage generally use data aggregated at a high level, the results of those procedures provide only a broad initial indication about whether a material misstatement of the financial statements may exist. However, they are helpful in identifying areas where audit work should be focused.

Analytical procedures at a planning stage can be explained in four phases, expectation, identification, investigation and evaluation, each of which is now explained.

Phase 1 Expectation Prior to commencing any analytical procedures, the audit team must have an expectation with which to compare fluctuations and trends. At the planning stage, this expectation will arise from their knowledge of the business and the industry in which the client operates. Expectations may also be derived from discussions with management.

Phase 2 Identification In performing the analytical procedures, the auditor will identify unusual trends and fluctuations from the prior year which are not in line with expectations. For example, from discussions with management, say the auditor's understanding was that staff numbers have not changed and staff costs should be similar to prior year. However, in preliminary analytical review, the auditor notes that staff costs have increased by 10% on prior year, this may indicate that the salary costs are misstated and therefore require further investigation during audit fieldwork.

Phase 3 Investigation For those fluctuations identified, the audit team considers the possible explanations for the differences.

Phase 4 Evaluation The evaluation stage involves obtaining information and explanations for the fluctuations, either self-generated within the audit team or through discussion with management. The extent of the evaluation depends on the type of analytical procedures being performed. During the risk assessment phase, auditors generally perform little, if any, follow-up work to evaluate an explanation. Instead, consistent with ISA 315, auditors typically use planning analytical procedures to improve their understanding of the client's business and to identify potential misstatements to allow them to develop the audit plan for the engagement.

For example, if analytical procedures performed on creditors during audit planning indicated the total creditor balance was higher than expected, the auditor would most likely adjust the audit plan by increasing the number of audit tests performed on creditors and inventory or assigning more experienced personnel to the audit of creditors.

Example 3.2 below illustrates the four phases of analytical review at the planning stage.

EXAMPLE 3.2: ANALYTICAL REVIEW AT THE PLANNING STAGE

Expectation	Identification	Investigation	Evaluation
The auditor has determined that the company's trading has declined in the current year and, as a result of initial discussions with management, finds out that management has reduced staff numbers by 15%. Staff costs are expected to be less this year than in the prior year.	Analytical review procedures demonstrate that salary costs are slightly higher than the prior year.	While staff numbers have decreased, the auditor finds that salary costs include redundancy costs.	The redundancy costs would explain why salary costs are higher than prior year and therefore does not pose a high risk of material misstatement. However, the audit team would include audit procedures that respond to the risk at the assertion level, e.g. occurrence and completeness of redundancy costs.

Expectation	Identification	Investigation	Evaluation
Following a discussion with management, the auditor determines that a number of the entity's clients are struggling to pay their invoices. Doubtful debt provisions should be higher.	Analytical procedures demonstrate that debtor days have increased by 30% and there does not appear to be any doubtful-debt provision.	In the current climate, as well as knowledge of the difficulties the clients are facing regarding payment by customers, the lack of a doubtful-debt provision may result in debtors being materially overstated in the financial statements.	Recoverability of debtors is an audit risk and the audit programme would include further audit procedures on the recoverability of debtors.

3.4.1.3 Observation and Inspection

Observation and inspection may support discussion with management and others, as discussed in **Section 3.4.1.1**, as it can be utilised to corroborate items discussed. Furthermore, it will also provide information about the entity and its environment. Examples of such audit procedures include observation and inspection of:

- the entity's operations, premises and plant facilities which will support the understanding of the entity as gained in discussions with management, e.g. the auditor may use a site visit to corroborate the fact that management invested in new equipment during the year as part of a planned expansion;
- internal documents such as business plans and internal control manuals. For example, the auditor may review internal control manuals to corroborate the internal control processes communicated by management;
- reports prepared by management, e.g. management accounts. For example, the auditor may review management accounts to corroborate the monthly gross margin that management indicated has increased steadily throughout the year;
- minutes of management meetings and board meetings, e.g. the auditor may review minutes to back-up the indication by management that there were slow paying debtors during the year and they agreed to provide for the debt.

3.4.1.4 Discussions among the Audit Team

The culmination of the risk assessment process is the meeting of the audit team to discuss the risk assessments. It allows sharing of knowledge with those who have carried out risk assessment procedures, as well as the knowledge of the members of the engagement team who have previously been involved in the audit.

Furthermore, ISA 240 requires these discussions to place particular emphasis on how and where the entity's financial statements may be susceptible to material misstatement due to fraud. (In **Chapter 4,** we discuss ISA 240 and the auditor's responsibilities in more detail.)

To look at this practically, **Example 3.3** provides a sample memo that includes extracts from an audit team meeting at the risk assessment stage.

EXAMPLE 3.3: MEMORANDUM DOCUMENTING AUDIT TEAM DISCUSSIONS AT PLANNING STAGE

MEMORANDUM

Discussions among the audit team at planning stage

To   Audit File – planning section
Date   12 February 2012
From   Audit Manager

A planning meeting with the engagement team was held on 12 February 2012. The following were in attendance:

Partner A   Engagement Partner
Manager B   Engagement Manager
In-charge C   In-charge Accountant

Areas discussed:

(a) **How and where the financial statements are susceptible to material misstatement due to errors or fraud. (This is discussed below under (f).)**

(b) **How IT processing may introduce specific risks relating to fraud or error occurring in the financial statements.**

The IT system in use by the company has not been a cause for concern in the past and there have been no instances of errors. No changes have been made to this system during the current year and therefore we do not believe that there are any specific risks.

The Directors are also closely involved in the day-to-day running of the company and would be aware of any discrepancies/anomalies in reported results compared to expectations.

(c) **How fair value measurements could result in material misstatements in the financial statements.**

There is no fair value accounting in this company.

(d) **Whether management override of internal control is a significant risk.**

Management override is possible in this system. However, we do not believe this to be a significant risk as a number of the directors are involved in running the business and, in a sense, oversee each other. Also, the actual accounts are compiled by the financial controller whose role does not include selling the product. The directors would only access the Sage Line 50 system for the purpose of reviewing the accounts.

However, we will carry out significant journal testing to assess any potential system over-rides.

(e) Whether contracts or agreements may contain embedded derivatives and, if so, the areas affected.

No embedded derivatives in place.

(f) How management could perpetrate and conceal fraudulent financial reporting.

First, there have been no instances of this in the past. We considered the following inherent risk factors under this heading:

- There is no domination of management by a single person or small group. All directors effectively oversee each other's work as results are monitored on a monthly basis.
- There is no high turnover of management – the directors have been in place for a significant number of years and this is the Financial Controller's second year-end.
- No complex accounting policies or treatments are adopted.
- Management does not display a significant disregard for regulatory authorities.
- There is no history of 'cut-off' issues.

Secondly, the audit procedures adopted to ensure that there is no risk of a material misstatement arising from fraudulent financial reporting are as follows:

- Review of journal entries and testing for appropriate authorisation and support.
- Review of Board minutes of review of results noting any issues of concern regarding performance raised by the Board.

(g) How assets of the entity could be misappropriated.

The most significant area subject to misappropriation would be fixed assets and debtors.

There are no individual fixed assets of a high value that would be an attractive asset for staff to misappropriate and sell. Therefore, we do not believe this to be a significant risk.

The cash receipts on debtors could be subject to misappropriation. However, the credit controller has close involvement in all outstanding amounts and most would be for repeat customers; thus, it would be difficult/too obvious for a staff member to misappropriate these proceeds.

(h) How journal entries (standard and non-standard) and other adjustments (eliminations, reclassifications and report combinations) could be used to manipulate the financial reporting process and override controls.

There has not been a history of non-routine transactions in the company. Journal entries will be reviewed as part of our audit procedures to ensure that these were correctly authorised, posted by an appropriate individual, and have appropriate support/explanations at all sites.

(i) Results of discussions with management, those charged with governance, and internal auditors, if any, regarding the existence or suspicion of fraud.

The Board of Directors are not aware of any instances of fraud.

(j) Whether others within the entity may be able to provide additional information or corroborate information gleaned in other discussions regarding fraud.

We have discussed this issue with Joe Bloggs, Financial Controller, and he is not aware of any issues of fraud.

Conclusion While we do not believe that the members of the management team possess the attitude, characteristics and ethical values that would allow them to knowingly and intentionally commit a fraudulent act, we are aware of the importance of maintaining a questioning mind and exercising professional scepticism throughout the audit. The engagement team has adequate knowledge of the business and its significant accounting cycles to be able to determine risk areas.

The understanding obtained by the audit team during this will be utilised to conclude if risks are evident and how they will be responded to, that is, what audit tests will be designed to address these risks. This is discussed below in **Section 3.4.3**.

3.4.2 Understanding Internal Controls

Internal control is a process effected by an entity's management, employees, other personnel and those charged with governance, and one that is designed to achieve three objectives:
- effective and efficient operations;
- reliable financial reporting; and
- compliance with laws and regulations.

Establishing and maintaining effective internal controls is an important management responsibility and requires regular monitoring by management to ensure that they are operating as intended and appropriately modified as needed.

An understanding of internal control assists the auditor in identifying potential misstatements which may occur due to weak controls which will then impact upon the design, nature, timing and extent of procedures.

ISA 315 notes the auditor's responsibilities in relation to internal control. These are covered in great detail in the standard at paragraphs A69–A103, however, they have been summarised in **Table 3.4** below:

TABLE 3.4: AUDITOR'S RESPONSIBILITIES AND EXAMPLES OF AUDITOR'S CONSIDERATIONS IN RELATION TO INTERNAL CONTROL

Auditor's Responsibilities	Auditor's Considerations
To obtain an understanding of the **control environment**	• Does management communicate and enforce integrity and ethical values? • Does management ensure that employees are competent to perform tasks, therefore reducing the risk of fraud and error? • Do those charged with governance scrutinise the internal control environment and ask questions as to its activities? Do they take appropriate action regarding any weaknesses in the internal control environment? • What is management's attitude towards risks and financial reporting? Do those charged with governance adopt conservative or aggressive accounting policies? • What is the entity's organisational structure? Is it suitably structured to ensure that a strong control environment exists? For example, if there are numerous locations, how is the internal control environment at each location monitored and maintained? • Are roles adequately assigned authorisation and responsibility? Are there approval levels in place for orders over a certain value? • Are there policies and procedures in place to ensure that competent people are recruited?
To obtain an understanding of the entity's **risk assessment process**	• How does management identify risks relevant to the financial reporting objectives? • If risks are identified, how do they estimate the significance of those risks? • How do they assess the likelihood of their occurrence? • How does management decide on actions to address those risks?

To obtain an understanding of the **financial reporting information system**, including the related business processes	• How are transactions initiated, recorded, processed, corrected as necessary, transferred to the general ledger and reported in the financial statements? • How are the above processes recorded in the accounting records? Is it automated or in paper form? • What is the financial reporting process used to prepare the financial statements? How are significant accounting policies and estimates agreed upon? • What are the controls surrounding non-standard journal entries?
To obtain an understanding of the **control activities relevant to the audit***	• Authorisation of transactions, e.g. what level of authorisation is permitted to purchase fixed assets? • Information processing, e.g. what are the controls surrounding the accuracy of inputting of the information? Are there any review processes? • Physical controls – what is the security surrounding fixed assets? Are they easily misappropriated? • Segregation of duties – are there different employees ordering fixed assets and paying for fixed assets? If not, is there a heightened risk of fraud?
An understanding of how the entity **monitors financial reporting** and initiates remedial actions in its controls	• How does the entity monitor activities? • Are there managerial levels reviewing reports on a regular basis for discrepancies? • Is there an internal audit function which monitors control activities?

* Control activities relevant to the audit will be at least those that relate to significant risks (**Section 3.4.5** below discusses when the auditor may define a risk as significant) and those that need to be tested because substantive tests alone will not provide sufficient appropriate audit evidence (ISA 315, paras. 29 and 30). They also include those that, in the judgement of the auditor, are relevant (e.g. control activities that address the areas where the auditor considers that the risk of error might be higher than other areas, but not necessarily a significant risk of material misstatement).

By understanding internal controls, the auditor can conclude as to what level of risk is present regarding material misstatement of the financial statements. All the considerations above in **Table 3.4** will allow the auditor to conclude if the level of control risk is high, and will require significant substantive testing, or the level of control risk is low and therefore the auditor can carry out controls testing.

The risks identified at this stage, along with the risks identified when the auditor is gaining an understanding of the entity and its environment, are then addressed by planning specific audit tests as discussed below in **Section 3.4.3**.

3.4.3 Relate the Identified Risks to Assertion Level and Financial Statement Level

Once the auditor has gained an understanding of the entity and its environment, including the internal control function, in line with ISA 315 the auditor is then required to assess the risks of material misstatement at:
- the financial statement level (risks that may affect several assertions); and
- the assertion level for classes of transactions, account balances and disclosures (risks that typically only affect a single assertion).

This assessment will provide a basis for designing and performing further audit procedures.

Example 3.4 shows risks at both the financial statement and assertion level.

EXAMPLE 3.4: RISKS AT ASSERTION LEVEL AND FINANCIAL STATEMENT LEVEL

Risk	Financial Statement Level or Assertion Level	Explanation
Changes in key personnel in the accounting department	Financial statement level	Change in key members of the accounting team may result in errors in the financial statements as the new members of staff may not understand the accounting systems, processes and controls sufficiently to process transactions correctly. This becomes a risk that relates more pervasively to the financial statements as a whole and potentially affects many assertions.

Significant transactions with related parties	Assertion level	Where an entity has significant related party transactions, the auditor can link this directly to the _completeness_ assertion; therefore audit tests will specifically be designed to target completeness of related party transactions.
Numerous customers are trading in difficult times and have breached their credit terms	Assertion level	Recoverability of debtors can be specifically linked to the _valuation_ assertion and specific audit tests designed to target this risk area.
Risk assessment indicated a weak control environment	Financial statement level	A weak control environment cannot be linked to one specific assertion, but relates more pervasively to the financial statements as a whole and potentially affects many assertions.

Once the auditor links the risk to assertion level or financial statement level, they must consider if it could result in material misstatement, and if so, develop audit tests to address the risk. This is discussed in **Section 3.4.4** below.

3.4.4 Consider if the Risks could Result in a Material Misstatement

When financial-statement-level risks are identified, they could potentially affect many assertions, so the auditor must carefully consider where these risks could manifest themselves, then consider the likelihood of misstatement, and whether the potential misstatement is of such magnitude that it could result in a material misstatement. The response for pervasive risks may not require a response in the audit plan, but rather an overall response in the audit strategy (as discussed in **Section 3.2**), such as using more experienced team members.

Assertion level risks that are more likely to be the cause of a material misstatement are further evaluated in order to understand whether:
• internal controls that address the risk have been established by the client;
• the controls are designed effectively;
• the controls are implemented; and
• the operating effectiveness of controls will be tested.

The answers to these questions will dictate the level of testing that is carried out. If, e.g. the completeness of revenue was identified as an assertion level risk but the audit team concluded that the entity had designed and implemented controls to address that risk (the operating effectiveness of which could be tested), then the audit testing will be largely tests of controls. However, if it was concluded that controls were not sufficient in this area, the audit testing would be largely substantive.

In identifying risks, the auditor should also consider if any of the risks are regarded as 'significant' as this impacts audit testing and communication of such risks. This is discussed in **Section 3.4.5** below.

3.4.5 Significant Risks

ISA 315 also requires the auditor to determine whether any of the identified risks are significant risks. Significant risks are identified (as is the assessed risk of material misstatement) that, in the auditor's judgement, require special audit consideration. Significant risks can often relate to significant non-routine transactions or judgemental matters. For example, the development of an accounting estimate may depend on management's judgement of the likelihood or otherwise of an event occurring (e.g. the outcome of pending litigation). Non-routine transactions are those that are unusual or infrequent for that entity, due to either its size or nature, e.g. a major redundancy programme.

When responding to significant risks, the auditor will develop audit tests specifically responsive to that risk. Responding to risks is discussed below in **Section 3.5**.

3.5 RESPONDING TO ASSESSED RISKS

In responding to assessed risks, we will look at financial-statement-level and assertion-level risks separately.

3.5.1 Financial Statement Level Risks

As noted above, financial statement risks affect the audit as a whole and cannot be linked to one specific assertion. Therefore, when addressing financial-statement-level risks, the auditor adopts procedures that will address the audit as a whole, rather than specific assertions. Examples of these procedures could be:
- adding more experienced team members to reduce the risk of not detecting potential misstatements. This may be appropriate if the finance team is deemed not to have sufficient experience, or has undergone significant changes.
- applying additional professional scepticism as the work progresses, i.e. asking more questions and always corroborating management's explanations. This may be appropriate if there is a higher fraud risk.

- providing additional review, e.g. an independent reviewer to reduce the risk of not detecting a potential error. This may be appropriate to compensate for a weak finance team.
- varying the nature and timing of the procedures, e.g. performing a stock count two months before the year end, or calling debtors to circularise rather than issuing letters. These procedures may be appropriate when there is a risk of fraud and the auditor suspects that management is manipulating the audit test results as they can predict the work that would be carried out.
- reconsidering continuance if there was considerable doubt over the integrity of management and/or those charged with governance.

3.5.2 Assertion Level Risks

In responding to risks at the assertion level, the auditor considers what level of audit testing is required, either by using tests of control, substantive testing, or a combination of both. In designing audit procedures to be performed, the auditor will consider:

- The significance of the risk, i.e. is the risk associated with a material transaction class or account balance in the financial statements. For example, if the transaction is below materiality, the level of testing to address the risk would be minimal compared with the testing required if the transaction class or account balance was material.
- The likelihood that a material misstatement will occur. For example, if the assertion level risk was the completeness of related party transactions, but there were minimal volumes of related party transactions during the year, the likelihood of a material misstatement occurring is low and therefore will impact upon the level of testing.
- Whether there are controls operating effectively in relation to the risk. For example, if there are controls operating effectively that relate to an assertion level risk, the auditor would develop tests of control, as opposed to substantive testing, to address the risk.

As a result of these considerations, the auditor will develop audit tests to address the risks. These audit tests will either be tests of control or substantive testing which are both addressed in detail in **Sections 3.5.2.1** and **3.5.2.2** below.

3.5.2.1 *Tests of Control*

Tests of control are used at the assertion level when the auditor has concluded in the risk assessment process that the relevant controls have been implemented and are expected to be operating effectively. Tests of controls can be used to significantly decrease substantive testing. However, if, in the risk assessment process, the auditor concluded that the entity has deficiencies in the control environment, there may be less scope to rely on the operating effectiveness of controls, and the auditor would obtain more extensive audit evidence from substantive procedures.

For example, the cash balance was identified as a risk area due to the fact that management told the auditor they had used their overdraft facility a couple of times during the year because of late lodgements. In the risk assessment process, the auditor identified controls that were likely to prevent cash balance being incorrect at the year end. The auditor carries out tests of control, examples of which might be:

- inspecting monthly bank reconciliations and confirming that they are being correctly prepared; and
- inspecting reconciliations for evidence of review by the account manager.

If the results of these tests are positive, the auditor can rely on the operating effectiveness of the controls and perform limited substantive tests.

In designing these tests of controls, there are a number of considerations the auditor should take into account:

- the *nature* of the tests of controls i.e. what *type* of test. For example, inquiry alone will not sufficiently test the operating effectiveness of bank reconciliation controls; therefore, the auditor should apply inquiry, combined with inspection or re-performance.
- the *extent* of the tests of controls i.e. how detailed will the test be or how frequently will the test be performed. For example, if the auditor was also carrying out substantive tests on the transaction cycle, the tests of control will be to a lesser extent; or, if the control is carried out on a frequent basis by the entity, how will that impact upon the extent of testing?
- the *timing* of tests of controls i.e. tests of control should obtain evidence on how the control performed throughout the year, and not just at a particular point in time, e.g. at the year-end. Therefore, the tests of control should be performed at relevant times during the period, as appropriate.

If the testing of these controls results in the discovery of deviations, the auditor needs to make specific enquiries to understand these matters and their potential consequences and determine:

1. if the tests of controls that have been performed provide an appropriate basis for reliance on the operating effectiveness of controls;
2. if additional tests of controls are necessary; and
3. if the operating effectiveness of controls cannot be relied upon and therefore additional substantive procedures are required to address the risks.

Tests of control are discussed in more detail in **Chapter 5**.

3.5.2.2 *Substantive Procedures*

Substantive procedures are performed when the auditor cannot rely on the operating effectiveness of controls. Furthermore, in accordance with ISA 330 (UK and Ireland) *The Auditor's Responses to Assessed Risks* ('ISA 330'), irrespective of the assessed risks of material misstatement, the auditor must design and perform substantive procedures for each material class of transaction, account balance and disclosure. This is due to the fact that:

- the auditor's assessment of risk is judgemental and so may not identify all the risks of material misstatement; and
- there are inherent limitations to internal control, such as management override.

Using the example in **Section 3.5.2.1** in relation to audit procedures for the cash balance, examples of substantive testing could be:

- obtaining the year-end bank statement and performing a reconciliation to the closing balance per financial statements and investigating any variances; and
- obtaining a bank confirmation letter to confirm the year-end bank balance recorded in the bank reconciliation.

In designing substantive tests, the auditor needs to consider the following:

- the *nature* of the substantive tests, e.g. substantive analytical procedures or tests of detail, or a combination of both (both of these tests are discussed in **Chapter 6**)
- the *extent* of the substantive tests, e.g. extract a sample of the debtors' year end balances to circularise, or circularise the full population;
- the *timing* of the substantive tests, e.g. the majority of substantive testing is carried out subsequent to the year-end. However, if the auditor is planning on performing substantive tests at a stock count at the client's premises, they should attend the year-end stock count. Alternatively, they could attend a stock count before the year-end and perform roll-forward procedures after the year-end.

Substantive tests are discussed in more detail in **Chapter 6**.

As well as developing audit tests to address the risks identified, the auditor must also consider the presentation and disclosure of the financial statements and assess if they are presented in line with their understanding and applicable law. This is discussed in **Section 3.5.2.3** below.

3.5.2.3 Adequacy of Presentation and Disclosure

After the controls and substantive procedures have been performed, the auditor must also consider the appropriateness of the overall presentation of the financial statements. This involves reviewing the financial statements and ensuring that they are presented in a manner that reflects the appropriate classification and description of the financial information, and the form, arrangement, and content of the financial statements and their notes. This includes an assessment as to whether they are presented in line with the financial reporting framework and company law.

In carrying out the audit tests discussed in this section, the auditor must ensure that they continually evaluate the sufficiency and appropriateness of the audit evidence utilised in the audit procedures to address the risks. This is discussed below in **Section 3.5.2.4**.

3.5.2.4 Evaluating the Sufficiency and Appropriateness of Audit Evidence

Based on the audit procedures performed and audit evidence obtained, the auditor concludes if the financial statements contain material misstatements and, if so, what impact this will have on the audit report.

If the auditor does not obtain sufficient audit evidence to conclude that an assertion is free from material misstatement, they should first obtain additional audit evidence by carrying out more procedures.

If the auditor is still unable to obtain sufficient appropriate audit evidence, the auditor is required to express a qualified opinion or disclaim an opinion. (See **Chapter 8** which covers audit reports.)

Consideration of the sufficiency and appropriateness of audit evidence is discussed in detail in **Section 7.3** of this text.

Finally in responding to assertion level risks, the auditor must ensure that they document the risks, responses to risks and conclusions of audit procedures adequately. This is discussed in **Section 3.5.2.5** below.

3.5.2.5 Documentation

As per the requirements of ISA 330, the auditor must include in the audit documentation:
- the responses to address the risks which were assessed during the risk assessment phase;
- the nature, timing and extent of audit procedures to be performed during the audit in response to the assessed risks;
- how the audit procedures link to the assessed risks and address the risks; and
- the results and conclusions of audit procedures which will ultimately feed into the audit opinion.

3.6 COMMUNICATION WITH THOSE CHARGED WITH GOVERNANCE

There are a number of requirements in the auditing standards regarding the auditor's responsibility to communicate certain matters to those charged with governance and management. The primary auditing standards that address communication are ISA 260 (UK and Ireland) *Communication With Those Charged With Governance* ('ISA 260') and ISA 265 (UK and Ireland) *Communicating Deficiencies in Internal Control to Those Charged with Governance and Management*[2] ('ISA 265').

ISA 260 includes requirements for communication with those charged with governance at the planning stage as follows:
- the auditor's responsibilities, including forming and expressing an opinion on the financial statements which have been prepared by management – this is usually communicated via an engagement letter (see **Chapter 2**, **Example 2.1**);

---

[2] Other communication requirements can be found in ISA 210, ISA 240, ISA 250, ISA 450, ISA 505, ISA 510, ISA 550, ISA 560, ISA 570, ISA 600, ISA 705, ISA 706, ISA 710 and ISA 720.

- the planned scope and timing of the audit, which may include how the auditor proposes to address significant risks, the auditor's approach to internal control and the application of materiality – this is usually communicated via a planning meeting or audit strategy document which would take place at the risk assessment stage; and
- for listed entities, the auditor also needs to communicate that all members of the engagement team, and member firms, where appropriate, have complied with relevant ethical and independence requirements – this is usually communicated via a planning meeting or audit strategy document.

ISA 260 and ISA 265 also include a number of requirements for communication at the completion stage of the audit and those are discussed in greater detail in **Chapter 7**.

3.7 CONCLUSION

Planning an audit is vitally important to ensure that the audit will be performed in an effective manner, and will ensure that the auditor can give an opinion on whether the financial statements are free from material misstatement due to fraud or error.

SUMMARY OF LEARNING OBJECTIVES

Learning Objective 1 To gain a detailed understanding of the concept of developing an audit strategy and audit plan in line with ISA 300 (UK and Ireland) *Planning an Audit of Financial Statements*

An audit strategy and plan are developed by the auditor to ensure that the audit is performed in an effective and efficient manner. The audit strategy is where the auditor ascertains the nature, timing and extent of *resources* necessary to perform the engagement and the audit plan is where the auditor sets out the *detailed procedures* required.

Learning Objective 2 To be able to calculate materiality and understand its purpose in line with ISA 320 (UK and Ireland) *Materiality in Planning and Performing an Audit*

The auditor is required to determine materiality at the planning stage of an audit as a basis for making judgements on identifying and assessing the risk of material misstatement; determining the nature, timing and extent of audit procedures; and evaluating the effect of uncorrected misstatements. Materiality is utilised at all stages of the audit.

Learning Objective 3 To be able to execute the risk assessment stage of an audit as required under ISA 315 (UK and Ireland) *Identifying and Assessing the Risks of Material Misstatement Through Understanding of the Entity and Its Environment*

Risk assessment procedures are performed to understand the entity and its internal control to allow the auditor to identify the risks that could cause the financial statements to be materially misstated, whether due to error or fraud.

Learning Objective 4 To develop appropriate responses to assessed risks in line with ISA 330 (UK and Ireland) *The Auditor's Responses to Assessed Risks*

Once the auditor performs risk assessment procedures, they then develop audit procedures to address these risks both at a financial statement level and assertion level. These audit procedures will allow the auditor to form an opinion as to whether the financial statements are free from material misstatement.

Learning Objective 5 To understand the auditor's responsibilities to communicate with those charged with governance at the planning stage as required by ISA 260 (UK and Ireland) *Communication With Those Charged With Governance*

The auditor has a responsibility to communicate the outcome of the risk assessment stage to those charged with governance, indicating the planned scope and timing of the audit, how the auditor proposes to address the significant risks, the auditor's approach to internal control and the application of materiality.

QUESTIONS

In each of the scenarios presented in the questions below, there is an issue/(s) which needs to be addressed by the auditor (an indicator) in relation to planning activities. You should read the questions and attempt to address the issues relating to planning activities.

(See **Appendix One** for Suggested Solutions to Review Questions.)

Review Questions

Question 3.1 (Based on Chartered Accountants Ireland, FAE Autumn 2011, Simulation 2)

Progressive Construction Limited

You are an Audit Manager with Foster, Freeman & Fitzgerald, Chartered Accountants and Registered Auditors. One of the Audit Partners has asked you to meet with him to discuss one of the firm's clients, Progressive Construction Ltd (Progressive Construction). The previous Audit Manager for this client has recently left the firm and the Partner, Sean Fitzgerald, needs some assistance in dealing with a difficult situation which has arisen with Progressive Construction.

He has received a letter from a legal firm (Corporate Solicitors) acting on behalf of the shareholders of Progressive Construction (reproduced at Appendix 1) and is preparing for a meeting with a representative from the legal firm. He requests that you prepare a Memo setting out what the firm needs to be concerned about in the context of the fraud which has been uncovered; particularly our responsibilities under auditing standards, the specific enquiries and procedures we ought to have performed and the specific aspects of our work on the 2009 audit that we should critically assess in preparation for the meeting with Corporate Solicitors.

Notwithstanding the issue above, the planning process for next year's audit is about to start and you have been reviewing the minutes of a planning meeting between your predecessor and the Financial Director of Progressive Construction (see Appendix 2). You are due to meet with Sean and the Audit Team next week for an audit planning meeting and need to draft an agenda, including the significant risks for this year's audit and any other general planning matters you would typically discuss at a planning meeting. Sean has also asked you to assess the information gleaned from the planning meeting with the client and to indicate any further work we should do or information we should obtain to identify risks and develop the audit plan.

APPENDIX 1

Corporate Solicitors
8 High Street
Dublin

18 October 2010

Foster, Freeman & Fitzgerald
Chartered Accountants
141 Low Street
Dublin

Dear Sirs

Progressive Construction Ltd

We act for the shareholders of the above company and wish to request a meeting with the Audit Partner responsible for the company's audit.

As you may be aware the company has been experiencing significant cash flow difficulties over the past few months largely as a result of losses incurred on the Castleford Shopping Centre project which formed part of the company's work-in-progress balance at 31 December 2009.

Following an investigation by the company's Board, it transpired that correspondence regarding a legal claim against the company being dealt with by the company's solicitors had been suppressed by one of the Quantity Surveyors and the company's Commercial Director, resulting in a failure to recognise a significant provision for losses in the Financial Statements for the year ended 31 December 2009.

The Board believes that this was driven by a desire to maintain the gross margin on the contract on which both individuals' bonuses were paid. Both the Quantity Surveyor in question and the Commercial Director have subsequently been dismissed.

The shareholders are concerned that the failure to recognise this provision for losses was not identified during the audit conducted by your firm for the year ended 31 December 2009 and have engaged us to explore this as a matter of urgency.

We should be obliged if you could make contact with our office to set up a meeting at a mutually convenient time.

Yours faithfully

James Dolan

James Dolan
for Corporate Solicitors

Appendix 2

Progressive Construction Ltd
Client Planning Meeting
for the Year Ended 31 December 2010

Date: 25 October 2010

In attendance:

James O'Rourke	Financial Director, Progressive Construction Ltd	JOR
Mary Carroll	Audit Manager, Foster, Freeman & Fitzgerald	MC

JOR welcomed MC and presented a copy of the company's September management accounts *(not illustrated here)*. These showed a profit of €/£12.2m before exceptional costs of €/£30m resulting from the Castleford Shopping Centre contract.

JOR indicated that the majority of the company's contracts had been performing well during the year and realising at least their budgeted margins. He also noted that work-in-progress balances at the year-end would be significantly lower than in previous years, simply as a result of the timing of contracts – a number of the current contracts would reach final account stage by then and a number of new contracts were not due to commence until January 2011.

JOR stated that the majority of the cash for the contracts should also be received by the year end although he was concerned with the €/£4.8m balance owed by Burgerway Restaurants, the rapidly expanding fast food company. MC indicated that she had heard that Burgerway was experiencing financial difficulties following some adverse press coverage regarding food hygiene in some of its restaurants.

MC asked about the difficulties surrounding the Castleford Shopping Centre contract. JOR said that this was causing real problems as the payment of the settlement awarded following the legal case had caused significant cash flow difficulties. Whilst the company has bank facilities in place until February 2012, he indicated that they were at risk of breaching one of their banking covenants and that the company's working capital facilities were extremely stretched at present.

MC enquired as to the bank's current position. JOR replied that he had not specifically discussed the current issues with the bank but that they had been supportive in the past when the company was seeking funds for expansion.

MC thanked JOR for his time and indicated that she would be in touch soon regarding the timing of the audit.

Question 3.2 (Based on Chartered Accountants Ireland, FAE Autumn 2011, Simulation 3)

RX Pharma

You are the Audit Manager of RX Pharmaceuticals Ltd (RX), a well-established, international, pharmaceutical company specialising in both contract manufacture of pharmaceutical products and the provision of services in connection with clinical trials.

It is February 2011 and the audit for the year ended 31 December 2010 is well underway. You have received a draft Income Statement from the client (Appendix A) and are currently focusing on the audit of revenue. You have just received a phone call from a member of the audit team who is auditing revenue for the first time and would like to meet with you to discuss the following:
1. the risks relating to revenue for RX;
2. the appropriate tests of controls and tests of details to perform and the basis of selection of the items to test to address the risks you have identified;
3. an appropriate materiality level to apply to the audit. NB: in the planning meeting the Partner suggested taking 5% of profit before tax (€/£ 1.1m) as materiality but asked you to consider if that was reasonable in the circumstances.

As you are meeting the audit team member first thing tomorrow, you decide to prepare some notes in advance to help structure your discussions.

To help prepare for the meeting, you have pulled out some notes that the team made on the company's revenue streams, processes and controls during the interim audit which was performed in November 2010 (Appendix B). It suddenly occurs to you that you have not yet drafted any management letter points arising from this work and resolve to do this immediately. You also remember an e-mail you received yesterday (Appendix C) from Jane Smith, another member of the team, who thinks she noted an error during the tests she was performing on creditors and decide to review it to see if any journal adjustments are required to the Financial Statements.

Appendix A

RX Pharmaceuticals Ltd
DRAFT INCOME STATEMENT
for the Year Ended 31 December 2010

	2010	2009	2008
	€/£000	€/£000	€/£000
Revenue	**225,836**	201,374	188,981
Cost of sales	**(140,813)**	(130,893)	(122,271)
Gross profit	**85,023**	70,481	66,710
Distribution costs	**(9,876)**	(8,821)	(8,654)
Administrative expenses	**(52,196)**	(49,264)	(47,245)
Operating profit	**22,951**	12,396	10,811
Finance costs	**(1,407)**	(983)	(854)
Finance income	**331**	502	567
Profit/loss before income tax	**21,875**	11,915	10,524
Income tax	**(6,125)**	(3,217)	(2,945)
Profit for the year	**15,750**	8,698	7,579

APPENDIX B

RX Pharmaceuticals Ltd   **Prepared by:** Audit Senior

Audit working paper – year ended   **Date:** 12 November 2010
31 December 2010

Notes on client's revenue streams, processes and controls

RX Pharmaceuticals Ltd (RX) has two key revenue streams:

- **Contract manufacture of pharmaceutical products** – the company manufactures tablets, capsules etc. under contract for large multinational pharmaceutical companies. The ingredients and manufacturing processes are tightly defined by the product licence owner.
- **Clinical trials services** – the company provides ancillary services to support large multinational pharmaceutical companies in conducting worldwide clinical trials. Services offered include packaging and distribution of trials materials, data capture and analysis of trials results and the sourcing of comparator products to be used as a placebo (a substance with no pharmacological effect but administered as a control in trials testing the efficacy of a new drug).

Revenue recognition for the contract manufacture side of the business is relatively straightforward with revenue being recognised on shipment of the manufactured product. Invoices are issued on a daily basis in respect of that day's despatches and are generated from the despatch notes. Each despatch note contains a barcode which is scanned as the shipment leaves the factory. This automatically generates an invoice using the quantity specified on the despatch note and the contracted price, both of which are derived directly from system records with no manual intervention.

Revenue recognition for the clinical trials services is more complex and occurs in a different manner depending on the service being provided:

- **Packaging** – RX receives loose tablets, capsules etc. from customers and packages these in bottles, blister packs etc. as required for use in clinical trials. Where necessary, packages are blinded so that active drugs and placebos cannot be distinguished, with RX maintaining records of the package contents on the customers' behalf.
  Revenue is recognised when the goods are packaged and is earned based on a contracted price per unit packaged. The Production Scheduler maintains a record of all packaging activities carried out during the month and forwards this to the Finance Department at month end for the purpose of raising customer invoices. A reconciliation is performed between the total invoice value raised and the total packaging activities performed, to ensure that all activities are invoiced.

- **Distribution** – customers' clinical trials are conducted worldwide and in some cases in remote locations. Certain drugs have to be maintained in temperature controlled environments. RX has a specialist logistics team that coordinates the clinical trials supply chain with external hauliers on its customers' behalf.
  Distribution is invoiced out at the third party haulier price, plus a margin of 5%, to cover the planning, organisation and administration performed by RX. Invoices are issued to customers on receipt of the invoice from hauliers. The time taken to receive the haulier invoices varies from one week to eight weeks depending on the haulier involved.
- **Data capture and analysis** – RX captures, tracks and collates the results of clinical trials on behalf of its customers. This service is generally priced on a per project basis and revenue is earned in stages as the project progresses. The contracts often specify key milestones when the customer is invoiced for the services performed to date. The Contracts Manager advises the Finance Department when a milestone on any of the contracts is reached. To ensure appropriate matching, costs of such worked are captured as work-in-progress until such time as the corresponding invoice is raised.
- **Sourcing of comparator products** – as all comparator products are sourced to specific customer requirements, RX does not carry any of these products in stock. When they are delivered to the company's premises and the Goods Received Note (GRN) is logged, the cost is accrued. The GRN is then immediately passed to the Sales Department from which an invoice is immediately issued to the customer incorporating a standard 10% mark-up to cover sourcing costs. As the accrual of the cost and the issue of the customer invoice should take place in the same period, comparator products are never held as stock. They are either forwarded immediately to the customer or used in a customer's clinical trials project.

Appendix C

E-mail from Jane Smith, team member responsible for creditors on RX Pharmaceuticals Ltd:

To: Anon, Audit Manager
From: Jane Smith
Received: 7 February 2011 16:02:45

Subject: Rx Pharmaceuticals – creditors testing

Whilst testing supplier statement reconciliations today I noted that RX Pharmaceuticals Ltd had not accrued for some invoices due from Medical Suppliers Inc. There were three invoices (numbers 16154, 16898 and 16900, total value €/£600,000). They were all dated pre-year end and related to goods delivered on 14, 16 and 21 December 2010.

I spoke with the Financial Controller who indicated that whilst the goods were received pre-year end this wouldn't be an issue as this related to the sourcing of comparator products and that the related revenue had not been booked either. He indicated that the company would make its usual 10% mark-up on comparators when the transactions were processed.

Are you happy with this response?

Kind regards

Jane

Question 3.3 (Based on Chartered Accountants Ireland, FAE 2011 Mock Paper, Simulation 2)

Perchant Hotels Limited

After a recent presentation by your firm to a potential audit client, to which you had an input, Jason Connolly, the Managing Partner of your firm, called you in this morning and advised you with some pleasure that the firm has been successful in obtaining the audit of the rapidly expanding Perchant Hotel Group ('Perchant'). He has also expressed his thanks to you for your input to the presentation made by the firm and, as a gesture of his appreciation, has confirmed that you will be assistant manager of the first audit.

You are aware that, based on the background investigation of the company you carried out prior to the presentation, Perchant has just recently opened their latest hotel and they currently operate seven hotels located in cities and large towns in both the Republic of Ireland and Northern Ireland.

Tom Hayden, Managing Director and principal shareholder of Perchant, regards the success of the group as being mainly due to the quality of its management at each property and incentivises local management to reward them for their continuing success in driving the business forward. Perchant's main accounting functions are based at its head office which operates a centralised room reservation service and also has purchasing responsibility for all non-perishable supplies for each of the hotel properties. On the other hand, each hotel purchases its own local services and perishable supplies and, in line with industry practice, also takes reservations directly.

The company's computer system at head office is connected on-line to PCs in each hotel property, and these PCs are, in turn, linked to terminals and point-of-sales terminals throughout the hotel chain. During the course of your presentation, you identified the New York property (which you hope to visit during the forthcoming audit!) is Perchant's only property outside of the Republic/Northern Ireland. The New York hotel is linked to the group's centralised reservation service; otherwise it operates independently from Head Office.

Based on your background knowledge, you understand that, in line with the hotel industry generally, Perchant derives its overall revenues principally from three main sources which are:

- Room lettings;
- Bars and restaurants; and
- Sundry extras including leisure and spa facilities, laundry services and telephone/internet charges.

During your background investigation prior to the recent presentation, you noted that each local hotel management is remunerated by way of a 'package' comprising a basic salary together with a bonus; the bonus is based on the surplus of hotel net revenue over direct costs at each of the company's seven hotel properties. Not surprisingly, and in line with industry practice, there is quite a high staff turnover coupled with a significant incidence of casual and student staff employed in the peak periods, i.e. summer and Christmas.

Arising from your congratulatory meeting with the firm's Managing Partner, Jason Connolly, this morning, he asked you to carry out some preliminary planning in relation to the first audit and, before preparing a detailed audit plan, he wants you to revert to him and advise on the potential areas of audit risk arising in the Perchant group to which you consider the firm should direct particular attention.

He mentioned to you during the course of his discussion this morning that, as the firm does not have any other significant hotel clients, he is somewhat unclear as to the internal controls that might be expected to exist in relation to the on-line computer system and the autonomy allocated within the group to the local hotel properties as regards the purchase of perishable supplies. He would like to be advised of the main considerations arising with respect to these matters.

You are aware, having just recently qualified, that the application of analytical procedures is a significant component of any risk assessment process and may assist in identifying aspects of your client of which you are unaware and may assist in assessing the risk of material misstatement. You understand that analytical procedures performed as risk assessment procedures include both financial and non-financial information. As part of your planning for the audit, Jason Connolly wants you to identify (and explain) the analytical review procedures you would adopt to obtain sufficient appropriate audit evidence with respect to room lettings and bar and restaurant operations.

You have just sat down at your desk and opened your 'inbox' and you see an e-mail that has been forwarded to you by Jason Connolly. In short, he received it this morning from Perchant's newly appointed financial accountant, Jill Kirby, who is located at head office. He has asked that you respond to him as a matter of urgency so that he can reply to her e-mail.

Her e-mail is attached in Appendix 1.

Appendix 1

From: Jill Kirby@perchant.com   Sent: 06/06/2011 10:15

To: Jason Connolly@xyxaccountants.com

Subject: Payroll System

Jason,

I refer to our recent meeting at which I had the pleasure of meeting with you for the first time since my appointment to the company approximately four weeks ago.

You are aware that, owing to the nature of our employees, many of whom are part-time, and, in addition to which, there is a significant staff turnover, weekly wages are paid in cash. You will, I trust, appreciate that this problem arises also from the fact that many of our employees are non-nationals and do not have bank accounts to which payment can be made directly.

I have just reviewed our payroll system and have established that, in previous years, the payroll was prepared by two elderly ladies who were due to retire towards the end of the current financial year. Prior to my appointment as company accountant, the company secretary hired a young graduate to learn the payroll system with the intention of taking over the payroll function, with an assistant if necessary, on retirement of the two ladies.

Shortly after his arrival, the new payroll clerk approached the company secretary with a suggestion that most of the drudgery in preparing the payroll could be avoided by using a well-known spreadsheet programme which, as an experienced user of such programmes, he felt he could set up very quickly. For example, it would do many of the straight-forward calculations and would do all of the adding-up automatically. PAYE and PRSI/NI would still have to be calculated manually but would then just be entered in the appropriate place in the calculation. Data such as hourly rates-of-pay, which would change infrequently, would carry forward from week-to-week.

The company secretary agreed to his suggestion and he went ahead and purchased and installed the applications. It saved so much clerical time that not only did he not need an assistant to help him when the ladies retired but he now has time to work for one/two days a week in the creditors' ledger section as well.

I have just been examining the payroll for last week and, despite adding up the payroll printout twice, the tots both times were €/£1,200 short of the grand totals shown on the printout for gross and net pay. I asked the payroll clerk about this and he assured me that there is some simple explanation and he would investigate it after his return from holiday in two weeks.

I am concerned that there may be something untoward occurring and would like your advice on how a payroll fraud might be perpetrated based on your experience of how payroll frauds are perpetrated together with your recommendations as to what steps I might take to detect if a payroll fraud is arising.

Question 3.4 (Based on Chartered Accountants Ireland, FAE 2011 Mock Paper, Simulation 3)

Pybex Limited

Refer to the scenario presented in **Question 2.2**.

Question 3.5 (Based on Chartered Accountants Ireland, FAE Autumn 2010, Simulation 1)

Daniels Stores Limited

Refer to the scenario presented in **Question 2.1**.

APPENDIX 3.1: EXAMPLE OF AN AUDIT PLANNING MEMORANDUM[3]

Amend the purple text throughout the document to suit the specific assignment details.

ENTER CLIENT NAME
Audit Planning Memorandum

ENTER YEAR END

---

[3] © Source: Procedures for Quality Audit 2010 (© Chartered Accountants Ireland, 2010).

Table of Contents

I. ENGAGEMENT OBJECTIVES, DELIVERABLES AND KEY DATES	Comments/ References
The audited financial statements for **CLIENT NAME** will be made available to the Directors at the end of our Audit (**INSERT ESTIMATE OF AUDIT COMPLETION DATE**). We will render an opinion on the true and fair presentation of the financial statements in accordance with accounting principles generally accepted in the (**Republic of Ireland, Northern Ireland, or otherwise**) and (**DELETE AS RELEVANT**) **COMPANIES ACTS 1963 to 2009/COMPANIES ACTS 2006** for the year ending **ENTER YEAR END DATE** Our audit of the financial statements is to be conducted in accordance with APB International Standards on Auditing (UK and Ireland) for audits of financial statements for periods ending on or after 15th December 2010. Please refer to engagement (**Attach and reference Engagement**) letter for further outline of the terms of our service deliverable to **CLIENT NAME.**	Engagement Letter is attached at _____
If the Engagement Letter outlines the provision of non-audit services, list here the ethical safeguards taken to ensure that Independence and Objectivity are not challenged. Refer to the Acceptance of Appointment or Reappointment section at B1, point 30. Consider safeguards **e.g.** When performing Accounts Preparation or Taxation services, the audit partner is/is not involved in making key management or judgmental decisions on behalf of the client and the client has acknowledged this in writing (incorporate into engagement letter).	
List the main reporting requirements of which you are currently aware e.g. Audit Report, Report to ODCE as consequence of breach of Section 31 of the Companies Act 1990 (ROI), Report under Criminal Justice Act 2003 (NI), etc.	
Outline the Key Dates on which deliverables **are expected** to be completed, for example (**Delete/Insert as required**): Client Work Programme or audit requirements delivered to client_____ Communication of Audit Plan to client_____ Management Representation Letter_____ Financial Statement Approval Date_____ Audit Report Date_____ Client's Annual Return Date_____ Corporation Tax Filing Date_____ Etc.	

II. KNOWLEDGE OF THE ENTITY – CONT.

Nature of the Entity:

Many of these details may be obtained by asking the client to complete the Client Work Programme. See Appendix 1.

The company operates in the **INSERT INDUSTRY** industry. Its main sources of income are from the **sale of/provision of**:

- **List main products or services that client provides/supplies**

The company has been in business since **INSERT YEAR** and has on average **INSERT EMPLOYEE NUMBER** employees. The average experience of the staff at management level is **X** years and the average overall experience of all staff is **X** years.

The client has a number of suppliers, the top 5 of which are:

- **List top 5 suppliers by Name and what they supply**

The clients customers mainly consist of **enter business type** and the majority of its revenue generating transactions are cash/credit sales. The clients top 5 customers are:

- **List top 5 customers by Name and what they buy**

The company operates out of **(number)** geographical locations including:

- **List geographical locations, e.g. Galway, Cork, Liffey Valley, Swords, Limerick**

The main business objectives of the client are:

- **List Business Objectives (Financial and Non-financial)**

Finance Factors:

The company is mainly financed by Internally Generated Capital (e.g. Revenues)/Bank Loans/Share Capital/Loans from Directors/Loans from Related Parties (e.g. Parent or subsidiary Company)/Venture Capital/Grant Giving Agencies/etc.

The Key Financial Indicators used by the **Directors/management** are:

- **List main Financial Indicators per discussion with management, e.g. Bank Balance and Cash Reserves, Gross Profit Margin, Net Profit Margin, Gearing Levels, Return on Capital Employed, Cost Levels, Revenue, etc.**

There **have/have not** been changes in Accounting Policies during the year. The following accounting policies were amended during the year:

- **List Accounting Policies that were changed and state management's reason for change**

A copy of the reviewed prior year signed financial statements is attached at **INSERT WORKING PAPER REFERENCE** and a copy of the reviewed Financial Statements filed with **CRO/Companies House** is attached at **INSERT WORKING PAPER REFERENCE.**

II. KNOWLEDGE OF THE ENTITY – Cont.

Ownership and Organisation Structure:

Directors	Date of Appointment	Holding at Period End		Holding at Start of Period	
		Ordinary shares	Preference shares	Ordinary shares	Preference shares

We have obtained the Share Register and reviewed on **INSERT DATE SHARE REGISTER WAS REVIEWED** and noted **no/the following** additional shareholdings:

- **List Names of other shareholders with holdings >15% and Number of shares held**
- Other Shareholders cumulatively hold **X** Ordinary Shares, representing **X** % of the shareholding

A list of the Key Management Staff and their responsibilities are as follows:

- **List Key Management Staff (including Directors), their respective job title, area of responsibility, number of staff reporting to them.**
- **List any exceptions noted.**

Main Audit Contacts in Client

We have agreed with the Board of Directors to communicate directly with **all directors/ INSERT NAME OF DIRECTOR.**

[Following in italics only applicable if not communicating with all directors] *It was agreed during our discussions with the* **INSERT NAME OF DIRECTOR** *on* **INSERT DATE OF DISCUSSION** *that all communications to* **INSERT NAME OF DIRECTOR** *will then be communicated by* **him/her** *to the rest of the board. All communications between us and the Board of Directors will be addressed to the Board of Directors and delivered to* **INSERT NAME OF DIRECTOR**. *This has been agreed in the Engagement Letter/letter dated* **INSERT DATE OF LETTER** *attached in working paper reference* **INSERT REFERENCE.**

During the course of the audit we will be dealing with:

- List client contacts and the area of the audit for which you will be dealing with them (e.g. AN Other – Payroll)

II. KNOWLEDGE OF THE ENTITY – Cont.

Industry Overview

The **INSERT CLIENT'S INDUSTRY** is currently experiencing **many economic challenges/economic growth**. In the past 12 months the industry has **contracted/expanded/experienced very little growth.**

The following general market conditions are most affecting the performance of the company:

- **List top 5 economic or industry factors affecting client (e.g. Credit Crunch has restricted availability of finance; increase in environmental protection legislation has fuelled demand for more green efficient product, etc.)**

The company has generally responded to these industry factors by:

- **List main responses from client in relation to challenges presented by industry (e.g. Restructured business to cut costs and reduce working capital requirements, disposed of non-essential assets, increased credit control activities, increased production of product to meet demand, etc.)**

The company has a number of competitors including:

- **List client's top 5 main competitors**

Other general industry information has been reviewed and attached at working paper reference **INSERT REFERENCE.**

Related Parties

We discussed with **management and/or Directors** on **INSERT DATE** and the following points were noted:

Date of Meeting/Discussion:	**INSERT DATE**
Meeting/Discussion Participants:	**INSERT ATTENDEES' NAMES**
Meeting Location/Discussion:	**INSERT LOCATION**

Obtained a schedule of related party transactions entered into during the year, attached at working paper reference **INSERT REFERENCE OR** No schedule of related party transactions was available, but **management and/or directors** were aware of the following related parties:

- **List related parties, e.g. Parent or subsidiary companies, transactions with family members and friends, etc. and purpose of transaction or business rationale for engaging in transaction**

- **All/Some** transactions **were/were not** on an arm's length basis

- **Director/management** approval was obtained for any transactions below an arm's length transaction

- We noted **Adequate/Inadequate** disclosures proposed for the Financial Statements for related party transactions (in accordance with GAAP (e.g. FRS 8) and Companies Acts requirements)

II.   KNOWLEDGE OF THE ENTITY – Cont.
We reviewed prior year financial statements attached at **INSERT REFERENCE** to ensure related party transactions identified are considered in current year audit. We will conduct our audit and be mindful of existence of other related party transactions based on reviewing minutes of meetings, scanning listings of transactions when selecting items for testing, further discussion with management, testing material transactions, reviewing solicitor confirmations and reviewing bank statements, etc. Related party transactions have been discussed with all members of the audit team on **INSERT DATE** (Not applicable if only one person on audit team in total, i.e. partner/ principal).

II. KNOWLEDGE OF THE ENTITY – Cont.

Consideration of Laws and Regulations

There are a number of regulatory factors relevant to the conduct of the company's business. A list of the main regulations include:

- **List the main Regulations affecting client, examples include:**
- **National minimum wage legislation (ROI: National Minimum Wage Act 2000. NI: National Minimum Wage Act 1998)**
- **Companies Legislation (ROI: Companies Acts 1963–2009. NI: Companies Act 2006)**
- **Tax Legislation**
- **Health and Safety Legislation**
- **Building Regulations**
- **Criminal and Anti-Money Laundering Legislation**
- **Etc.**

We discussed with **management and/or Directors** on **INSERT DATE** and the following points were noted:

Date of Meeting/Discussion: INSERT DATE

Meeting/Discussion Participants: INSERT ATTENDEES' NAMES

Meeting Location/Discussion: INSERT LOCATION

There were no breaches of laws and regulations identified during the year **OR** the following breaches of laws and regulations were noted by **directors/management** during the year.

- **List breaches and state whether or not auditor has duty to issue further report and/ or impact on audit work**

Financial Performance – Planning Analytical Review:

We obtained the draft financial figures for the reporting period (draft Financials or Trial Balance) and for the period up to **INSERT CURRENT DATE** (e.g. latest management accounts) from the client and attached at **INSERT REFERENCE.** Based on this financial data we have conducted a preliminary analytical review and our workings are attached at **INSERT REFERENCE.**

Based on knowledge accumulated to date, review of supplementary information (e.g. budgets/forecasts prepared by client, review of minutes, review of bank statements, etc.) and discussions with management on **INSERT DATE** the following main performance issues have been identified:

- **List main reasons for performance in reporting period and to date (e.g. sales have decreased due to significant customer going into liquidation, margins have increased due to increased efficiencies as result of investment in new machine, etc.)**

The key financial ratios of the company are:

- ◦ Gross Profit Margin
- ◦ Acid Test Ratio

These financial ratios have/have not changed in accordance with our expectations.

II. KNOWLEDGE OF THE ENTITY – Cont.

Based on review of budgetary information and discussion with management, the company **has/has not** performed as expected.

Based on preliminary analytical review we will carry out the following audit work:

Enter specific tests which will be carried out as a result of the planning analytical review.

Or

See the Risk Assessment below where these are set out.

Financial Performance – Preliminary Assessment of Going Concern:

Based on the above planning analytics, the fact that the company **has/has not** performed as expected, consideration of industry factors identified above and objectives of the business the following matters will be considered as part of Going Concern:

List any matters that arise that may cast doubt on going concern, for example:

- **Management's expectations and consideration of going concern for a period of 12 months from the date of signing the audit report.**
- **The Credit Crunch and the unavailability of finance is a matter of concern for the directors.**
- **There are significant distributable reserves available to meet any short-term short-fall in expectations.**
- **Etc.**

As a result of planning analytics and consideration of going concern to date, the following areas will be determined a key risk affecting going concern, dependent upon materiality:

- **List Key Risks affecting Going Concern, e.g. Revenue/Turnover, Bad Debts, Impairment of Investment Properties, etc.**

III.   INTERNAL CONTROL ENVIRONMENT

Understanding the Entity's Internal Control Environment

Section C is used to record the accounting systems in a way that is sufficient for the purposes of complying with Auditing Standards and legislation.

The following aspects of the business operations provide an overview of the internal control environment in the company:

List main factors of client's control environment, for example:

- Management are experienced and have been with the company for X years and hold INSERT QUALIFICATIONS
- Finance Staff/Bookkeeper has been with the company X Years and is a INSERT QUALIFICATION
- The organisational structure identified in Part II above is/is not complex and management and/or Directors are involved in the daily operations of the business
- Etc.

Management attitude to internal control **is/is not** positive. Management demonstrate their attitude to internal controls by:

List the key controls operated by the company over these key areas:

1. Completeness of Income
2. Approval of Expenses
3. Payment of Wages
4. Other key areas

Conclusion: Based on results of testing performed above as at **INSERT DATE**, we will rely on **some/all** of the controls above. Any control deficiencies have been discussed with management and any significant deficiencies have been communicated in writing to the directors.

List the controls on which you intend to place reliance in your audit.

See the Risk assessment below where our testing of key controls is considered.

Summary of Controls review (subject to test results) and substantive audit procedures:

We have planned our audit procedures to place **some/no** reliance upon controls (See Controls to be tested above) and perform substantive procedures on the areas of risk identified above .

IV. RISK ASSESSMENT	Schedule/ References
Consideration of matters forward from prior years The following matters forward were noted in the prior year working papers: • **List prior year matters noted in prior year, for example:** • **It was noted that debtors' balances relating to XYZ Ltd and ABC Ltd were over one year old and had not been written off on the basis that management were confident that payment would be forthcoming.** We have reviewed the prior year summary of adjusted and unadjusted differences and noted errors arising in the following areas: • **List areas where error was noted in prior year, for example:** • **Sales** In performing our audit procedures we will pay particular attention to the areas where misstatement occurred in the prior year in order to determine if there are any similar errors in the current year.	

| **Risk of Fraud:**

Our audit will be conducted with professional skepticism and using sampling and testing procedures that are in accordance with International Standards on Auditing. Based on our understanding of the client obtained above and from our previous audit and non-audit experience with this client, there **is/is not** a history of fraud occurring in the company.

The risk of Fraud was discussed with the audit team on [insert date]

We discussed fraud with **Management/Directors** on [insert date]

Based on discussion with management, **the following/no** occurrence(s) of fraud **were/was** suspected, alleged or actually transpired in the company during the year.

Based on a similar understanding we have identified the following areas with a higher potential risk of fraud:

1. Revenue Recognition (Completeness of Income)
2. Risk of management over-ride of controls
3. **List any other areas identified as fraud risk here. If a fraud were to occur in this company, how would it most likely happen?** | |

Risk Assessment:

Review all of the information in the plan so far including your understanding of the client, the industry and the control environment. On this basis, list at least 5* key risks that you have identified and detail how they will be addressed in the audit.

119

Risk Identified	Level of Risk	Controls Testing	Response to Risk	Ref
	H/M/L	*Yes/No*		
Example Risks:				
Debtors may not be recoverable. Planning analytics indicate that debtors have increased significantly	High	No	We will review management's provision against bad debts. We will challenge the assumptions made and consider the outturn of last year's provision. We will ensure that we have sufficient for specific large debtors including Z Limited and Y Limited.	H1:Tests 5, to 12
All **sales** may not be recorded	Med	Yes	We will test controls over income completeness such as supervision by management. We will also test sales orders to completed sales.	N1: Tests 3 and 4
Stock levels of the company's key product may be too high and may not be saleable	High	No	We will review post-year end sales volumes and sales prices. We will review future sales budgets and forecasts.	G1: Test 13

*It is suggested that five risks should be identified. This number may vary in accordance with the circumstances of the engagement. Even on very straightforward audits, risks arising from completeness of income, recoverability of debtors and relationships with related parties may arise. On more complex or regulated audits, the risk assessment will be much more extensive.

Materiality
Materiality has been calculated as follows (See B2 for detailed documentation):

	Amount	Area
Overall Materiality		
Planning Materiality		
Specific Materiality		e.g.: Directors' loans
Clearly Trivial		

[Delete if not testing controls] If our tests of controls produce results that deem the controls unreliable, we will revisit the planning section to amend the extent of substantive testing that is required.

If, during the course of our audit, we identify any additional risks we will revisit planning and make a note of the matter in section A3 (Matters Forward).

V. NATURE, TIMING AND EXTENT OF THE AUDIT

Overall Approach to Audit

Task	Detail	Person Responsible
Discuss Audit Plan with Directors	Insert date of discussion here (or reference copy of letter sent to directors)	
Assignment Approach and Tailoring the work program	Summarise approach and indicate what areas are to be tailored for this client	
Stocktake attendance	Insert date of stocktake	
Issue of Confirmation Letters	Complete Point 3 of the Audit Planning Checklist at B1.2	
Number of Locations	Insert client's locations to be visited during the audit – refer to part ii for list of all client's locations	
Resource Planning	Summarise timetable, budget and staff to be involved on this engagement	
Expected content of Significant Matters Memorandum	Based on planning and prior year matters forward, summarise any issues that you expect to be included in significant matters memorandum	
Post-balance sheet events	Is a significant delay expected between the audit fieldwork and the approval of the financial statements or the signing of the audit report? Do any special arrangements have to be made for this?	
Independent Partner Review if appropriate	Insert who is conducting hot file review and reasons why one is required (ref firms ISQC1 procedures)	

Audit Sampling

Summarise planned approach to sample selection for Tests of Controls here (or attach and refer to firm's overall sampling strategy), e.g. judgemental approach

Summarise planned approach to sample selection for Tests of Detail or Substantive Tests here (or attach and refer to firm's overall sampling strategy), e.g. judgemental approach

VI. ETHICAL AND OTHER MATTERS	Schedule/Reference
Consider the timing and nature of other reports that may be required by the client or by statute	e.g. Internal Control Report, Grant Application, Full and Abridged Audit Report, etc.
Consider any issues for possible inclusion in the letter to those charged with governance	e.g. Significant weakness in Internal Controls, etc.
Consider any issues for possible inclusion in the letter of representation	e.g. In addition to points noted in Planning Memorandum above, existence of contractual arrangements/agreements, disclosure of related party transactions, etc.
Consider and ensure documentation of any safeguards to be taken in order to satisfy independence and objectivity requirements under the Ethical Code	e.g. Provision of Non-audit Services and Safeguards taken as a result, etc.
Ensure Ethical requirements have been discussed with team members and confirmations of independence have been obtained	Obtain independence confirmations from team members and reference on working papers
Summarise any other matters arising	

VII. AUDIT PLANNING MEMORANDUM SIGN-OFF

I have read the above Audit Planning Memorandum and related attachments and understand the broad approach to the areas on which we need to obtain audit evidence so that the audit is performed in an effective manner and have shared it with key engagement team members as deemed appropriate.

All significant risks identified have been appropriately assessed and an adequate response has been reflected in the audit testing strategy outlined above.

Materiality has been accurately calculated and the assumptions applied fairly represent the risk associated with this client.

Name   **Date**

Before Start of Audit

Prepared By:

Reviewed By:

Audit Plan read by other
Audit Team Members

Name

Name

Name

Post-audit Review of Audit Planning Memorandum – Revisit
Materiality, Analytical Review and Risk Assessment (Audit Partner
Completion Only)
I have reviewed our preliminary assessments of the above in the context of the final results of our audit work. I am of the opinion that our original assessments are still valid (if not, please reference re-assessment).

Reviewed By:

4

FRAUD, LAWS AND REGULATIONS IN AN AUDIT OF FINANCIAL STATEMENTS

4.1 Introduction
4.2 Fraud
4.3 Laws and Regulations in an Audit
4.4 Reporting to Regulators in the Financial Sector (ROI Only)
4.5 Duty of Auditors in ROI to Report to ODCE
4.6 Conclusion

LEARNING OBJECTIVES

In reading and studying this chapter, your objectives will be to:
- understand and execute the auditor's responsibilities in relation to fraud; and
- understand and execute the auditor's responsibilities in relation to laws and regulations.

4.1 INTRODUCTION

Fraud, laws and regulations in an audit of financial statements were mentioned in **Chapter 3** in relation to their relevance to the risk assessment process. As the auditor has a responsibility in relation to fraud, laws and regulations throughout the audit, this chapter discusses the area in greater detail.

4.2 FRAUD

4.2.1 Introduction

In **Chapter 3** we noted the requirements of ISA 240 *The Auditor's Responsibilities Relating to Fraud in an Audit of Financial Statements* in the risk assessment process and responses to assessed risks.

The term *'fraud'* refers to intentional acts of one or more individuals that result in a material misstatement of financial statements. As noted in **Chapter 3**, in assessing risks, the audit team needs to be alert to the possibility of fraud. The audit team should plan and perform the audit to determine that the financial statements are free of material errors, including those due to fraud. Furthermore, the audit team should consider whether factors are present that could indicate fraud. This involves considering where in the business or in the financial statements fraud could be occurring. If fraud factors are present, audit procedures should be designed to obtain reasonable assurance that material fraud will be identified.

Auditors in general are aware of fraud more than ever due to the high profile cases that have occurred over the last few years. Some examples of these are noted below:

Enron Through the use of accounting loopholes, special purpose entities, and poor financial reporting, Enron was able to hide billions in debt from failed deals and projects. The uncovering of this fraud led to the bankruptcy of Enron and the dissolution of one of the world's five largest accounting practices at the time, Arthur Andersen.

Worldcom The financial reporting of Worldcom overstated profits by US$4 billion by recognising operating leases and other expenses as capital items. The uncovering of this fraud led to the bankruptcy of Worldcom. Again, the auditors did not discover this fraud.

Lehman Brothers The investment bank accounted for debt off balance sheet. The uncovering of this fraud led to the collapse of Lehman Brothers and the investigation is still on-going into the role and responsibility of the auditors.

4.2.2 Types of Fraud

For audit purposes, two types of misstatements are relevant when considering fraud:
1. misstatements arising from **fraudulent financial reporting**; and
2. misstatements arising from **misappropriation of assets**.

Fraudulent financial reporting is the intentional manipulation, falsification or alteration of records or documents. It involves management and/or those charged with governance intentionally producing financial statements that contain errors for some particular reason. For example, if an application for bank funding by an entity depended on the level of profits reported in the year-end financial statements, management and/or those charged with governance may inflate the profits by omitting to apply the cut-off principle accurately, that is, including revenue in the incorrect period.

Misappropriation of assets may be accomplished by embezzling funds, stealing assets and causing the entity to pay for goods or services that have not been received. For example, an unhappy employee in the accounts payable department may be using the entity's money to pay for personal bills; or the stock manager may be stealing items of stock and selling them independently.

Three conditions are normally present when fraud occurs. First, management or employees have an **incentive** or are under pressure, which provides a reason to commit fraud.

Secondly, **circumstances** exist that provide an opportunity for a fraud to be perpetrated, e.g. the absence of controls, ineffective controls, or the ability of management to override controls.

Thirdly, those involved are able to **rationalise** committing a fraudulent act. Some individuals possess an attitude, character or set of ethical values that allow them to knowingly and intentionally commit an act of fraud.

These three conditions outlined above are known as the **fraud triangle** (as noted in *Nolan,*[1] Chapter 6) and all three elements are present in frauds. While the auditor cannot read minds to evaluate the rationalisation or attitude of the individual(s) committing the fraud, the incentives or pressures and opportunities are often red flags that could indicate fraud. These would be considered in the risk assessment process.

4.2.3 Assessing the Risk of Fraud in the Financial Statements

Certain information should be obtained and evaluated to assess fraud risks at the planning stage of the audit, such as:
- Considering the presence of one or more of the fraud risk factors, which are classified according to the conditions that are always present in frauds:
  - **incentives** to perpetrate fraud, e.g. do management bonuses depend on the level of profit reported?
  - **opportunity** to carry out the fraud, e.g. are there significant levels of related party transactions where it may be easy to hide the incorrect transactions?

---

[1] Martin Nolan, *External Auditing and Assurance: An Irish Textbook* (1st Edition, Chartered Accountants Ireland, 2010)

- o **rationalisation** to justify the fraudulent action, e.g. is there low morale among senior management, therefore making them more susceptible to committing fraud?

ISA 240, Appendix 1 contains further examples of incentives, opportunities and rationalisations.

- Inquiring of management and others within the entity (including those charged with governance, internal auditors, and others, such as in-house legal counsel and lower-level employees) to obtain their views about the risks of fraud and how they are addressed. For example, if management has very strong controls and a zero-tolerance attitude to fraud, the auditor would consider the risk of fraud to be low.
- Inquiring of internal auditors as to whether management has satisfactorily responded to findings resulting from their procedures and whether they have knowledge of any fraud or suspected fraud.
- Considering any unusual or unexpected relationships that have been identified in performing analytical procedures. Analytical procedures for revenues are required, while planning the audit as well as during the audit fieldwork, on every engagement.
- Considering information obtained from:
  - o discussions among audit team members;
  - o procedures relating to the acceptance and continuance (re-acceptance) of clients and engagements;
  - o reviews of interim financial statements; and
  - o other risk assessment procedures.

This information should enhance the audit team's ability to identify areas (assertions, accounts, classes of transactions or disclosures) where fraud could occur and to develop an appropriate response. This identification process includes considering the type, significance, pervasiveness, and likelihood of the risk of fraud.

As a result of fraud risk-assessment discussed in **Chapter 3**, the audit plan will include tailored substantive tests of detail to address areas of fraud risk. Alternatively, the timing or scope of the audit may be adjusted to address any indications that an identified misstatement may be the result of suspicions of fraud. Below are some examples of fraud risks and how these would be addressed.

EXAMPLE 4.1: FRAUD RISKS AND RESPONSES TO THESE RISKS

Fraud Risk	Testing
Example A Management has informed the audit engagement partner that they suspect the stock manager is misappropriating items of stock	• The audit team would attend the stock count and perform a high number of sample checks on stock from floor to sheet, and sheet to floor • The audit engagement partner would assign the most senior team member to audit stock as it is a high risk area
Example B Understanding of the internal control environment concluded that there is a high risk of management override	• High level of substantive testing minimising reliance on controls • Journal entry testing to determine if there have been any unusual entries to the system – this may indicate fraudulent financial reporting if, e.g. there are numerous non-standard journal entries posted by management • Detailed cut-off testing to ensure that all income and expenses are recorded in the correct period – exceptions to this may indicate fraudulent financial reporting

Example C
 	
Management suspects that the sales manager is in collusion with customers regarding payment of rebates
	• The audit engagement partner would assign the most senior team member to audit sales rebates as it is a high risk area
	  o A sample of rebates should be selected and calculations checked, noting the following:
	  o Obtain signed rebate agreements
	  o Ensuring the sales took place and trace to payment of invoice
	  o Review credit notes after the year end to ensure that the sales were not returned after the rebates were claimed

Furthermore, at all times during the audit, the auditor should apply professional scepticism, recognising the possibility that a material misstatement due to fraud could exist. This requires on-going questioning, always considering the reliability of audit evidence received. For example, if the auditor obtained the debtors' listing from the accounting system, are the controls surrounding the provision of this information strong so that the auditor can rely on the information received? Furthermore, when the auditor is concerned about the authentication of documents they should confirm directly with the third party, e.g. when confirming the existence of debtors, the auditor requests the response be sent directly to them rather than the entity being audited.

4.2.4 Detection of Fraud

If, during the course of the audit, the auditor detects fraud, they should firstly inform the appropriate level of management, the directors or those charged with governance. Secondly, if a material fraud is discovered that affects the financial statements, the auditor seeks to correct the error or considers the impact on the auditor's report; and finally the auditor should consider reporting obligations to third parties, e.g. if the auditor discovers fraud carried out by the directors, the auditor should consider reporting to policing bodies. The auditor should seek legal advice in this regard.

4.2.5 Documentation

ISA 240 also requires the auditor to document all considerations in relation to fraud. Specifically, auditors should include in their audit file the:
- significant decisions reached during the discussion among the members of the audit team regarding the risk of fraud in the financial statements;
- identified and assessed risks of material misstatement due to fraud at assertion and financial statement level;
- response to assessed fraud risk, including the nature, timing and extent of audit procedures and how these link to the assertion level; and
- results of audit procedures, including those designed to address the risk of management override of controls.

4.3 LAWS AND REGULATIONS IN AN AUDIT

4.3.1 Introduction

ISA 250A *Consideration of Laws and Regulations in an Audit of Financial Statements* details the auditor's responsibilities in relation to laws and regulations and their potential impact on the financial statements. In order to assess the impact on the financial statements, the standard requires that the auditor obtain an understanding of the legal and regulatory framework of the entity. This may be achieved by, e.g.:
1. using the auditor's existing understanding of the entity's industry, regulatory and other external factors to assess if they are complying with all the relevant laws and regulations, e.g. if the entity was paying a dividend, the auditor would be aware that company law requires the entity to have sufficient distributable reserves to make this payment;
2. assessing if there is any potential impact of those laws and regulations upon the reported amounts and disclosures in the financial statements, e.g. in relation to the

example above, the auditor would assess that this payment may result in a material misstatement to reserves;

3. inquiring of management as to other laws and regulations that may be expected to have a fundamental effect on the operations of the entity, e.g. laws and regulations in relation to patents or licences that the auditor is not directly aware of;

4. inquiring of management about the entity's policies and procedures regarding compliance with laws and regulations to ascertain the controls surrounding the entity's compliance with laws and regulations, and so allowing the auditor to assess any potential risks of material misstatement; and

5. inquiring of management regarding the policies or procedures adopted for identifying, evaluating and accounting for litigation claims to allow the auditor to ascertain if the financial statements are materially misstated in relation to potential legal provisions.

Once this information is received, the auditor's responsibilities differ depending on the type of laws and regulations, that is, 'direct' laws and regulations; or 'other' laws and regulations.

4.3.2 Direct Laws

'Direct' laws and regulations are defined in ISA 250A as those that have a direct effect on the determination of material amounts and disclosures in the financial statements, e.g. tax and pension laws and regulations. Examples of these are:
- the form and content of financial statements as required by company law;
- the provision or recognition of tax or pension costs;
- company law requirements that determine the circumstances under which a company is prohibited from making a distribution except out of distributable profits; and
- company law provisions requiring auditors to report non-compliance, e.g. inadequate books and records, illegal directors' loans and disclosure of directors' remuneration.

4.3.2.1 Auditor's responsibilities in relation to direct laws and regulations

The auditor must obtain sufficient audit evidence regarding the compliance with those provisions, and if such evidence cannot be obtained, this may impact upon the audit report. Furthermore, if the audit evidence received concludes that the entity is not complying with these direct laws and regulations, this may also have an impact on the audit report.

4.3.3 'Other' Laws and Regulations

'Other' laws and regulations are defined by ISA 250A, paragraph 6(b), as those that do not have a direct effect on the determination of the amounts and disclosures in the financial statements, but compliance with which may be fundamental to the operating aspects of the business, to an entity's ability to continue its business, or to avoid material penalties. For example, non-compliance with regulatory solvency requirements or with environmental regulations may have a material impact on the financial statements if, e.g. the entity could not continue as a going concern, or a regulatory fine needs to be accrued in the financial statements.

4.3.3.1 Auditor's responsibilities in relation to other laws and regulations

The auditor must undertake specified audit procedures to help identify non-compliance with those laws and regulations that may have a material effect on the financial statements. These procedures will involve:

- inquiring of management, and, where appropriate, those charged with governance, as to whether the entity is in compliance with such laws and regulations; and
- inspecting correspondence, if any, with the relevant licensing or regulatory authorities.

When determining the type of procedures necessary in a particular instance, the auditor takes account of the particular entity concerned and the complexity of the regulations with which it is required to comply. In general, a small company that does not operate in a regulated area will require few specific procedures compared to a large multinational corporation carrying on complex, regulated business.

An example of an audit programme for testing of compliance with laws and regulations is included below in **Appendix 4.1**.

4.3.4 Instance of Non-compliance

When instances of non-compliance are identified by the auditor, they should take the following steps:
1. obtain an understanding of the non-compliance and obtain further information to evaluate the impact on the financial statements, e.g. is there potential exposure from a legal perspective and, as a result, is a provision required?
2. discuss with management or those charged with governance;
3. if the auditor cannot obtain sufficient information from management or those charged with governance, they must consider legal implications and seek legal advice;
4. if insufficient audit evidence is obtained, the auditor must consider the impact on the audit report; and

5. the auditor must consider if they have any obligations to report to regulatory and enforcement authorities, e.g. money laundering offences must be reported to the policing bodies in the UK and Ireland.

4.4 REPORTING TO REGULATORS IN THE FINANCIAL SECTOR (ROI ONLY)

4.4.1 Introduction

ISA 250 – Section B *The Auditor's Right and Duty to Report to Regulators in the Financial Sector* deals with the circumstances in which the auditor of a financial institution subject to statutory regulation (a regulated entity), i.e. a bank, is required to report directly to the Central Bank of Ireland (the regulator) on information that comes to their attention during their work as auditor.

In conjunction with ISA 250 – Section B, *M46 Reporting to the Financial Regulator under The Central Bank and Financial Services Authority of Ireland Act 2004* (M46) provides auditors of Irish regulated entities guidance in this regard.[2]

4.4.2 Reporting responsibilities

The auditor of a regulated entity generally has special reporting responsibilities in addition to the audit report as follows:

1. **A Responsibility to Provide a Report on Matters Specified in Legislation or by a Regulator** – this is where the auditor has additional statutory reporting responsibilities over and above the audit report.

   In Northern Ireland, the duty to report to the regulator is included in the Financial Services and Markets Act 2000. In the Republic of Ireland there are numerous acts for different entity types – these are listed in Appendix 1 of M46.

   An ROI example of such statutory reporting is that section 47 of the Central Bank Act 1989 requires auditors of banks to report to the central bank if they:
   "(a) have reason to believe that there exist circumstances which are likely to affect materially the holder's ability to fulfil his obligations to persons maintaining deposits with him or meet any of his financial obligations under the Central Bank Acts, 1942 to 1989, or
   (b) have reason to believe that there are material defects in the financial systems and controls or accounting records of the holder, or
   (c) have reason to believe that there are material inaccuracies in or omissions from any returns of a financial nature made by the holder to the Bank, or

---

[2] Institute of Chartered Accountants in Ireland/CCAB-I September 2006, revised January 2008. See www.charteredaccountants.ie (CHARIOT).

> *(d) proposes to qualify any certificate which he is to provide in relation to financial statements or returns of the holder under the Companies Acts, 1963 to 1986, or the Central Bank Acts, 1942 to 1989, or*
>
> *(e) decides to resign or not seek re-election as auditor".*

Appendix 2 to M46 includes an example statutory duty confirmation to the financial regulator.

2. **A Statutory Duty to Report Certain Information, Relevant to the Regulator's Functions, that Comes to the Auditor's Attention in the Course of the Audit Work** – this is where the auditor is not required to carry out additional specific procedures, but should report to the regulator when the auditor concludes that there is reasonable cause to believe that a matter may be of material significance to the regulator.

Whilst precise matters which may result in a report vary depending on relevant legislation, in general, a duty to report arises when an auditor becomes aware that:
* The regulated entity is in serious breach of:
  ○ requirements to maintain adequate financial resources, or
  ○ requirements for those charged with governance to conduct its business in a sound and prudent manner (including the maintenance of systems of control over transactions and over any client's assets held by the business); or
* there are circumstances which give reason to doubt the status of those charged with governance of senior management as fit and proper persons.

4.4.3 Auditor's responsibilities

In order to comply with these reporting requirements, the auditor must ensure the following points are addressed at each stage of the audit:

Planning As well as gaining an understanding of the entity and its environment as required by ISA 315 *Identifying and Assessing the Risks of Material Misstatement Through Understanding of the Entity and Its Environment*, the auditor must ensure that they understand applicable statutory provisions, the rules of the regulators and all auditor's reporting responsibilities in relation to the regulatory requirements. In gaining an understanding of the control environment, the auditor should take account of the entity's higher level procedures for complying with the requirements of the regulator.

Fieldwork In directing and supervising the performance of the audit, the engagement partner must ensure that all members of the engagement team are alert to the possibility that a report to its regulator may be required, and are able to identify reportable situations when they arise. Therefore, they need to ensure that all team members have an understanding of the provisions of the applicable legislation; the regulator's rules and any guidance issued by the regulator; and any specific requirements which apply to the particular regulated entity.

Where an apparent reportable situation arises, the auditor shall:

1. Obtain evidence to assess its implications for the auditors reporting responsibilities. For example:
   (a) Though minor, does the breach cast doubt over the status of those charged with governance as fit and proper persons?
   (b) If the breach occurred prior to the auditor's visit, has it been corrected so that no breach now exists? Or did those charged with governance take corrective action?
2. Determine whether the breach is of material significance to the regulator. '*Material significance*' is defined in the standard as "a matter or group of matters is normally of material significance to a regulator's functions when, due either to its nature or its potential financial impact, it is likely of itself to require investigation by the regulator". Obviously, this requires interpretation in the context of the specific legislation applicable to the regulated entity.
3. Consider if the breach is criminal conduct and should be reported to the specified authorities, e.g. money laundering needs to be reported to the Garda Bureau of Fraud Investigation and the Revenue Commissioners.

Reporting If the auditor concludes that a matter has come to the auditor's attention that gives rise to a statutory duty to report, the auditor shall bring the matter to the attention of the regulator as soon as is practicable. Where possible, the auditor should agree with those charged with governance the circumstances giving rise to the report. However, where the report is a statutory duty, the auditor has no obligation to inform those charged with governance of the circumstances giving rise to the report.

When the reportable matter is in relation to the integrity or competence of those charged with governance, the auditor shall make the report to the regulator as soon as is practicable without informing those charged with governance.

Where the auditor considers that a matter which does not give rise to a statutory duty to report is, nevertheless, in the auditor's professional judgement, such that it should be brought to the attention of the regulator, it is normally appropriate for the auditor to request in writing from those charged with governance of the regulated entity to draw it to the attention of the regulator. If those charged with governance have not properly informed the regulator of the matter, the auditor shall make a report direct to the regulator as soon as practicable.

When making, or confirming in writing, a report direct to the regulator, as per ISA 250B, the auditor shall:

1. State the name of the regulated entity concerned;
2. State the statutory power under which the report is made;
3. State that the report has been prepared in accordance with ISA 250B;
4. Describe the context in which the report is given;
5. Describe the matter giving rise to the report;

6. Request the regulator to confirm that the report has been received; and
7. State the name of the auditor and date.

4.5 DUTY OF AUDITORS IN ROI TO REPORT TO ODCE

4.5.1 Introduction

ISA 250 – Section A *Considerations of Laws and Regulations in an Audit of Financial Statements* notes that the auditor should plan and perform the audit with an attitude of professional scepticism, recognising that the audit may reveal conditions or events that could lead to questioning whether an entity is complying with laws and regulations.

In order to do this, the auditor must obtain an understanding of the legal and regulatory framework applicable to the entity and the industry.

In the Republic of Ireland, section 194 (as amended) of the Companies Act 1990 (CA 1990) sets out specific auditor's responsibilities to make disclosures to regulatory authorities in the public interest. Therefore, auditors of Irish companies should be familiar with the requirements of the section and the related reporting responsibilities.

APB Bulletin 2007/2 *The Duty of Auditors in the Republic of Ireland to Report to the Director of Corporate Enforcement* discusses these reporting responsibilities in detail. Below is a summary of the auditor's responsibilities.

4.5.2 Section 194 of the Companies Act 1990 (as amended by subsequent legislation)

Section 194 CA 1990 is reproduced in Appendix 1 of APB Bulletin 2007/2 *The Duty of Auditors in the Republic of Ireland to Report to the Director of Corporate Enforcement.*

In summary the auditor's responsibilities can be split into two areas:
1. books of account, and
2. indictable offences.

Books of Account Section 194 CA 1990 states that, if the auditors form an opinion that the company does not maintain proper books and records as required by section 202 CA 1990, the auditors must report on this to the Director of Corporate Enforcement.

Proper books of account are defined in section 202 but, in summary, proper books of account should:
- correctly record the transactions of the company;
- enable the financial position of the company to be determined at any time;
- enable the accounts to be readily and properly audited;
- include all day-to-day entries of all monies received and expensed;
- record all assets and liabilities;
- record all goods/services purchased and sold and sufficient details of suppliers and buyers; and
- include statements of stock held at the end of the financial year.

For example, if an auditor commenced an audit and it came to their attention that six months of financial records were not available or posted onto the financial accounting system, the auditor would conclude that the company has not maintained proper books and records and is required to report this to the Director of Corporate Enforcement.

Details on reporting are covered later in this section.

Indictable Offences If the auditor, in the course of carrying out their audit, is of the opinion that the company appears to have committed an indictable offence under the Companies Act 1990, the auditor is obliged to report this to the Director of Corporate Enforcement.

A current list of indictable offences can be found on the Office of the Director of Corporate Enforcement (ODCE) website at www.ODCE.ie. Included here in **Appendix 4.2** to this chapter is a list of indictable offences which are the subject of reporting obligations by auditors under section 194 CA 1990.

For example, if an auditor, during the course of their work, discovered that the entity had a loan due from a director of an amount greater than 10% of the previous year's net assets this would constitute a breach of section 31 CA 1990. As this is an indictable offence, the auditor is obliged to report to the ODCE.

The key point to note in this legislation is that it is based on information that the auditor becomes aware of '**during the course of the audit**'. Therefore, the auditor is not expected to seek out possible indictable offences as part of their audit process.

4.5.3 Reporting Responsibilities

If the auditor suspects that the company has not complied with laws and regulations which fall into an indictable offence, the auditor considers two areas:
1. report to ODCE; and
2. impact on financial statements.

4.5.3.1 Report to ODCE

Where an auditor detects a suspected breach of the Companies Act 1990 they should obtain sufficient information to enable the formation of the opinion as to whether there are reasonable grounds to conclude that an indictable offence has been committed.

ISA 250 – Section B provides guidance in this regard and paragraph A28 notes that the auditor should use their professional judgement in concluding if the matter is reportable by undertaking appropriate investigations to determine the circumstances. However, these procedures do not require the same degree of evidence as audit procedures forming an opinion on the financial statements. Examples of such procedures would be:
• enquiry of appropriate level of staff;
• review correspondence and documents relating to the transaction or event; and
• discuss with those charged with governance or management, as appropriate.

Any report to the ODCE should be made as soon as is practical after the offence is discovered. In reporting to the ODCE, the auditor should include:
• auditor's details;
• statutory authority under which the report is being made;
• details of the company/persons subject to the report;
• whether the issue has been discussed with the directors;
• details of the suspected indictable offence;
• details of the grounds on which the auditor has formed the opinion that an indictable offence has been committed;
• any other information considered relevant by the auditor;
• auditor's signature; and
• date of report.

Following this submission, the auditor is also obliged to furnish the ODCE with any further information they require to carry out their investigations, including access to working papers.

4.5.3.2 Impact on Financial Statements

If the auditor has made a report to the ODCE on the above grounds, the auditor must obtain an understanding of the nature of the non-compliance and evaluate the possible effect on the financial statements. This may be, e.g. any potential fines that need to be accrued, or the impact of insufficient books and records on the audit report.

This can be illustrated in two examples:
• If the company did not maintain adequate books and records, this may have led to a limitation of scope upon the auditor as they could not obtain all the financial records to form an opinion. As a result, the audit report may have to be qualified on this basis and, depending on the materiality of the omission, the opinion will either be 'except for' or disclaimer.

- If the company entered into an illegal director's loan, the auditor needs to consider the financial consequences. For example, an illegal loan may result in a potential fine from the ODCE and therefore the auditor needs to consider if this should be provided for, as well as the potential disclosure requirements, in the financial statements.

4.5.4 ODCE Response to Auditor's Reports

The ODCE will consider each report and request additional information from the auditor if necessary. The Director will then make a decision on action which may include a fine and/or imprisonment depending on the seriousness of the breach of the Companies Act 1990.

4.6 CONCLUSION

The auditor has responsibilities to ensure that the risk assessment process and addressing of those risks in an audit takes into consideration the risk of material misstatement through fraud or non-compliance with laws and regulations. These not only impact upon the audit, but also may result in reporting obligations that the auditor must comply with by law.

SUMMARY OF LEARNING OBJECTIVES

Learning Objective 1 To understand and execute the auditor's responsibilities in relation to fraud

There are two main types of fraud that an auditor should consider when planning an audit: misappropriation of assets and fraudulent financial reporting. The auditor should identify and assess the risk of fraud at the risk assessment stage, and develop audit procedures to address these risks. The auditor should also ensure that they meet their reporting obligations to third parties, should a fraud be detected.

Learning Objective 2 To understand and execute the auditor's responsibilities in relation to laws and regulations

An auditor has responsibilities to identify and assess non-compliance with laws and regulations that may have an impact on the financial statements. The risk of non-compliance should be assessed at the risk assessment stage and audit procedures developed to address this risk. The auditor should also ensure that they meet their reporting obligations to third parties, should non-compliance with laws and regulations be detected.

QUESTIONS

On each of the scenarios presented in the questions below, there is an issue/(s) which needs to be addressed by the auditor (an indicator) in relation to fraud, laws and regulations. You should read the questions and attempt to address the issues relating to fraud, laws and regulations.

(See **Appendix One** of this text for Suggested Solutions to Review Questions.)

Review Questions

Question 4.1 (Based on Chartered Accountants Ireland, FAE Autumn 2011, Simulation 2)

Progressive Construction Limited

Refer to the scenario presented in **Question 3.1.**

Question 4.2 (Based on Chartered Accountants Ireland, FAE Autumn 2010, Simulation 3)

Castleford Credit Union

> *Note: The role of 'supervisor' is mentioned in the case study.*
> *'Supervisors' perform a monitoring role within credit unions, conducting tests on the credit union's processes and controls and reporting their findings to those charged with governance.*

You are the audit senior on Castleford Credit Union Ltd for the year ended 30 September 2009.

Castleford Credit Union Ltd has about 2,000 members, all of whom reside in Castleford and many of whom are employed in the local car assembly plant. The credit union has been established for eight years and your firm has provided audit services throughout this period. It has typically had a very strong balance sheet although this year you are aware that many of its members have been placed on short-time working arrangements due to a significantly reduced demand for new cars.

You have just attended a progress update meeting with the audit partner. At the meeting you reviewed the credit union's draft financial statements and discussed the work performed by your team to date. Minutes of the meeting are attached at Appendix A.

APPENDIX A

Castleford Credit Union

NOTES OF AUDIT PROGRESS MEETING
Held on 25 October 2010

In attendance:

Kevin Maguire (KM) – audit engagement partner

Anon (AA) – audit senior

Jennifer Connelly (JC) – audit associate

AA indicated that the team was making good progress with the audit fieldwork and that the testing of controls and testing on members' shares was complete. The credit union had net assets of €/£10,000,000 at the year end and materiality has been determined as €/£100,000 as discussed and approved at the audit planning meeting.

AA indicated that the controls testing hadn't raised any significant issues, although they had been unable to obtain evidence over the work performed by the supervisors as specified by the supervisors' handbook as working papers and related conclusions had not been retained. Based on enquiry and independent corroboration they concluded that the supervisors had been performing their duties and had not raised any significant concerns as a result of their testing.

KM said that given the current economic environment and specifically the short-time working implemented by the local factory he was concerned about the collectability of members' loans (which are unsecured). It was concluded that AA would pull together a work programme to address these risks for KM's review. KM also asked if AA would consider the scenario in which they were unable to satisfy themselves surrounding the collectability of members' loans and to consider the implications for the audit report.

JC updated AA and KM on the results of the testing on the annual dividend. She stated that there was a formula error in the spreadsheet used to calculate the interim dividend which resulted in the dividend being based on only five months' average shareholding as data from October 2008 was not included. This resulted in the dividend being understated by €/£20,000. KM asked AA to propose a correcting journal entry for this error and also to consider the impact on the audit report if the directors refused to post the journal entry.

KM enquired as to whether the team had noted any further internal control points for inclusion on the management letter. JC indicated that she noted that the bank reconciliations had not been completed during May and June due to staff illness but that they had been brought up to date by the year end. KM added that he would like AA to draft all the management letter points noted for him to review at their next meeting.

KM also stated that the credit union is updating its procedures manual to ensure compliance with money laundering regulations and asked if AA could review the draft (attached as Appendix B) and suggest any improvements necessary to ensure it is accurate and comprehensive.

APPENDIX B

Castleford Credit Union Limited

ANTI-MONEY LAUNDERING PROCEDURES TO ENSURE
COMPLIANCE WITH ALL APPLICABLE LEGISLATION

Background Money laundering is a form of fraud. It is essentially a process where the perpetrator attempts to legitimise the proceeds of any crime. Proceeds of crime can include proceeds from activities such as drug trafficking, terrorism, shoplifting, theft, tax evasion and other financial criminal activity. As a form of fraud the emphasis is on concealing the illegal source of the money which makes it difficult to detect especially given that the transactions are rarely linked to one country.

Many countries have now taken measures to criminalise money laundering and related issues. In the UK and Ireland there are various statutes relating to this issue, making it illegal to:

- Possess, deal with or conceal the proceeds of any crime;
- Attempt, assist or incite money laundering; and
- Fail as an individual in the regulated sector to inform relevant parties of a knowledge or suspicion of money laundering.

The procedures outlined in this document are designed to ensure that both you and the credit union fulfil their respective obligations deriving from this legislation.

Member identification When a new member applies to join the credit union the teller must verify their identity by undertaking the following procedures:

Request evidence of identity – this must comprise one item of government issued photographic identification (e.g. passport, EU/EEA driving licence, EU/EEA national identity). Request evidence of address – this must comprise one of the following items showing the applicant's name and address – utility bill, tenancy agreement, confirmation of address from employer (including address-bearing payslip). Confirmation that an appropriate document has been examined must be noted on the reverse of the membership application form.

No membership applications may be accepted without the above evidence being presented.

Suspicious transactions If you have concerns regarding any suspicious transactions then you should inform the manager immediately without alerting the member as to your concerns. Managers will then raise the issue with the board of directors.

APPENDIX 4.1: EXAMPLE OF AN AUDIT PROGRAMME FOR TESTING COMPLIANCE WITH LAWS AND REGULATIONS[3]

Insert Client Name on Frontsheet

R1

31 December 2010

	Initials	Date
Prepared by:		
Reviewed by:		

Compliance With Laws and Regulations

Return to Index

	Audit Programme	Schedule/ Comment	Initials	Date
	ISA 250A distinguishes the auditor's responsibilities in relation to compliance with two different categories of laws and regulations as follows: (a) The provisions of those laws and regulations generally recognised to have a direct effect on the determination of material amounts and disclosures in the financial statements such as tax and pension laws and regulations; and (b) Other laws and regulations that do not have a direct effect on the determination of the amounts and disclosures in the financial statements, but compliance with which may be fundamental to the operating aspects of the business, to an entity's ability to continue its business, or to avoid material penalties (for example, compliance with the terms of an operating lease, compliance with regulatory solvency requirements, or compliance with environmental regulations); non-compliance with such laws and regulations may have a material effect on the financial statements.			
	In ISA 250A, differing requirements are specified for each of the above categories of laws and regulations. For the category referred to in (a) above, the auditor's responsibility is to obtain sufficient appropriate audit evidence regarding compliance with the provisions of those laws and regulations. For the category referred to in (b) above, the auditor's responsibility is limited to undertaking specified audit procedures to help identify non-compliance with those laws and regulations that may have a material effect on the financial statements. ISA(UK&I)250A(6)(7)			
	Ensure the audit plan is reflected in the following. The following steps are suggestions only and should be removed or added to as necessary to address the risks of material misstatement identified at the risk assessment stage.			

---

[3] Source: Procedures for Quality Audit 2010 (© Chartered Accountants Ireland, 2010).

	Audit Programme	Schedule/ Comment	Initials	Date
1.	Request copies of any letters or reports from regulatory authorities including those arising from visits to the client's premises ISA(UK&I)250A(14)(15), for example: (i) Health and safety; (ii) Environmental health; (iii) Fire inspectors; (iv) Licensing officers; or (v) Other: specify (these will vary depending on the industry in which the client operates).			
2.	Inspect legal fee invoices to identify any legal advice taken regarding breaches arising during the year.	**L1**		
3.	If any breaches have occurred consider: (i) Advising management forthwith; and (ii) the impact on the financial statements. ISA(UK&I)250A(18)(19)(25)			
4.	Record any breaches in the record of significant matters.	**A6**		
5.	Consider whether we have grounds for suspicion of money laundering and the need to report in accordance with the firm's internal anti-money laundering procedures as required by money laundering legislation. In this context have due regard to the risk of the 'prejudicing an investigation' offence in the Republic of Ireland or the 'tipping off' offence in the United Kingdom/Northern Ireland. ISA(UK&I)250A(28)	**A14**		
6.	In the Republic of Ireland, consider the reporting requirements of an accountant or auditor under S.59 of the Criminal Justice (Theft and Fraud Offences) Act 2001 where he becomes aware that theft, fraud or other related offences, as defined by that Act, may have been committed. ISA(UK&I)250A(28) Copyright Chartered Accountants Ireland	**A14**		

	Audit Programme	Schedule/ Comment	Initials	Date
7.	In the Republic of Ireland, ensure that due consideration has been given to the reporting requirements of auditors under the Companies Acts 1963–2009. Specifically consider whether we have become aware, in the course of our audit, of any indictable offences committed by the company or an officer or an agent of it which are reportable to the Director of Corporate Enforcement under S.194 of the Companies Act, 1990 as amended by S.74 of the Company Law Enforcement Act, 2001. In this context refer also to the Auditing Practices Board Bulletin 2007/02, "The Duty of Auditors in the Republic of Ireland to Report to the Director of Corporate Enforcement". ISA(UK&I)250A(28) The ODCE has compiled a list of the indictable offences it considers most likely to come to the attention of auditors in the course of their work. This list is as follows (Information Notice I/2009/4 Reporting Company Law Offences): (a) Giving of financial assistance by a company for the purchase of its own shares; (b) Fraudulent trading; (c) Not holding an EGM where net assets are half or less of the company's called up share capital; (d) Wilfully providing false information in any return, report, certificate, balance sheet or other document under the 1986 Act; (e) Substantial property transactions/loans to directors or connected persons, including Section 31 loans; (f) Directors' and secretary's notification of interest in the company; (g) False statements to auditors, delay in providing information; (h) Failure to keep proper books and records; (i) Furnishing false information under the Acts, including to electronic filing agents; (j) Destruction, mutilation, falsification of documents; (k) Omission from balance sheet of directors' statement claiming audit exemption; (l) Wilfully false statements in accounts and returns; (m) Company to have a director resident in the European Economic Area.			

	Audit Programme	Schedule/ Comment	Initials	Date
8.	In the Republic of Ireland, ensure that due consideration has been given to reporting requirements which arise under S.1079 of the Taxes Consolidation Act 1997.			
9.	Determine any other whistle blowing obligations imposed on auditors by statute and whether there have been any breaches of law and regulations which must be reported to regulators as a consequence. ISA(UK&I)250A(28)ISA(UK&I)250B			
10.	Include in the audit documentation identified or suspected non-compliance with laws and regulations and the results of discussions with management and, where applicable, those charged with governance and other parties outside the entity. ISA(UK&I)250A(29)			
11.	Include confirmation of actual or suspected breaches of laws and regulations, or lack of such breaches, in the letter of representation. ISA(UK&I)250A(16)	**A8**		
12.	When adequate information about the suspected non-compliance with laws and regulations cannot be obtained, the auditor should consider the effect of the lack of sufficient appropriate audit evidence on the auditor's report. (ISA(UK&I)250A(20)(25)(26)(27)			
13.	If as a result of work you suspect any breach of laws and regulations, revisit your overall audit risk assessment. ISA(UK&I)250A(21)			
14.	Consider whether the relevant local data protection legislation has been complied with as regards 'data controllers' and 'data processors'.			
15.	Ensure financial statements comply with the appropriate legislation and applicable accounting standards.			
16.	Additional tests/test areas to ensure planning criteria have been met.			

Conclusion

Subject to the matters noted for the reviewer, nothing has come to our attention to indicate serious non-compliance by the company that would require disclosure in, or amendment to, the financial statements.

Name:		Accountant in Charge
Date		
Name		Reviewer
Date		

APPENDIX 4.2: INDICTABLE OFFENCES UNDER SECTION 194 OF THE COMPANIES ACT 1990[4]

OFFENCE	SECTION[5]
EXEMPTION FROM THE USE OF THE WORD 'LIMITED' OR 'TEORANTA'	
1. Provision of incorrect, false or misleading information under 63/24(1)(c).	63/24(7) -IN 2001/88
2. Alteration of memorandum or articles of association in contravention of 63/24(4).	63/24(7) -IN 2001/88
3. Failure to comply with a direction from the Registrar under 63/24(5) to change a company's name.	63/24(7) -IN 2001/88
PROSPECTUS, STATEMENT IN LIEU	
4. Delivering a statement in lieu of a prospectus to the Registrar containing any untrue statement.	63/35(7) -AM 83/ Sch 1, para 6
5. Inclusion of any untrue statement in issued prospectus.	63/50(1)
6. Delivery to Registrar of statement in lieu of prospectus containing false statement.	63/54(5)
FINANCIAL ASSISTANCE FOR THE PURCHASE OF A COMPANY'S OWN SHARES	
7. Giving of financial assistance for the purchase of a company's own shares without observing the requirements of section 60 of the 1963 Act.	63/60(15)
SHAREHOLDER, PERSONATION OF	
8. False and deceitful personation of owner of share/interest in company/share warrant/coupon and obtaining or endeavouring to obtain rights thereto.	63/90
ANNUAL RETURN	
9. Failure to file annual return once per year.	63/125(2) -IN 2001/59

[4] Source: Decision Notice D/2002/2 *The Duty of Auditors to Report to the Director of Corporate Enforcement.* Copyright ODCE. See http://www.odce.ie/
[5] See page 160 for key to abbreviations of legislative references.

10.	Failure to file annual return on time.	63/127(12) -IN 2001/60
BANKRUPT		
11.	Undischarged bankrupt acting as officer, liquidator or examiner or directly or indirectly being involved in the promotion, formation or management of any company without court approval.	63/183 -IN 90B/169
12.	Failure to produce to the ODCE a sworn statement of all facts relevant to a director's financial position, where the director is an undischarged bankrupt.	63/183A -IN 2001/40(4)
REGISTER OF DIRECTORS AND SECRETARIES		
13.	Failure to supply a member or any other person with a copy of the register, or any part thereof, within 10 days of request.	63/195 (10A) -IN 2001/91
14.	Failure by a director or secretary to give written notice to company of information required for register.	63/195 (14) -IN 90B/51
WINDING-UP, EXAMINATION		
15.	Obstruction of persons entering property pursuant to a Court order or obstruction of persons taking possession of company property pursuant to such an order.	63/245A (5) -IN 2001/45
WINDING-UP, VOLUNTARY CREDITORS		
16.	Failure by a liquidator to call meeting of creditors when he forms the opinion that the company will be unable to pay its debts.	63/261(7) -IN 90B/129
WINDING-UP, VOLUNTARY (BOTH KINDS)		
17.	Failure by a liquidator to summon a general meeting at the end of the first year from the commencement of the winding-up and each succeeding year to lay before it an account of his/her acts and dealings and of the conduct of the winding-up and to send a copy of the account to the Registrar within seven days of the meeting.	63/262(2) -AM 90B/145
18.	Obstruction of persons entering property pursuant to a Court order or obstruction of persons taking possession of company property pursuant to such an order.	63/282C (5) -IN 2001/49

WINDING-UP, OFFENCES BY OFFICERS (ALL MODES)	
19. Offences as listed in the section i.e. any person who is a past or present officer of the company who:	63/293(1)
(a) does not to the best of his knowledge and belief fully and truly disclose to the liquidator when he requests such disclosure all the property, real and personal, of the company and how and to whom and for what consideration and when the company disposed of part thereof, except such part as has been disposed of in the ordinary way of the business of the company, or	
(b) does not deliver up to the liquidator, or as he directs, all such part of the real and personal property of the company as is in his custody or under his control, and which he is required by law to deliver up, or	
(c) does not deliver up to the liquidator, or as he directs, all books and papers in his custody or under his control belonging to the company and which he is required by law to deliver up, or	
(d) within 12 months next before the commencement of the winding up or at any time thereafter conceals any part of the property of the company to the value of €12.70 or upwards, or conceals any debt due to or from the company, or	
(e) within 12 months next before the commencement of the winding up or at any time thereafter fraudulently removes any part of the property of the company to the value of €12.70 or upwards or makes any material omission in any statement relating to the affairs of the company, or	
(f) makes any material omission in any statement relating to the affairs of the company, or	
(g) knowing that a false debt has been proved by any person under the winding up, fails for the period of one month to inform the liquidator thereof, or	
(h) after the commencement of the winding up prevents the production of any book or paper affecting or relating to the property or affairs of the company, or	
(i) within 12 months next before the commencement of the winding up or at any time thereafter conceals, destroys, mutilates or falsifies or is privy to the concealment, destruction, mutilation or falsification of any book or paper affecting or relating to the property of the company, or	
(j) within 12 months next before the commencement of the winding up or at any time thereafter makes or is privy to the making of any false entry in any book or paper affecting or relating to the property of the company, or	
(k) with 12 months next before the commencement of the winding up or at any time thereafter fraudulently parts with, alters or makes any omission in, or is privy to the fraudulent parting with, altering or making any omission in, any document affecting or relating to the property or affairs of the company, or	
(l) after the commencement of the winding up or at any meeting of the creditors of the company within 12 months next before the commencement of the winding up attempts to account for any part of the property of the company by fictitious losses or expenses, or	

(m)	has within 12 months next before the commencement of the winding up or at any time thereafter, by any false representation or other fraud, obtained any property for or on behalf of the company on credit which the company does not subsequently pay for, or	
(n)	within 12 months next before the commencement of the winding up or at any time thereafter, under the false pretence that the company is carrying on its business, obtains on credit for and on behalf of the company, any property which the company does not subsequently pay for, or	
(o)	within 12 months next before the commencement of the winding up or at any time thereafter pawns, pledges or disposes of any property of the company which has been obtained on credit and has not been paid for, unless such pawning, pledging or disposing is in the ordinary way of business of the company, or	
(p)	is guilty of any false representation or other fraud for the purpose of obtaining the consent of the creditors of the company or any of them to an agreement with reference to the affairs of the company or to the winding up.	
20.	Where offence is committed under section 293(1)(o), in that company property has been pawned, pledged or disposed of by a past or present officer of a company, which property was obtained on credit and not paid for, it is also an offence to receive the property knowing it to be pawned, pledged or disposed of in such circumstances.	63/293(3)
WINDING-UP, FRAUD BY OFFICERS (ALL MODES)		
21.	Fraud by an officer of a company which is ordered to be wound-up or which passes a resolution for voluntary winding-up.	63/295
FRAUDULENT TRADING		
22.	Knowingly carrying on the business of the company with intent to defraud creditors or for any fraudulent purpose.	63/297 -IN 90B/137
LIQUIDATOR, DISQUALIFIED PERSON		
23.	Disqualified person acting as liquidator.	63/300A(4) -IN 90B/146
WINDING-UP, INFORMATION (ALL MODES)		
24.	Failure by liquidator where liquidation is not concluded within two years to send to the Registrar particulars about the progress of the liquidation.	63/306(2) -AM 90B/145
RECEIVER		
25.	Acting as receiver when disqualified by being an undischarged bankrupt; officer of company within 12 months; parent, spouse, brother, sister, or child thereof; partner or employee of officer or servant of company; auditor of company.	63/315(5) -IN 90B/170

RECEIVER, NOTIFICATION	
26. Failure by receiver to: • send notice of appointment to the company forthwith; • send to the Registrar within two months of receiving it a statement of affairs prepared in accordance with section 320 of the 1963 Act; • failure to send at cessation of receivership a statement to the Registrar as to the solvency of the company.	63/319(8) -AM 2001/52
27. Failure by receiver to send abstract of receipts and payments to the Registrar every six months.	63/319(8) -AM 90B/145 -AM 2001/52
RECEIVER, STATEMENT OF AFFAIRS	
28. Failure by officers of the company, promoters, employees to prepare and submit the statement of affairs to the receiver within 14 days of receipt of the notice of the appointment of the receiver.	63/320(5)
RECEIVER, ABSTRACTS	
29. Failure by receiver to deliver to the Registrar within one month abstract of receipts and payments made up every six months.	63/321(2) AM 90B/145
30. Failure by receiver to furnish books, answer questions or give assistance to ODCE.	63/323A(4) -IN 2001/53
FOREIGN COMPANIES, PROSPECTUS	
31. Issue, circulation or distribution of prospectus of a foreign company knowingly in contravention of sections 361 to 364 of 1963 Act.	63/365
'LIMITED', IMPROPER USE	
32. Improper use of 'limited' or 'teoranta' by person or persons not incorporated with limited liability.	63/381(1) -IN 2001/98
ALLOTMENT, AUTHORITY REQUIRED	
33. Allotment by directors of shares without authority from the company in general meeting or the articles of association.	83/20(7)

SHARES, PRE-EMPTION RIGHTS	
34. Knowingly or recklessly permitting inclusion of any matter which is misleading, false or deceptive in a material particular in a director's statement circulated with a special resolution to propose the allotment of shares without applying pre-emption rights.	83/24(6)
NON-CASH CONSIDERATION, EXPERTS' REPORTS	
35. Knowingly or recklessly making a misleading, false or deceptive statement to any expert carrying out a valuation or making a report in respect of non-cash consideration before the allotment of shares.	83/31(3)
CONSIDERATION	
36. Failure to observe the requirements of sections 26 to 30, 32 and 35 of the 1983 Act i.e.: 26. subscription of share capital 27. prohibition on allotment of shares at a discount 28. payment for allotted shares 29. payment of non-cash consideration 30. experts' reports on non-cash consideration before allotment of shares 32. experts' reports on non-cash assets acquired from subscribers, etc. 35. special provisions as to issue of shares to subscribers.	83/36(1)
CAPITAL, MAINTENANCE OF	
37. Knowing and wilful failure by directors to convene extraordinary general meeting to be held not later than 84 days of becoming aware that the net assets of the company are half or less of the amount of the company's called-up share capital.	83/40(2)
ACQUISITION OF OWN SHARES	
38. Acquisition of own shares by company limited by shares or by guarantee and having a share capital, whether by purchase, subscription or otherwise in contravention of S41.	83/41(3)
ACCOUNTS, FALSE STATEMENT	
39. Knowingly and wilfully making a statement false in any material particular in any return, report, certificate, balance sheet or other document required or for the purposes of the 1986 Act.	86/22(3)

COURT PROTECTION	
40. Failure by petitioner to deliver notice of petition to Registrar within three days of its presentation.	90/12(5)
41. Failure by examiner to publish notice of his appointment within 21 days in *Iris Oifigiúil.*	90/12(5)
42. Failure by examiner to publish notice of his appointment within three days in at least two daily newspapers.	90/12(5)
43. Failure by examiner to deliver notice of appointment within three days to the registrar.	90/12(5)
44. Failure to publish statement 'under the protection of the court' on invoices, orders or business letters.	90/12(5)
45. Person acting as examiner who is not qualified to act as liquidator of the company.	90/28(2)
INVESTIGATION	
46. Failure to give information required or knowingly making a statement false in a material particular or recklessly making a statement false in a material particular in relation to the ownership of shares in or debentures of a company.	90B/15(3)
47. Where Ministerial/Directorial notice has been given to restrict shares under 90B/16, exercising or purporting to exercise any right to dispose of such shares, or option thereon, or voting in respect of such shares; failing to notify restriction to person entitled to vote in respect of such shares, entering into agreement to sell shares or attached rights.	90B/16(14)
48. Issuing shares in contravention of restrictions.	90B/16(15)
49. Failure to comply with direction of ODCE to produce books or documents or provide an explanation or make a statement.	90B/19(6) -IN 2001/29
50. Providing an explanation or making a statement knowing it to be misleading in any material respect.	90B/19(8) -IN 2001/29
51. Destruction, mutilation, falsification or concealment of books or documents the subject of a direction.	90B/19(9) -IN 2001/29
52. Destruction, mutilation, falsification, concealment or disposal of books or documents when an investigation is being or is likely to be carried out.	90B/19A -IN 2001/29
53. Obstruction of exercise of right of entry or search under warrant or right to take possession of any books or documents or failure to give proper name address or occupation to officer or failure to produce to officer information in his custody or possession.	90B/20(6) -IN 2001/30

54.	Unauthorised publication of any information, book or document.	90B/21(2) -AM 2001/31
DIRECTORS		
55.	Dealing in right to call for or to make delivery at specified price, time, and number of relevant shares or debentures.	90B/30(1)
56.	Failure by director to repay surplus business expenses advanced within six months of expenditure.	90B/36(3)
57.	Making a prohibited loan to a director or connected person.	90B/40(1)
58.	Procuring a company to make a prohibited loan to a director or connected person.	90B/40(2)
59.	Failure by licensed bank to maintain register of substantial contracts with directors which are excluded from publication by 90B/41(6).	90B/44(8)
60.	Failure by licensed bank to permit inspection of register of substantial contracts with directors.	90B/44(8)
DISCLOSURE OF INTERESTS IN SHARES		
61.	Failure by director, shadow director or secretary to notify company in writing within the proper period of interests in shares and debentures of the company.	90B/53(7)
62.	Failure by director, shadow director, or secretary, without reasonable excuse, to ensure notification by agent of acquisitions or disposals of shares or debentures in the company.	90B/58(7)
63.	Failure to amend index following removal of register entry.	90B/61(3)
64.	Improper deletion of register entry.	90B/62(3)
65.	Failure to restore improper deletion.	90B/62(3)
66.	Failure by director, shadow director or secretary to notify company in writing of grant of right to subscribe for shares or debentures of the company to spouse or minor child or the exercise of such right.	90B/64(6)
67.	Failure by company whose shares are dealt in on recognised stock exchange to notify that stock exchange of acquisitions and disposals by director, shadow director, secretary or spouse or minor child thereof.	90B/65(3)
ACQUISITION OF PLC SHARE		
68.	Failure to make disclosure within proper period of acquisition of relevant share capital equal to or exceeding the notifiable level (5%).	90B/79(7) -AM 2001/35
69.	Failure of persons acting together to acquire interests in public limited company (concert parties) to keep each other informed.	90B/79(7) -AM 2001/35
70.	Failure of purchaser to ensure immediate notification to purchaser by his agent of acquisitions or disposals.	90B/79(7)

INVESTIGATION OF INTERESTS ACQUIRED		
71.	Failure to prepare report of investigation requisitioned by members to investigate purported acquisition of interests in shares in the company and to make the report available at the company's registered office (and where the investigation is not completed within three months, an interim report); and notifying the requisitionists within three days of the report becoming available.	90B/84(7)
72.	Failure to comply with a notice served by the company.	90B/85(3)
REGISTER OF INTERESTS IN SHARES		
73.	Failure to notify within 15 days person notified by third party as having interests in the shares of the company.	90B/86(7)
74.	Failure to make within 14 days any necessary alterations in any associated index of any removal from the register.	90B/86(7)
75.	Making unauthorised deletion from register.	90B/87(3)
76.	Failure to restore unauthorised deletion.	90B/87(3)
77.	Refusal to permit inspection of register or report made under 90B/84 or to supply a copy thereof.	90B/88(4)
INSIDER DEALING		
78.	Unlawfully dealing in securities in contravention of 90B/108.	90B/111
79.	Dealing within 12 months of conviction by person convicted of insider dealing.	90B/112(3)
80.	Dealing on behalf of another person with reasonable cause to believe deal would be unlawful under 90B/108.	90B/113(2)
81.	Failure to observe professional secrecy.	90B/118(3) -AM 2001/38
WINDING UP, VOLUNTARY CREDITORS		
82.	Exercise, without Court sanction, of liquidators' powers, as conferred by section 276/63, before the creditors' meeting. Failure by the liquidator to attend the creditors' meeting under section 266/63 and to report to the meeting on any exercise by him of his powers.	90B/131(7)
WINDING UP, REPORT OF OFFENCES		
83.	Failure by liquidator or receiver to include in periodic returns a report relating to any past or present officer or member of the company who is the subject of a disqualification order or who has been made personally responsible for debts of a company.	90B/144(2)

WINDING-UP, PERIODIC RETURNS	
84. Failure by liquidator or receiver to make or file any return, etc. required by the Companies Acts.	90B/145(1)
DIRECTORS OF INSOLVENT COMPANIES, NOTIFICATION BY LIQUIDATOR	
85. Failure of liquidator to notify the court of his opinion that the interests of any other company or its creditors may be placed in jeopardy because a director of the insolvent company is acting as a director or is involved in the promotion or formation of such other company.	90B/151(3)
86. Failure by liquidator to notify creditors and contributories of receipt of notice of intention of director of insolvent company to apply to court for relief from 90B/150.	90B/152(5)
DISQUALIFIED DIRECTOR	
87. Person acting in contravention of disqualification order.	90B/161(1)
88. Director or other officer or member of committee of management or trustee of any company knowingly acting in accordance with the directions or instructions of a disqualified person.	90B/164(1)
89. Failure by director or shadow director charged with alleged fraud or dishonesty to give written advance notice to the court of required particulars of directorships.	90B/166(3)
AUDITORS	
90. Failure by auditor to notify Registrar of Companies within 14 days of service of notice of resignation on company.	90B/185(6)
91. Failure by auditor to include required material in notice of resignation.	90B/185(6)
92. Failure to give, within 14 days, notice to persons entitled to receive documents under 63/159(1) of an auditor's written notice of intention to resign in which are set out the circumstances connected with the resignation which should be brought to the notice of the members or creditors of the company.	90B/185(7)
93. Failure to convene a general meeting within 14 days of service of notice by auditor for the purpose of receiving and considering an account and explanation of the circumstances connected with the auditor's resignation.	90B/186(6)
94. Failure to send to persons entitled to receive documents under 63/159(1) and to the Registrar a copy of any further statement by auditor to members.	90B/186(6)
95. Failure to send to the auditor notices of the meeting and all other documents relating thereto and to permit him to attend and be heard on any part of the business which concerns him as former auditor.	90B/186(6)
96. Failure to vacate office as auditor or public auditor on becoming disqualified and to give written notice of this to the company, society or friendly society.	90B/187(9)

97.	Failure by person acting as auditor or as a public auditor to furnish to ODCE, following request, evidence of his qualifications to act as such within 30 days of the demand.	90B/187 (12) -IN 2001/72
98.	Failure by body of accountants to provide a report to ODCE as soon as possible where its disciplinary committee has reasonable grounds for believing that an indictable offence under the Companies Acts may have been committed by a person while a member of the body.	90B/192(7) -IN 2001/73
99.	Failure by auditor to serve notice on company and to notify Registrar within seven days of such notice of his opinion that company is contravening or has contravened requirement to maintain proper books of account.	90B/194(4) -AM 2001/74
100.	Failure by auditor to furnish ODCE with explanations or to give access to documents.	90B/194 (4) -IN 2001/74
101.	Failure by auditor to notify ODCE of his opinion as to the commission of an indictable offence.	90B/194 (4) -IN 2001/74
102.	Person who is subject of disqualification order becoming or remaining partner in firm of auditors; giving directions or instructions in relation to conduct of audit; working in any capacity in conduct of audit of accounts of a company.	90B/195(1)
103.	Failure by subsidiary company or its auditor to give to the auditors of the holding company such information and explanations as may be required.	90B/196(2)
104.	Failure of holding company to obtain from its subsidiary information needed for purposes of audit.	90B/196(2)
105.	Knowingly or recklessly making a statement to the auditor, when an officer or employee of the company, which is misleading or false or deceptive in a material particular.	90B/197(1)
106.	Failure to provide to auditor within two days of requisition any information or explanations required.	90B/197(3)
107.	Failure by recognised body of accountants to deliver within one month of renewal/recognition to the Registrar a list of members qualified for appointment as auditors.	90B/199(4)
108.	Failure by recognised body of accountants to deliver within one month of their qualification list of members qualified for appointment as auditors.	90B/200(4)

BOOKS OF ACCOUNT	
109. Failure to keep, on a continuous and consistent basis, proper books of account.	90B/202 (10)
110. Failure to keep proper books of account being considered to have contributed to a company's insolvency.	90B/203(1)
PURCHASE OF OWN SHARES	
111. Failure to retain and permit inspection of contracts for purchases of own shares.	90B/222(3)
112. Failure to deliver to registrar within 28 days return relating to purchase of own shares.	90B/226(4)
113. Failure to comply with Ministerial regulations relating to purchase of own shares.	90B/228(3)
114. Failure by quoted company to notify recognised stock exchange.	90B/229(3)
115. Contravention of provisions, 90B/207-211, 218, 222-224 i.e.: 207 – power to issue redeemable shares; 208 – cancellation of shares on redemption; 209 – treasury shares; 210 – power to convert shares into redeemable shares; 211 – power to purchase own shares; 218 – incidental payments with respect to purchase of own shares; 222 – retention and inspection of documents; 223 – dealings by company in its own securities, or; 224 – holding by subsidiary of shares in holding company.	90B/234
FALSE INFORMATION	
116. Furnishing false information in any return, report, certificate, balance sheet, etc. in purported compliance with the Companies Acts. (In certain circumstances, the maximum prison term on indictment may be increased.)	90B/242(1) -AM 2001/106
DOCUMENTS	
117. Destroying, mutilating or falsifying any book or document or being privy thereto.	90B/243(1)
118. Fraudulently parting with, altering or making an omission in any book or document or being privy thereto.	90B/243(2)
CLASSIFICATION	
119. Failing to comply with any system of classification required by Ministerial regulation for documents to be filed with the registrar.	90B/247(4)

UCITS/INVESTMENT COMPANIES		
120.	Contravention of 90B/252-261; any regulation made thereon; or any condition laid down under 90B/257 by Central Bank of Ireland, namely: 253 – share capital of investment companies; 254 – power of company to purchase own shares; 255 – treatment of purchased shares; 256 – authorisation of Central Bank of Ireland; 257 – powers of the Central Bank of Ireland; 258 – adaptation of certain provisions of UCITS regulations; 259 – default of investment company; 260 – amendment and restriction of certain provisions, or 261 – supplementary regulations.	90B/262
ACCOUNTS-EXEMPTION FROM AUDIT REQUIREMENT		
121.	Failing to include statement in balance sheet in accordance with 99/33 (4) and (5) i.e. directors' statement.	99/33(6)
122.	Wilfully making a false statement in any return, balance sheet or other document required for the purposes of 99/Part III.	99/37(1)
RESIDENT DIRECTOR		
123.	Failure of a company to have a resident director or bond or a certificate under 99/44.	99/43(13)
LIMITATION ON NUMBER OF DIRECTORSHIPS		
124.	Becoming or remaining a director or shadow director in breach of 99/45(1) i.e. of more than 25 companies, exclusive of statutory exemptions.	99/45(8)
DISCLOSURE OF INFORMATION		
125.	Disclosure, except in accordance with law, of information obtained by the Director of Corporate Enforcement which has not otherwise come to the notice of the public.	2001/17(4)
OBLIGATION TO REPORT ON CONDUCT OF DIRECTORS		
126.	Failure by liquidator of insolvent company to provide report to ODCE, or to apply to Court for the restriction of directors under 90B/150 unless relieved by ODCE of obligation.	2001/56(3)

EXAMINATION OF LIQUIDATOR'S BOOKS	
127. Failure by liquidator to produce books to the ODCE for examination or to answer questions as to the content of the books and give such assistance in the matter as is reasonable.	2001/57(4)
REPORTING TO ODCE OF MISCONDUCT BY LIQUIDATORS OR RECEIVERS	
128. Failure of a professional body to report to the ODCE a finding by its disciplinary committee or tribunal that a member conducting a liquidation or receivership has failed to maintain appropriate records, or that it has reasonable grounds for believing that a member has committed an indictable offence under the Companies Acts during the course of a liquidation or receivership.	2001/58

Key to abbreviations:

63:     Companies Act, 1963

82:     Companies (Amendment) Act, 1982

83:     Companies (Amendment) Act, 1983

86:     Companies (Amendment) Act, 1986

90:     Companies (Amendment) Act, 1990

90B: Companies Act, 1990

92R: European Communities (Companies: Group Accounts) Regulations, 1992

99:     Companies (Amendment) (No 2) Act, 1999

01:     Company Law Enforcement Act, 2001

DCE: Director of Corporate Enforcement

AM: As amended by

IN: Inserted by

REP: Replaced by

5

TESTS OF CONTROL

5.1   Introduction
5.2   Types of Tests
5.3   Timing of Tests
5.4   Drawing Conclusions from Tests of Control
5.5   Conclusion

LEARNING OBJECTIVES

- To be able to develop tests of control and recognise that there are different tests that can be designed;
- To assess the suitability of timing of tests of control; and
- To be able to assess the results of the tests of control and initiate the necessary action.

5.1 INTRODUCTION

As discussed in **Chapter 3**, tests of control are used in an audit when, following the auditor's evaluation of the design of those controls, and whether they have been implemented, there is an expectation that the controls are operating effectively. In this case, the auditor will use tests of controls to test the operating effectiveness of controls which will reduce the level of substantive testing required.

Chapter 5 "Controls and Testing" of **Nolan**[1] covers tests of control in detail and you should refer to that chapter and ensure you are familiar with its contents. As a reminder, **Nolan**, Section 5.2, sets out the four stages in reviewing and testing controls:

---

[1] Martin Nolan, *Auditing and Assurance: An Irish Textbook* (1st Edition, Chartered Accountants Ireland, 2010).

1. **Identify risks and objectives within each financial cycle**, i.e. link financial statements assertions to each transaction class and account balance, e.g. completeness of revenue transactions; cut-off of receivables balance, and so on.
2. **Ascertain systems and internal controls**, i.e. observe and document the internal control environment for each financial cycle, where applicable, e.g. revenue and receivables.
3. **Assess the systems and internal controls**, i.e. are they effective or ineffective? Effective controls will result in controls testing, ineffective controls will result in substantive testing.
4. **Test the system and internal controls** – the auditor will test the controls, *only* if the controls are deemed effective. If the controls are ineffective, the auditor develops substantive procedures and does not rely on the controls.

Steps 1, 2 and 3 form part of the risk assessment process and Step 4 is the response to assessed risks.

It should be noted that the responses to assessed risks do not have to be either tests of control or substantive tests; they can be a combination of both. For example, the auditor may conclude that the controls surrounding the bank cycle are expected to be operating effectively and therefore use tests of control, whereas the other cycles are audited using substantive testing as the controls were not expected to be operating effectively.

However, it is important to remember that, irrespective of the operating effectiveness of controls or otherwise, substantive testing must be performed on all material balances and transactions. To illustrate this, let's say the trade receivables balance amounts to €1.2m (materiality is set at €500,000) and since the auditor has concluded that the controls surrounding receivables are effective, is testing the controls. However, in line with ISA 330, as the trade receivables balance is over materiality, the auditor also must carry out substantive testing. For example, the auditor may test valuation of debtors by testing the controls surrounding aged receivables; or test the existence of receivables by testing the controls surrounding generation of invoices. However, in testing the completion of receivables, the auditor would use substantive testing such as substantive analytical procedures to address the risk of material misstatement.

As noted above, *Nolan*, Sections 5.3 to 5.7, covers these stages for the following cycles:
- revenue and receivables;
- purchases and payables and payroll;
- bank and cash;
- inventory; and
- investments.

At this stage you should therefore be very familiar with tests of control in each of these areas.

This chapter will build on the control testing discussed in **Nolan**, Chapter 5, "Controls and Testing" by indicating some key factors that should be considered by the auditor when designing tests of control:
- types of tests – enquiry and observation, re-performance, computer-assisted audit techniques;
- timing of tests; and
- drawing conclusions from tests of control.

5.2 TYPES OF TESTS

The type of test used by the auditor will vary depending on the nature of the control, whether the control is documented or undocumented, and the judgment of the audit team. Some key testing techniques are as follows:
- enquiry and observation;
- re-performance; and
- computer-assisted auditing techniques (CAAT).

Each of these is explained below.

5.2.1 Enquiry and Observation

When performing enquiry and observation procedures, the audit team assesses the performance of the control through the enquiry of appropriate entity personnel and through observation of the application of the control. For example, observing certain controls that are in place at the quarter-end physical stock-takes. Tests of control performed using enquiry and observation often include re-performance, e.g. the auditor re-performing a control such as a stock count or stock reconciliation. Re-performance is discussed in **Section 5.2.2** below. Enquiry, observation and re-performance allow the audit team to assess the correctness of the information subject to the control by inspecting the pertinent data, documents, reports, or electronic files.

When performing enquiry and observation, the audit team ordinarily considers all of the following:
- What control procedures are operated by the entity?
- Has the control been in operation throughout the period?
- Is the control consistently applied, including confirming with others within the entity that the control procedure is applied consistently and effectively?
- What alternative procedures operate in unusual circumstances (e.g. holidays and sickness)?
- Have the control procedures identified any errors?
- How and when are the errors corrected?
- What circumstances might cause the control to fail, be overridden, or be ineffective?

- What are the rights and security levels for personnel using automated systems?
- Are breaches of segregation likely or common?

For manual controls, observation and enquiry procedures are usually carried out only once during the year, provided there are no conflicting observations (e.g. observing that a control is not being performed or that documents subject to the control are erroneous). In such instances, further observations or inquiries (or other tests of control) are necessary in considering the effectiveness of the key control in question.

Examples of enquiry and observation tests of control are:
- observe the customer-receipts process and ensure no part of it is being performed by individuals responsible for posting to the ledgers or customer account maintenance; and
- observe the receipting process to ensure goods are inspected on arrival, compared with purchase order details, and discrepancies are noted on the GRN prior to signing.

5.2.2 Re-performance

When re-performance is used as a testing method, the audit team executes (or re-performs) the control to test if the control is performing adequately. In other words, the audit team selects items that the control was applied to and re-performs the control to determine whether it was operating effectively during the period under review.

Re-performance is a testing method ordinarily applicable to manual controls that operate on an infrequent basis. For example, re-performance may be used to test the operating effectiveness of monthly bank reconciliations. Such tests may have the following aspects:
- ascertaining whether 12 timely reconciliations were performed;
- testing or reviewing certain of the reconciling items; and
- re-performing at least one reconciliation to determine how the control was performed and the correctness of the information subject to the control, including appropriate follow-up of amounts in the reconciliation.

As discussed in **Section 5.2.1**, re-performance may form part of inquiry and observation as well as CAAT procedures. In order to observe the control taking place, the auditor may need to re-perform it, e.g. reconcile the monthly stock report to the general ledger.

5.2.3 Computer Assisted Auditing Techniques

In an automated environment, Computer Assisted Auditing Techniques (CAAT) can be used to test controls. CAAT procedures vary, but always involve interrogating electronic data using Microsoft Excel or a more advanced data interrogation tool.

An example of a CAAT would be if the entity implemented a control that the CEO approves all transactions over €/£100,000, a population of transactions over €/£100,000 can be extracted from the accounting system using a data interrogation tool. The audit team can then use the extracted population to select items to test the control procedure.

Another example would be a control over employees entered in the payroll application. Using a data interrogation tool, the audit team can extract, from an electronic file of employees at the end of the period, a population of new hires by identifying those individuals with hire dates during the period tested. The audit team can then test the control procedure applied to these employees on commencement of their employment, e.g. are controls in place to prevent fictitious employees being entered on the system and paid?

The benefits of using CAAT in performing tests of controls will be maximised if computer audit tools are used to assist in the execution of substantive procedures. The use of CAAT for individual audit tests, whether tests of controls or substantive tests, may not be cost effective. However, when several audit tests relating to one or more audit areas are aggregated, utilisation of CAAT is generally quite economical. In addition, the benefit can also be maximised when CAAT are used from year to year. For instance, files from the prior audit year can be merged with files from the current audit year to identify changes or new items. This comparison may assist in narrowing the population to which substantive procedures would be applied.

5.3 TIMING OF TESTS

The results of tests of control affect the nature, timing, and extent of substantive procedures relating to risks of material misstatement. For example, if the auditor developed tests of control and the results of these tests indicated that the controls were not operating effectively, the auditor would have to revert to substantive testing to gain assurance that the financial statements are free from material misstatement. Therefore, the tests of control should be completed and evaluated as early as possible, preferably before starting substantive testing.

Furthermore, when testing controls, the auditor requires audit evidence of controls operating effectively over the period, not just at year end. Therefore, very commonly, controls are tested at an interim period during the year and then updated at the year end to ensure that the controls are still operating effectively.

It is important to note that, whether interim testing is carried out or not, controls should be tested at various stages throughout the period. For example, if the auditor was testing controls over the bank reconciliations, they may choose four reconciliations for different months of the year.

5.3.1 Using Audit Evidence obtained in Previous Audits

In certain circumstances, audit evidence obtained from previous audits may be relevant to the current audit if the auditor performs audit procedures to establish its continuing relevance. For example, in performing a previous audit, the auditor may have determined than an automated control was functioning as intended. The auditor may obtain audit evidence to determine whether changes to the automated control have been made that affect its continued effective functioning. This audit evidence may be obtained through, e.g. inquiries of management and the inspection of logs to indicate what controls have been changed.

However, in determining whether it is appropriate to use audit evidence about the operating effectiveness of controls obtained in previous audits, the auditor needs to consider:

1. the effectiveness of other elements of internal control, including the control environment, the entity's monitoring of controls, and the entity's risk assessment process, e.g. if the control environment in the current year is weak, the auditor would not consider it appropriate to rely on audit evidence obtained in previous years as it is not reflective of the current year control environment;
2. the risks arising from the characteristics of the control, including whether it is manual or automated, e.g. if the control was manual bank reconciliations, the auditor would be less likely to rely on previous years' testing of the control as there is an increased risk of human error over this control; however, if the control was an automatic stop on customer accounts should they reach a certain credit limit, as this is automated, and on the basis that the auditor enquires if there has been any change to the automation, it may be appropriate for the auditor to rely on the results of the testing of that control in the previous year;
3. the effectiveness of general IT-controls, e.g. if the control tested in the previous year relied on a strong IT control environment, and the auditor concludes that the IT control environment is weak in the current year, the auditor would not rely on the prior testing of this control;
4. the effectiveness of the control and its application by the entity, including the nature and extent of deviations in the application of the control noted in previous audits, and whether there have been personnel changes that significantly affect the application of the control, e.g. if the nature of the control or the individual initiating the control has changed since the prior year, the auditor would not rely on the prior year testing on the basis that it is not reasonable to assume that it would still be operating effectively;
5. the risks of material misstatement and the extent of reliance on the control, e.g. if the risk of material misstatement in the valuation of debtors was regarded as significant, the auditor would not rely on a control tested in the prior year to obtain reasonable assurance that it is not materially misstated in the current year.

In many cases, tests of control provide an opportunity to accelerate audit work before the year-end by reducing substantive procedures performed after the year-end and allowing for a more efficient audit strategy. That is, by carrying out some of the testing before the year end, the amount of time required for the audit after the year end can be reduced, therefore resulting in a more efficient audit.

5.4 DRAWING CONCLUSIONS FROM TESTS OF CONTROL

After performing tests of control, the audit team should determine whether or not the results provide sufficient evidence that the tested controls operate effectively to achieve the intended control reliance, and therefore the auditor can rely on the control to conclude that the related transaction class or balance is free from material misstatement.

When a test of a key control shows the control has failed to operate effectively, the audit team may determine that the control over the process is ineffective and the intended control reliance cannot be achieved for the particular risk.

Where the auditor concludes that the tests of control support the intended control reliance, but there were some deviations noted in the testing, the audit team should evaluate all deviations to determine their cause. This evaluation should consider whether the deviation indicates the presence of more significant issues such as a pervasive control failure, fraud or override of controls, as it may impact other controls. The effect of the deviation is not mitigated even when it is isolated to a specific type of transaction, a specific time period, or to a specific employee. To illustrate this, let's say the auditor was testing the controls surrounding monthly bank reconciliations and, in the testing of six reconciliations, there were minor deviations in two reconciliations caused by human error. The auditor should investigate whether this deviation may impact other controls, e.g. if the individual responsible for the errors was also responsible for the stock reconciliations, the auditor should consider if this may result in a weak control environment relating to stock.

The audit team then determines, as a result of the failed test of control, the required substantive procedures to be carried out to ensure that the auditor obtains sufficient appropriate audit evidence that the financial statements are free from misstatement. For example, if the tests of control on the valuation of trade receivables failed, the auditor has to develop substantive procedures to address this assertion. Examples of such substantive procedures would be review of aged receivables listing and post-year-end cash receipts.

Furthermore, all internal control weaknesses should be communicated to management and/or those charged with governance in line with ISA 265.

5.5 CONCLUSION

Tests of control are very effective and efficient audit procedures in an audit, but their relevance depends on the effectiveness of the entity's internal control system. Whilst tests of control can be utilised to test operating controls, an auditor cannot form an opinion as to whether or not the financial statements are free from material misstatement solely using tests of control. The results of tests of control affect the nature, timing and extent of substantive procedures. Substantive testing will be discussed in **Chapter 6**.

SUMMARY OF LEARNING OBJECTIVES

Learning Objective 1 To be able to develop tests of control and recognise that there are different tests that can be designed

Tests of control developed by the auditor will depend on the control being tested. The majority of tests of control will be enquiry and observation, re-performance or computer assisted auditing techniques. Practical applications of these testing techniques are illustrated in *Nolan*, Chapter 5.

Learning Objective 2 To assess the suitability of timing of tests of control

Unlike substantive testing, tests of control will not be performed at one set period of time, e.g. just at year end. When testing controls, the auditor requires audit evidence of controls operating effectively during the period, not just at year end. Therefore, commonly, controls will be tested at various points during the year. Furthermore, tests of control should occur early in the audit process as the output of the tests of control affect the nature, timing and extent of substantive procedures.

Learning Objective 3 To be able to assess the results of the tests of control and initiate the necessary action

After performing tests of control, the audit team determines whether or not the results provide sufficient evidence that the control is operating effectively and can be relied upon. When a test of control shows a failure of a control, the auditor will either perform further testing on compensating controls, or develop substantive procedures to address the risk of material misstatement.

QUESTIONS

In each of the scenarios presented in the questions below, there is an issue/(s) which needs to be addressed by the auditor (an indicator) in relation to tests of controls. You should read the questions and attempt to address the issues relating to tests of controls.

(See **Appendix One** of this text for Suggested Solutions to the Review Questions.)

Review Questions

Question 5.1 (Based on Chartered Accountants Ireland, FAE Autumn 2006)

Comcomp Limited

Comcomp Limited is a very successful company that manufactures high quality computer components. It employs 200 staff and has had an average annual turnover of €/£25 million over the past three years. Your firm has acted as auditors for Comcomp for a number of years and you are the senior on the audit of the financial statements for the year ended 31 December 2011. As this is your first involvement in the audit of Comcomp, you review the prior year's file in detail and note that there were no significant problems identified.

Your audit assistant has been working on the audit of purchases and payables. As the first step she has documented the purchases systems in four stages below. In order for your audit assistant to carry out controls testing on the controls, identify four key specific controls tests for her to perform in order to obtain sufficient audit assurance over the operation of the control activities as described.

Furthermore, Mark Kelly, the audit engagement partner has asked you to provide him with the relevant paragraph for inclusion in the management letter advising Comcomp of three key weaknesses that exist in the cash cycle. As well as the weakness, he has asked you to include the related risk and recommendation for improvement.

Purchases System

Stage 1

The system automatically flags when pre-determined re-order levels are reached. These requisitions are printed by the purchasing supervisor and forwarded to the buying department which verifies that the requisition has been properly approved.

All goods requisitions must be authorised by an appropriate level of management depending on the value of the order. The procedural manual stipulates the following approval levels:

Purchases up to €/£1,000	Purchasing Supervisor
Purchases over €/£1,000 and below €/£25,000	Purchasing Manager
Purchases over €/£25,000	Finance Director

Comcomp has a list of preferred suppliers for different categories of purchases. Once a suitable supplier has been selected, and the purchase price agreed, the order is processed on the computer and dispatched.

Stage 2

The goods inwards clerk receives all goods into the goods inwards warehouse, views the order on the system and ensures that there are no discrepancies between the order and the goods received and signs the GRN. Any discrepancies are physically marked on the GRN and the system updated to record the actual quantities received. A copy of the signed GRN is then filed by the goods inwards clerk.

Stage 3

All invoices are stamped on receipt and given a unique sequential reference number. The purchases ledger clerk checks the arithmetical accuracy of the invoice, verifies it against the goods received information on the computer and matches the GRN to the invoice. The purchases ledger clerk prepares a daily batch control sheet detailing all invoices and the total amount payable. Once the stamp is completed on each invoice, the purchasing supervisor signs it off as approved before forwarding it on to the input clerk to record the invoice on the purchase system. Once all invoices for the day have been inputted into the system, the input clerk produces a batch total from the system and this is agreed to the daily batch control sheet. This reconciliation is signed off as agreed by both the input clerk and the purchasing supervisor.

Stage 4

Cheques are generated at the end of each month to clear the full outstanding balance on the purchases ledger. The purchasing supervisor then approves these cheques for payment and has them signed by the appropriate cheque signatory as given in the procedural manual (same approvals as Stage 1).

Question 5.2 (Based on Chartered Accountants Ireland, FAE Autumn 2008)

Coal Limited

Coal Limited is a coal merchant, and it sells coal to domestic customers using a network of depots throughout Ireland. The company's Accounts Department, including the Financial Controller and Financial Director, is located at its Head Office.

You have just completed the interim audit fieldwork for the year ended 31 December 2011 and are reviewing the systems notes for the cash and treasury cycle that you have documented.

The engagement partner, Paula Flynn, is meeting the client and would like to discuss weaknesses already identified along with tests of control that the audit team intend to perform at year end to obtain sufficient audit assurance over the operation of the control activities identified. She has requested that, for each weakness, identify the related risk and suggest a recommendation for improvement. Furthermore, she has recommended that you develop four key specific controls tests.

Cash and Treasury Cycle Systems Notes

Receipts

Money is received into all depots in the form of cash and cheques from customers. A number of accounts are paid by direct debit and via the internet. Any such receipts are identified by the Financial Controller at Head Office during a daily review of the bank statements.

Money can also be received from the delivery men who deliver coal directly to customers' doorsteps. Each delivery man records sales in his book, and takes receipt of cash and issues a receipt to the customer for the sale. The delivery men return to the depot every evening and their books are reconciled to the cash receipts, and the sales ledger and cash book are updated. For those customers who will send the payment directly to the depot only the sales ledger is updated.

Each depot prepares a daily report detailing all receipts including a breakdown of cash/cheques and the customer accounts to which they relate. The depots make daily lodgements to the bank into the 'Coal No 1' account.

A daily report is faxed by each depot through to the Head Office supervisor which details the receipts that have been posted at the depots. The supervisor prepares a summary sheet on a daily basis which collates receipts from all the depots.

Statements are sent out from Head Office to customers on a monthly basis and all queries are followed up by the Head Office supervisor.

Purchases

There is one purchases ledger maintained, which is used to record payments being made for all the depots. All purchase invoices are received into Head Office either directly from the supplier, or via the individual depots which forward them directly to Head Office.

At Head Office, the supervisor records all invoices on the purchase ledger as soon as they are received. The invoices are placed on hold awaiting authorisation for payment. The invoices are returned to the respective depots where they must be reviewed and agreed for payment by the respective managers, who authorise the payment by signing the face of the invoice.

Following authorisation, the invoices are returned to the supervisor in Head Office, who checks that the appropriate approval has been given and then lifts the block on their payment, allowing them to form part of the next payment run.

Payment runs are made on a weekly basis by the supervisor. All payments are made by cheque. All cheques must be signed by at least two authorised signatories.

Reconciliation

Bank reconciliations are prepared by the Financial Controller on a monthly basis. All bank reconciliations are reviewed by the Financial Director on a timely basis.

6

SUBSTANTIVE TESTING

LEARNING OBJECTIVES

In reading and studying this chapter, your objectives are to be able to:
- design and apply audit tests which will give appropriate audit evidence to support the financial statements assertions, taking into account the identified risks;
- choose appropriate sampling techniques;
- design and apply audit tests to transactions and balances as required by the auditing standards.

6.1 INTRODUCTION

As explained in ISA 330 *The Auditor's Responses to Assessed Risks*, substantive procedures (or testing) are audit procedures designed to detect material misstatements at the assertion level.

There are two types of substantive procedures:
1. substantive analytical procedures (see **Section 6.2**); and
2. tests of detail (see **Section 6.3**).

When carrying out substantive procedures, the auditor has to ensure that the procedure is appropriately aimed at a particular assertion. This can be illustrated as below:

EXAMPLE 6.1: APPLYING AUDIT TESTS TO ASSERTIONS

ASSERTION	PROCEDURES	
	Relevant to the Assertion	**Not Relevant to the Assertion**
Existence of creditors at year end	*Test of creditor payments made after the year end –* this tests if the payments made after the year end relating to costs incurred during the year are appropriately accrued at year end	*Test of creditor payments made during the year –* no impact on the year end liability and therefore not relevant to the existence assertion
Valuation of debtors at year end	*Test of debtor receipts after the year end –* this confirms whether the year-end debtor balance has been received since the year end, or if a provision for bad or doubtful debts is necessary	*Debtors' confirmations –* offers little evidence whether the customer is likely to pay the debt or not and, therefore, irrelevant to the assertion
Existence of stock at the year end	*Attendance at stock count –* confirms whether stock recorded exists	*Trace stock items back to purchase invoices during the year –* does not test the stock actually exists at the year-end

In addition, when designing substantive tests, the auditor should always think about the audit evidence that will be derived from carrying out the substantive tests. The quantity of audit evidence required is affected by the risk of material misstatement (the greater the risk, the more audit evidence is likely to be required) and also by the quality of such audit evidence (the higher the quality, the less audit evidence is likely to be required). This does not mean, however, that large quantities of audit evidence will compensate for low quality audit evidence. (Audit evidence is discussed in more detail in **Chapter 7**.)

In this chapter, we will examine the key elements of substantive testing as directed by auditing standards.

6.2 SUBSTANTIVE ANALYTICAL PROCEDURES

We discussed in **Chapter 3** how analytical procedures are used for risk assessment in the planning stage. ISA 520 *Analytical Procedures* sets out the requirements for, and guidance on, analytical procedures utilised during fieldwork (substantive analytical procedures) and at completion (discussed in **Chapter 7**).

As substantive procedures, analytical procedures can provide evidence about one or more assertions related to an account balance or class of transaction. At this stage, analytical procedures provide all or a portion of the evidence required to respond to a risk.

Substantive analytical procedures may be appropriate when the balance involves a large volume of transactions that are predictable over time. For example, wages and salaries figure in an entity which has 500 employees, and pays salaries on a weekly basis, is going to include a large number of transactions. Furthermore, the cost can be predicted over time based on movement of employees, or pay increases. Therefore, based on discussions with management and knowledge of the business the auditor can easily set an expectation of what the salary cost should be. In this case, substantive analytical procedures may identify unexpected variances which may indicate a potential misstatement.

A key requirement to allow the auditor to perform substantive analytical procedures effectively is that reliable data are available to perform relevant analytical procedures and an expectation can be reasonably predicted. For example, referring to the example above, whilst an expectation can be reasonably predicted, the auditor should assess the accuracy of the information contained in the wages and salary costs. This will form part of the risk assessment procedures when the auditor is reviewing the controls and, e.g. performing walkthroughs on the payroll process. If the results of these procedures conclude that the controls surrounding the payroll process are weak, the auditor may carry out some additional tests on the accuracy of the payroll cost prior to carrying out substantive analytical procedures. This may involve, e.g. extracting a sample of employees and tracing their salary cost from the payroll system to nominal ledger.

In contrast to the use of analytical procedures as risk assessment procedures, those applied as substantive procedures involve more extensive data gathering, analysis and evaluation, and the judgements involved are more objective than the analytical procedures performed during risk assessment. For example, the results of the substantive analytical procedures will determine if, in the auditor's opinion, the balance or class of transactions is free from material misstatement. Accordingly, the tests need to be well-defined and structured.

When substantive analytical procedures are performed, the audit team should document the following:

1. the *expectation* and the factors considered in the development of that expectation, e.g. salary costs should have increased by 5% because the entity gave employees pay rises of 5% in the year;
2. the *results* of the comparison between the expectation and the entity's recorded amount, e.g. the comparison of the two showing that employee costs are even higher;
3. any *additional auditing procedures* performed in response to material (or unexpected) differences and the results of those procedures. For example, if the analytical procedures illustrated that the salary costs were higher than the expected amount, the audit team would carry out further audit procedures such as discussing the differences with management and corroborating management's explanations; and
4. any *corroborating evidence* obtained to support any large or unusual variances between actual figures and expectations.

It should be noted that ISA 520 specifically requires auditors, when carrying out substantive analytical procedures, to ensure the following:

1. The substantive analytical procedure is *suitable* for addressing the relevant assertion. For example, analytical procedures are suited to testing the accuracy assertion regarding payroll expense as the auditor can develop an expectation and test against that expectation. However, analytical procedures would not satisfy the existence assertion in relation to the payroll liability.
2. The data used for analytical procedures is *reliable*. For example, the auditor would need to be satisfied that the controls surrounding the production of the payroll schedule are adequate before they could use the schedule as a basis for corroborating the explanations. This may require some testing of the accuracy of the report produced.
3. An expectation can be developed to a level of *accuracy* which, when compared to the actual result, will identify a misstatement. For example, the auditor would develop an expectation that salary costs have increased by 5% from the prior year based on their discussions with management and knowledge of the business, that all employees received a 5% increase, and there has been no movement in employee numbers. If the actual results of the analytical review then result in a variation of greater than 5%, the auditor can identify a misstatement.
4. The *acceptable* amount of difference from the expectation is determined in advance. This will be based on materiality as well as the auditor's experience and judgement on what is reasonable. For example, a 10% variance on the prior year may be accepted without further investigation, however, anything above this amount may indicate material misstatement.

If the auditor identifies unacceptable variances which are inconsistent with expectations, they should perform alternative substantive procedures.

6.3 TESTS OF DETAIL

Substantive tests of detail involve selecting specific classes of transactions, account balances, and disclosures and performing testing on that particular class of item, e.g. selecting debtors and performing debtors' circularisations. Tests of detail are discussed in **Nolan**,[1] Chapters 8 to 14, for all audit areas as follows:

- tangible fixed assets,
- inventories,
- revenue and receivables,
- bank and cash,
- investments,
- purchases and payables, and
- share capital and reserves.

This chapter will discuss some more advanced audit areas and the relevant tests of detail that would be appropriate.

6.3.1 Rebate Accrual

To illustrate the risks and appropriate responses to those risks in relation to the audit of a rebate accrual, an example is noted below.

EXAMPLE 6.2: AUDIT OF REBATE ACCRUAL

Your client pays rebates to various customers based on agreed rates once the customer purchases a certain amount of goods. The rebate amounts are agreed verbally and there are no rebate agreements in place. The rebate accrual in the financial statements amounts to €/£123,000 and is regarded as material.

6.3.1.1 Risks

When auditing a rebate accrual at the year end, the auditor should be aware of the risk that the rebate accrual is not complete at the year-end, is incorrectly calculated and therefore the valuation is also incorrect (risk of error); or of a potential collusion between the finance team and customers in payment of rebates (risk of fraud).

6.3.1.2 Audit Procedures

1. Select a sample of rebate accruals and:
    (a) review past rebate payment percentage for consistency of rebate percentage applied in the current year;
    (b) check that the sales on which the rebate has been calculated have been invoiced and paid to ensure that the rebate is based on actual sales;

---

[1] Martin Nolan, *External Auditing and Assurance: An Irish Textbook* (1st Edition, Chartered Accountants Ireland, 2010)

   (c) review post-year-end credit notes to ensure that the items sold used to calculate the rebate accrual have not been returned; and

   (d) review post-year-end rebates paid and compare to amounts posted as rebate accruals to test the accuracy of the accrual.

2. Consider circularising customers for confirmation of the agreed rebate percentage and the amounts due to them.

6.3.2 Investment Property Valuation

To illustrate the risks and appropriate responses to those risks in relation to the audit of investment properties, an example is noted below.

EXAMPLE 6.3: AUDIT OF VALUATION OF INVESTMENT PROPERTY

> Your client acquired a property for redevelopment three years ago for a price of €/£3.5 million and adopts the fair value model of valuation under IAS 40 Investment Property. In the current year's financial statements the directors have written down the investment property to €/£1.5 million on the basis that the market is not as active as it previously was. They have based their valuation on the potential sales value of houses they can build on the land.

IAS 40 *Investment Property* requires that investment properties should be included in the balance sheet at fair value. The standard does not require the valuation to be made by a person(s) qualified to perform property valuations, e.g. a Chartered Surveyor.

6.3.2.1 Risks

The risks for the auditor when testing the valuation of investment properties are the accuracy of the valuations.

ISA 540 *Auditing Accounting Estimates, Including Fair Value Accounting Estimates, and Related Disclosures* includes requirements and guidance for auditors in this regard. Some of the substantive tests of detail the auditor would carry out are included below.

6.3.2.2 Audit Procedures

Audit procedures in relation to the audit of the valuation of investment property are as follows:

1. Discuss with management the valuation basis and assumptions:

   (a) compare assumptions with actual post-year-end events;

   (b) obtain evidence to support management's valuation basis with regard to the asset in question, and upon which the assumptions are based;

   (c) compare the basis of the valuation with the industry and marketplace norm; and

   (d) assess whether or not significant assumptions used by management are reasonable;

2. Consider the requirement to include an expert to value the property;
3. If uncertainties exist, consider the need to include an emphasis of matter paragraph in the audit report;[2] and
4. Ensure the disclosures in the financial statements are adequate in line with IAS 40.

6.3.3 Warranty Provision

To illustrate the risks and appropriate responses to those risks in relation to the audit of warranty provisions, an example is noted below.

EXAMPLE 6.4: AUDIT OF WARRANTY PROVISION

Your client is a car manufacturer and on sale of a new car the car manufacturer issues a free two-year warranty. As a result, the client includes a warranty provision in the financial statements which is considered to be material.

6.3.3.1 Risks

In auditing the warranty provision, the risks are that the provision is incomplete or valued inaccurately as it is based on unreasonable or inappropriate assumptions.

Similar to valuation of properties, ISA 540 *Auditing Accounting Estimates, Including Fair Value Accounting Estimates, and Related Disclosures* includes requirements and guidance for auditors in this regard. Some of the substantive tests of detail the auditor would carry out are included below.

6.3.3.2 Audit Procedures

Audit procedures in relation to the audit of warranty procedures are as follows:
1. Discuss the basis of the warranty provision with management:
   (a) evaluate the reasonableness of the provision; and
   (b) review warranty claims and costs after the year end and compare to the level of the provision.
2. Select a sample of warranty provisions from prior year(s) and compare to actual warranty claims made against those provisions to assess the accuracy of management's assumptions.
3. Assess the adequacy of the provision and determine if an adjustment is required.

---

[2] Emphasis of matter paragraphs are discussed in **Chapter 8**.

6.3.4 Going Concern

To illustrate the risks and appropriate responses to those risks in relation to the audit work carried out to determine whether an entity can continue as a going concern, an example is noted below.

EXAMPLE 6.5: AUDIT OF GOING CONCERN

Your client has made a net loss for the year and has been in a net liability position for the last two years. They have prepared cash flow projections which illustrate that the company can continue as a going concern.

6.3.4.1 Risk

The risk is that the company cannot actually maintain the going concern basis for 12 months from the date of signing the audit report, as cash flow forecasts are based on unreasonable or inappropriate assumptions.

ISA 570 *Going Concern* includes requirements and guidance in this regard. Some of the substantive tests of detail the auditor would carry out are included below.

6.3.4.2 Audit Procedures

Audit procedures in relation to the audit of going concern are as follows:
1. Obtain management's cash flow projections and discuss the basis of assumptions:
   (a) compare the assumptions to actual post-year-end events, and
   (b) compare targets to the industry norm and marketplace.
2. Review prior-year cash flow projections and compare to actual to assess the accuracy of management assumptions.
3. Review loan agreements and banking facilities for any covenant breaches which may indicate a risk of non-renewal of facilities.
4. Review minutes of meetings which may indicate any financial difficulty during the year.
5. Review subsequent events for further indications of going concern difficulties.
6. Consider the impact on the audit report:
   (a) if uncertainties exist, consider including an emphasis of matter paragraph in the audit report; or
   (b) if the auditor does not agree with the going concern basis, consider modification of the audit report.

6.4 SAMPLING TECHNIQUES

When carrying out substantive tests of detail as discussed at the beginning of this chapter, it may not always be practical to perform procedures on all of the population. For example, if the auditor was testing the debtors' listing for existence, and the debtors' listing was made up of two million balances, it would not be practical or cost effective to test the existence of every single balance. Therefore, when carrying out substantive tests of detail on transactions and balances, the auditor should use a sampling technique to test a representative sample and extend the results of that test over the full population.

ISA 530 *Audit Sampling* defines sampling as "the application of audit procedures to less than 100% of items within a population of audit relevance such that all sampling units have a chance of selection in order to provide the auditor with a reasonable basis on which to draw conclusions about the entire population".

There are two types of sampling that an auditor can apply:
• **Statistical Sampling** This method is a random selection of a sample from a population. It is normally achieved using tailored software. This method of sampling ensures that each item has an equal chance of being selected.
• **Non-statistical Sampling** This method is not random and is based on the judgement of the auditor. For example, the sample may be chosen based on every 10th item, or all items over a certain value.

When an auditor uses sampling as a technique, the process can be explained in the following steps:
Step 1 *Define the population* – for example, creditors' listing, debtors' listing, or post-year-end payments.

Step 2 *Determine the sampling technique* – statistical or non-statistical.

Step 3 *Determine the sample size* – the level of sampling risk that the auditor is willing to accept affects the sample size required. The lower the risk the auditor is willing to accept, the larger the sample size will need to be.

As noted in ISA 530, sampling risk is the risk that the auditor's conclusion based on a sample may be different from the conclusion if the entire population were subjected to the same audit procedure.

The sample size can be determined by the application of a statistically based formula, usually based around materiality, or through the exercise of professional judgement. Appendix 2 and Appendix 3 of ISA 530 give illustrative examples of when a sample size should be increased or decreased.

Step 4 *Select items for testing* – using either statistical or non-statistical methods.

Step 5 *Perform audit procedures* – for example, if the sample was selected to test the existence of trade debtors, the auditor would issue a debtor confirmation for each item in the sample or, if the sample was selected to test the valuation of stock, the auditor would trace each item to its corresponding purchase invoice to verify cost.

Step 6 *Identify the nature and cause of deviations and misstatements* – if the auditor finds an error when testing the valuation of stock, they may determine that the error only arises in one particular line of stock. On this basis, the auditor may decide to extend the testing of that particular stock item, rather than testing the full stock listing.

Step 7 *Project the misstatements* – when the auditor finds errors in a sample used for substantive testing, e.g. stock valuation, the error should be extrapolated over the entire population. For example:

	€
Total Stock Value	800,000
Sample tested (40% of entire population)	320,000
Error in sample	30,000
Extrapolated over total population	75,000

If the auditor concludes that the error was a once-off, they would not extrapolate over the full population. For example, if the valuation testing highlighted one stock item (say out of a sample of 20) where the cost per invoice was input incorrectly into the system, the auditor may conclude that this was an unintentional human error and therefore not necessary to extrapolate the error over the population. Compare this to a situation where, e.g. the valuation testing discovered numerous pricing errors (say 9 errors out of a sample of 20), the auditor might conclude there could be further errors in the stock listing and therefore extrapolate the error over the full population.

Step 8 *Evaluate results* – the auditor should compare any extrapolated error to performance materiality and determine if there is a risk of material misstatement. If so, the auditor may request management to investigate misstatements, and propose an adjustment. Alternatively, the auditor may tailor further audit procedures to gain the required level of assurance.

6.5 OTHER SUBSTANTIVE TESTING

The auditor is always required to perform substantive procedures on all material balances. However, there are additional substantive tests of details that the auditor is required to perform in all instances details of which are included in:

ISA 501 *Audit Evidence – Specific Considerations for Selected Items*
ISA 540 *Auditing Accounting Estimates, Including Fair Value Accounting Estimates and Related Disclosures*
ISA 550 *Related Parties*

ISA 610 *Using the Work of Internal Auditors*
ISA 620 *Using the Work of an Auditor's Expert*

We will discuss these below.

6.5.1 Audit Evidence – Specific Considerations for Selected Items

ISA 501 specifies audit procedures for three specific audit assertions:
1. existence and condition of inventory;
2. completeness of litigation and claims involving the entity; and
3. presentation and disclosure of segment information.

6.5.1.1 Existence and Condition of Inventory

The standard notes that, if inventory is material to the financial statements, the auditor should obtain sufficient appropriate evidence of its existence and condition by attending the physical inventory count. At this count, the auditor should:
1. Evaluate management's instructions for controlling and recording the results of the physical count;
2. Observe the physical inventory count performed;
3. Inspect the inventory for existence and evidence of any damaged or obsolete items; and
4. Perform test counts.

An example of an audit programme for attendance at inventory to meet these objectives is included below at **Appendix 6.1**.

6.5.1.2 Completeness of Litigation and Claims involving the Entity

ISA 501 notes that the auditor shall design and perform audit procedures in order to identify litigation and claims involving the entity which may give rise to a risk of material misstatement. These procedures are required, irrespective of whether or not this was identified as a risk at the risk assessment stage. These procedures are required to ensure that the financial statements contain adequate provisions for any potential claims or legal expenses.

Examples of such audit procedures are:
1. Enquire of management if there are any legal issues in progress;
2. Review minutes of meetings for any indications of legal issues; and
3. Review profit and loss expenses for any legal expenses.

The auditor may also consider issuing a letter to the entity's legal advisors requesting confirmation of any current litigation, and any unpaid legal expenses.

6.5.1.3 *Presentation and Disclosure of Segment Information*

Under certain financial reporting frameworks, there is a requirement to include segmental disclosures in the financial statements. For example, IFRS 8 *Operating Segments* requires entities to disclose segment information to enable users of the financial statements to evaluate the nature and financial effects of the business activities in which it engages and the economic environment in which it operates.

The auditor should ensure that the required disclosures are prepared in accordance with the requirements of the relevant financial reporting framework. Examples of these procedures are as follows:

1. Obtain an understanding of the methods used by management in determining segment information and evaluate if this is in line with IFRS 8;
2. Review the minutes of management meetings to ensure that the information used by the decision makers is similar to the segmental information included in the financial statements; and
3. Perform a reconciliation of the segmental information to the financial statements.

6.5.1.4. *Auditing Accounting Estimates, Including Fair Value Accounting Estimates and Related Disclosures*

When the financial statements contain accounting estimates and the auditor concludes that there are risks of material misstatement, ISA 540 dictates the audit procedures that the auditor should undertake in relation to these estimates.

Audit procedures in relation to the audit of accounting estimates are as follows:

1. Review the basis of management's assumptions in calculating the accounting estimate:
   (a) test the data on which the accounting estimate is based for accuracy, completeness and relevance and whether the accounting estimate has been properly determined using the relevant data and management assumptions;
   (b) consider the source, relevance and reliability of external data used to make the accounting estimate;
   (c) review information and assumptions used to form the accounting estimate and determine if it is consistent with the audit team's understanding of the entity; and
   (d) recalculate the accounting estimate.
2. Develop a point estimate or a range to evaluate management's point estimate.
3. Ensure that the recognition and disclosure of the estimate is in line with the requirements of the relevant accounting standard.
4. Obtain written representations where significant assumptions have been made by management in making the accounting estimate.

6.5.2 Related Parties

ISA 550 *Related Parties* requires the audit team to perform specific audit procedures to obtain evidence regarding management's identification, proper accounting for and disclosure of related parties and related party transactions. In order to meet these objectives, a sample of a related party audit programme is included below at **Appendix 6.2**.

6.5.3 Using the Work of Internal Auditors

When an internal auditor has been involved in the audit and the external auditor wishes to rely on the internal auditor's conclusions, the external auditor shall evaluate and perform audit procedures on the work of the internal auditor to determine its adequacy for the external auditor's purposes.

Examples of such procedures are:
1. Determine that the internal auditor has adequate technical training and proficiency to carry out the work by requesting evidence of membership of a professional body and details of any regulatory compliance procedures.
2. Review the work carried out by the internal auditor and determine that:
   a) the work was properly supervised, reviewed and documented;
   b) adequate audit evidence has been obtained to reach the conclusions drawn by the internal auditor;
   c) the reports prepared by the internal auditor are consistent with the work performed; and
   d) any exceptions or significant findings disclosed by the internal auditors have been appropriately resolved.
3. Communicate to those charged with governance the extent of reliance on the internal auditor's work.

6.5.4 Using the Work of an Expert

In some circumstances the auditor may need to seek an individual with expertise in a field other than accounting or auditing to obtain sufficient appropriate audit evidence.

Experts are people with special skills or knowledge in a particular field other than accounting or auditing, such as actuaries, valuation experts, solicitors, engineers and environmental consultants.

The audit team may encounter complex or subjective matters potentially material to the financial statements that require special skills or knowledge and may require using the work of an expert to obtain sufficient audit evidence. For example, the use of an expert should be considered in matters involving:
• valuation issues (such as appraised valuations of property and stock options);
• fair value determinations (such as defined benefit pension schemes);

- the determination of physical characteristics relating to the quantity and condition of assets (such as mineral reserves);
- the determination of amounts derived by using specialised techniques or methods (such as actuarial calculations); and
- the interpretation of technical requirements, regulations and agreements (such as legal determinations as to whether or not a contract is binding or an engineer's determination of whether or not technical specifications have been met).

As per ISA 620 *Using the Work of an Auditor's Expert*, when engaging with an expert there are a number of procedures that the auditor needs to carry out. These are listed below along with the audit procedures that would be carried out to meet the requirements of ISA 620.

FIGURE 6.1: AUDIT PROCEDURES REQUIRED WHEN USING THE WORK OF AN EXPERT

Requirement	Procedure
That the expert has the necessary competence and capabilities for the auditor's purposes	1. Obtain proof of the expert's membership of a professional body 2. Discuss with other professionals within or external to the audit firm who are familiar with the expert's work; obtain references 3. Rely on previous experience with the expert
That the expert is objective and can carry out the work independently	1. Inquire from the client if they have any previous relationship with, or interest in, the expert 2. Discuss with the expert any relationship or financial interests they may have with or in the client 3. Discuss the ethical requirements that apply to the expert as a member of their relevant professional body 4. Conclude as to whether or not there are risks to objectivity and, if there are such risks, if there are sufficient safeguards in place
That the auditor obtains an understanding of the expert's field of expertise so they can determine the nature, scope and objectives of the work, and evaluate the adequacy of the work for the auditor's purposes	1. Discuss with the expert 2. Gain an understanding of the assumptions used and if they are suitable for financial reporting purposes 3. Gain an understanding of the internal and external data that the expert utilises

The auditor agrees with the expert the scope, roles and responsibilities, and timeliness and forms of communication expected from the expert; also agree confidentiality requirements	1. Issue an engagement letter or service agreement to the expert
Evaluate the expert's work for relevance and reasonableness, including assumptions and methods used	1. Review assumptions used by the expert to ensure they are generally accepted in the expert's field and consistent with financial reporting requirements 2. Review the expert's working papers and reports 3. Examine any external data utilised and check them to reliable sources 4. Confirm relevant matters with third parties 5. Perform detailed analytical procedures 6. Re-perform calculations 7. Discuss with another expert for reasonableness 8. Discuss the report with management

If the auditor concludes that the work of the expert is not adequate for the auditor's purposes, they should agree further work to be carried out by the expert, or carry out further audit procedures. If the auditor cannot resolve the matter through additional work and the matter is material, the auditor should modify the audit opinion.

The auditor should not make reference to the work of an expert in the auditor's report unless it is relevant to an understanding of a modified audit report, e.g. if the results of the expert's work led to a modified opinion, the auditor may wish to include details of the expert's work in the audit report if it helped the user to understand the issue.

An example of an audit programme for testing the work of an auditor's expert is included below at **Appendix 6.3**.

6.5.5 Opening Balances

In some circumstances, the auditor will be carrying out an audit where they have not audited the comparative figures and, as a result, the opening balances. This could occur where either it is a new audit where another auditor audited the prior period figures or where a previously audit-exempt client falls within the requirements for an audit for the first time.

ISA 510 *Initial Audit Engagements – Opening Balances* requires that on the aforementioned initial audit engagement it is the auditor's responsibility to obtain sufficient appropriate audit evidence as to whether or not the opening balances contain material misstatements which affect current-year figures; and appropriate accounting policies have been consistently applied to opening balances and current-year financial statements, or changes in accounting policies have been adequately presented.

In order to achieve these objectives, the auditor should carry out the following substantive tests of detail procedures on opening balances:

1. Check if prior-period closing balances have been correctly brought forward to the current period;
2. Determine if the opening balances reflect the current year accounting policies;
3. Where prior-period figures were audited, review the predecessor's working papers and conclude if sufficient evidence of accuracy of opening balances can be obtained; and
4. Where prior-period figures were not audited, or sufficient appropriate evidence could not be obtained from the predecessor's working papers, perform specific audit procedures to obtain evidence regarding opening balances.

6.5.5.1 Audit Procedures

Examples of specific audit procedures to test opening balances are listed below:

EXAMPLE 6.6: SPECIFIC AUDIT PROCEDURES FOR OPENING BALANCES

Opening Balance	Assertion	Test
Fixed Assets	Existence	1. Physically inspect assets
	Valuation	1. Re-inspect purchase invoices for cost of asset 2. Consider if any impairment indicators were in place at the end of the previous period
Stock	Existence	1. Carry out a stocktake and perform roll back procedures based on sales and purchases for the relevant period
	Valuation	1. Using stock records at the end of the prior period, select a sample of stock and trace the items to purchase invoices before that year end to verify cost, and sales invoices in the current year to verify net realisable value 2. Assess that each stock item selected was valued at the lower of cost and net realisable value

Debtors	Existence	1. Select a sample of debtors at the end of the prior period and issue debtors' circularisations for the balance at the end of the prior year
	Valuation	1. Review cash receipts for the period and compare to the list of opening debtors' balances 2. Consider the need for a provision to be created against opening balances
Creditors	Existence	1. Review cheque payments and invoices received at the beginning of the year to ensure that all liabilities were correctly included in the prior period
	Valuation	1. Review cheque payments at the beginning of the year and compare with the liabilities to ensure the correct balance was recorded
Bank	Existence	1. Obtain bank statements for both the prior and the current years to ensure that the year-end balance was correctly recorded

If the auditor is unable to obtain sufficient appropriate audit evidence regarding opening balances, they shall express a modified opinion based on limitation of scope.

6.6 CONCLUSION

Substantive procedures are developed by the auditor to address risks of material misstatement as identified at the risk assessment stage. In addressing these risks, the auditor must also comply with the requirements of the International Standards on Auditing (UK and Ireland) as referred to throughout this chapter. The sufficiency and accuracy of the audit evidence obtained to complete the audit procedures will determine whether the auditor can form an opinion as to whether the financial statements are free from material misstatement. These conclusions are drawn at the completion stage of the audit which is discussed in **Chapter 7**.

SUMMARY OF LEARNING OBJECTIVES

Learning Objective 1 To be able to design and apply audit tests which will give appropriate audit evidence to support the financial statements assertions, taking into account the identified risks

Substantive procedures will either be analytical procedures or tests of detail. Whether analytical procedures or tests of detail are chosen will be determined by the assertion being addressed and the level of risk of material misstatement identified at the risk assessment stage.

Learning Objective 2 To be able to choose appropriate sampling techniques

Sampling techniques are used to enhance the efficiency and effectiveness of the audit by applying audit procedures to less than 100% of the population. Sampling can either be statistical or non-statistical and the results of the audit procedures are then extrapolated over the entire population.

Learning Objective 3 To be able to design and apply audit tests to transactions and balances as required by the auditing standards

An auditor will design and apply audit procedures to address risks of material misstatements, as well as to comply with requirements set by the auditing standards.

QUESTIONS

In each of the scenarios presented in the questions below, there is an issue/(s) which needs to be addressed by the auditor (an indicator) in relation to substantive testing. You should read the questions and attempt to address the issues relating to substantive testing.

(See **Appendix One** of this text for Suggested Solutions to Review Questions.)

Review Questions

Question 6.1 (Based on Chartered Accountants Ireland, FAE 2010, Simulation 3)

Castleford Credit Union

Refer to the scenario presented in **Question 4.2**.

Question 6.2 (Based on Chartered Accountants Ireland, FAE 2011, Simulation 3)

RX Pharma

Refer to the scenario presented in **Question 3.2**.

APPENDIX 6.1: EXAMPLE OF AN AUDIT PROGRAMME OF ATTENDANCE INVENTORY[3]

Insert Client Name on Frontsheet

31 December 2010

G2

Audit Materiality		0
Performance Materiality		0
	Initials	Date
Prepared by:		
Reviewed by:		

Stock and Work in Progress – Attendance Substantive Tests

Return to Index

	Test	Schedule/ Comment	Initials	Date
If stock is material to the financial statements, obtain sufficient appropriate audit evidence regarding the existence and condition of the stock. ISA(UK&I)501(4)				
Preliminary Work				
1	Obtain and evaluate details of the client's planned stocktake procedures. ISA(UK&I)501(4) Review and confirm that: (i) Client staff are properly briefed; (ii) Proper controls have been set up to cover stock movements and cut-off; and (iii) The overall procedures are adequate and will result in the accurate recording of stock and work in progress.			
2	Review the prior period's audit file and/or the Audit Planning Memorandum for major stock lines held, their location and any special knowledge required for identifying stock, its condition etc.			
3	Consider whether it will be efficient to combine stocktake attendance with physical verification of fixed assets and material cash counts.			
4	Attend the client's physical stock counting, unless impracticable.			

---

[3] Source: Procedures for Quality Audit 2010 (© Chartered Accountants Ireland, 2010).

	Test	Schedule/ Comment	Initials	Date
	At the client's premises			
5	Note conclusions drawn from observing count, as to: (i) Care taken by client staff; (ii) Accuracy of recording results; (iii) The execution of the count and the manner in which instructions were followed; (iv) Control of stock movements; (v) Control over issue of count sheets and their return, including ruling off of stock sheets after last item and cancellation of issued but unused sheets; (vi) Recording of damaged, obsolete or slow-moving goods; and (vii) Control over counting to ensure that stock is not double counted or omitted and the manner in which problems were cleared.			
6	Select a sample of items from the stock on hand and: (i) Count items and trace to the count sheets, note and reconcile any differences; (ii) If an item looks obsolete or damaged ensure a note is made to this effect; and (iii) Check that enough detail is recorded on the test schedule to ensure that the item can be traced to the final stock sheets.			
7	Select a sample of items from the count sheets and: (i) Check to physical stock, note and reconcile any differences; (ii) If an item looks obsolete or damaged ensure a note is made to this effect; and (iii) Check that enough detail is recorded on the test schedule to ensure that the item can be traced to the final stock sheets.			
8	Review procedures taken to record the current stage of completion of work in progress and confirm that these are being followed.			
9	Inspect stock area, and make enquiries of the staff to determine if there are slow-moving or obsolete items of stock. In particular, enquire about and document items stored in relatively inaccessible areas, dirty or damaged items and items with previous year's stock tickets still attached.			

	Test	Schedule/ Comment	Initials	Date
10	Enquire into stocks held on behalf of third parties and make sure that these are recorded separately.	**G1**		
	Also ascertain if there is any stock held by third parties and, if material, obtain sufficient appropriate audit evidence regarding the existence and condition of that stock. ISA(UK&I)501(8)	**G1**		
11	Where the client uses numbered goods inward and outward dockets, note the last numbers used before the count commences. Where these are not in use consider and document what other cut-off controls exist. (See also point 15 below.)	**G1**		
12	Obtain a list of completed despatch documents for goods not despatched at the stocktake date and ascertain whether these were included in the stock count.			
13	Determine whether items in the goods inward area are included in the stock count.			
14	Note the numbers of the count sheets used to ensure that none is added or removed at a later date.			

15	Note for audit use:
	  (i) Last sales invoice number;
	  (ii) Last credit note number;
	  (iii) Last cheque number issued on each account;
	  (iv) Last deposit made to each bank account; and
	  (v) Any cheques written but not issued.			

16	If the physical counting is conducted at a date other than the date of the financial statements perform additional audit procedures to obtain audit evidence about whether changes in stock between the count date and the date of the financial statements are properly recorded. ISA(UK&I)501(5)			
17	If unable to attend physical stock counting make or observe some physical counts on an alternative date and perform audit procedures on intervening transactions. ISA(UK&I)501(6)			
18	If attendance at the physical stock counting is impracticable, perform alternative procedures to obtain sufficient appropriate audit evidence regarding the existence and condition of the stock. ISA(UK&I)501(7)			

	Test	Schedule/ Comment	Initials	Date
19	Note any apparent new, missing or idle fixed assets and put on fixed assets section of the file.			
20	Prepare a file note and commentary on the conduct of the stocktake and include the information obtained above.			

Conclusion

Subject to the matters noted for the reviewer, in my opinion sufficient audit assurance has been obtained to enable us to conclude that the stock count was appropriately carried out.

Name:		Accountant in Charge
Date		
Name		Reviewer
Date		

APPENDIX 6.2: EXAMPLE OF RELATED PARTY AUDIT PROGRAMME[4]

Insert Client Name on Frontsheet   Q1
31 December 2010

Audit Materiality		0
Performance Materiality		0
	Initials	Date

Related Parties

	Initials	Date
Prepared by:		
Reviewed by:		

Return to Index

	Audit Programme	Schedule/ Comment	Initials	Date
	Ensure the audit plan is reflected in the following steps. The following steps are suggestions only and should be removed or added to as necessary to address the risks of material misstatement identified at the risk assessment stage.			
1	Assess the appropriateness of the accounting policy and the accounting estimates method for this area. Ensure that the accounting policy is in accordance with accounting standards and applicable law, and that the methods used for making the accounting estimates are appropriate.			
2	Ensure the engagement team's discussion at the audit planning stage included specific consideration of the susceptibility of the financial statements to material misstatement due to fraud or error that could result from the entity's related party relationships and transactions. ISA(UK&I)550(12)			
3	Enquire of management regarding: (i) the identity of the entity's related parties, including changes from the prior period; (ii) the nature of the relationship between the entity and these related parties; (iii) whether the entity entered into any transactions with these related parties during the period and, if so, the type and purpose of the transactions. ISA(UK&I)550(13)			
4	Obtain a schedule of transactions and balances with related parties.			

---

[4] Source: Procedures for Quality Audit 2010 (© Chartered Accountants Ireland, 2010).

	Audit Programme	Schedule/ Comment	Initials	Date
5	Review and inspect bank confirmations, legal confirmations and minutes of meetings, to identify possible related party transactions.			
6	Remain alert when inspecting other records or documents for arrangements or other information that may indicate the existence of related party relationships or transactions. Examples of these records include the following: Third party confirmations (in addition to bank and legal confirmations); Share register; Tax returns; Returns to any regulators; Correspondence/invoices with lawyers; Pension schemes; Trusts for the benefit of employees; and Other relevant documentation. ISA(UK&I)550(15)			
7	If any significant transactions outside the entity's normal course of business are identified during the audit enquire of management about the nature of these transactions and whether related parties may be involved. ISA(UK&I)550(16)			
8	Share relevant information obtained about the entity's related parties with other members of the engagement team. ISA(UK&I)550(17)			
9	Identify and assess the risks of material misstatement associated with related party relationships and transactions and determine whether any of those risks are significant risks. In making the determination, treat identified significant related party transactions outside the entity's normal course of business as giving rise to significant risks. ISA(UK&I)550(18)			

	Audit Programme	Schedule/ Comment	Initials	Date
10	If fraud risk factors are identified (including circumstances relating to the existence of a related party with dominant influence) when performing the risk assessment procedures and related activities in connection with related parties, consider such information when identifying and assessing the risks of material misstatement due to fraud in accordance with ISA(UK&I)) 240. ISA(UK&I)550(19)			
11	If related party transactions are identified that were not disclosed by management: (i) promptly communicate the relevant information to the other members of the engagement team; (ii) request management to identify all transactions with the newly identified related parties; (iii) enquire as to why the entity's controls over related party transactions failed to enable the identification or disclosure of the related party relationships or transactions; (iv) perform appropriate substantive audit procedure relating to such newly identified related parties or significant related party transactions, for example: – compare transactions identified to other normal transactions to ascertain if at arm's length – obtain supporting documentation, e.g. invoice, dispatch note, etc. – review post-year-end transactions to identify if transaction was subsequently cancelled (v) reconsider the risk that other related parties or significant related party transactions may exist that management had not previously identified and perform additional audit procedures as necessary; (vi) If the non-disclosure by management appears intentional (and therefore indicative of a risk of material misstatement due to fraud) evaluate the implications for the audit. ISA(UK&I)550(22)			

	Audit Programme	Schedule/ Comment	Initials	Date
12	For identified significant related party transactions outside the entity's normal course of business:			
	(a) inspect the underlying contracts or agreements and evaluate:			
	(i) whether the business rationale (or lack thereof) of the transactions suggests that they may have been entered into to engage in fraudulent financial reporting or to conceal misappropriation of assets;			
	(ii) whether the terms of the transactions are consistent with management expectations; and			
	(iii) whether the transactions have been appropriately accounted for and disclosed in the financial statements.			
	(b) obtain audit evidence that the transactions have been appropriately authorised and approved. ISA(UK&I)550(23)			
13	If management has made an assertion in the financial statements to the effect that a related party transaction was conducted on terms equivalent to those prevailing in an arm's length transaction, obtain sufficient appropriate audit evidence about the assertion. ISA(UK&I)550(24)			
14	Evaluate whether the identified related party relationships and transactions have been appropriately accounted for and disclosed in the financial statements. ISA(UK&I)550(25)			
15	Obtain written representations from management and, where appropriate, those charged with governance that they have disclosed the identity of the entity's related parties and all the related party relationships and transactions of which they are aware and they have appropriately accounted for and disclosed such relationships and transactions. ISA(UK&I)550(26)	__A8__		
16	Communicate with those charged with governance significant matters arising during the audit in connection with the entity's related parties. ISA(UK&I)550(27)	__A7__		

	Audit Programme	Schedule/ Comment	Initials	Date
17	Document the names of the identified related parties and the nature of the related party relationships. ISA(UK&I)550(28). Also include in Matters forward for next period's audit (A3).			
18	In the Republic of Ireland, consider the legality of related party transactions and any reporting obligations which may arise in accordance with the Company Law Enforcement Act 2001 – for example in the event of an illegal loan to a director in contravention of Section 31 of the Companies Act 1990 and the Companies (Amendment) Act 2009. (See also A10.2(a). H1 & R1)			
19	For ROI, ensure that the disclosure requirements of Section 41 to 43 of the Companies Act 1990 are complied with in relation to the disclosure of related party transactions. (See also A10.2(a))			
20	Consider if there is any evidence of 'window dressing' transactions around the period end. Follow up any such transactions and ensure that any related party transactions are disclosed.			
21	Ensure that none of the audit evidence obtained from other audit procedures is in any way inconsistent with the schedule of related parties obtained.			
22	Ensure financial statements comply with the appropriate legislation and applicable accounting standards.			
23	Additional tests to ensure planning criteria have been met.			

Conclusion

Subject to the matters noted for the reviewer, in my opinion sufficient audit assurance has been obtained to enable us to conclude that the financial statements are not materially misstated in respect of related party disclosures.

Name:		Accountant in Charge	
Date			
Name		Reviewer	
Date			

APPENDIX 6.3: EXAMPLE OF AN AUDIT PROGRAMME FOR TESTING THE WORK OF AN AUDITOR'S EXPERT[5]

Insert Client Name on Frontsheet
31 December 2010

Appendix 5		
Audit Materiality		0
Performance Materiality		0
	Initials	Date
Prepared by:		
Reviewed by:		

Using the Work of an Auditor's Expert

Return to Index

	Audit Programme	Schedule/ Comment	Initials	Date
	The following work programme will not be applicable in audits where the engagement auditor has not obtained the services of an auditor's expert.			
	If expertise in a field other than accounting and auditing is necessary to obtain sufficient appropriate audit evidence the auditor shall determine whether to use the work of an auditor's expert. This may be required in relation to such matters as the valuation of complex financial instruments, fixed assets and intangible assets. ISA(UK&I)620(7)			
1	Determine in what areas the use of an auditor's expert is required. ISA(UK&I)620(8)			
2	Evaluate whether the auditor's expert has the necessary competence, capabilities and objectivity for the auditor's purposes. This shall include inquiry regarding interests and relationships that may create a threat to that expert's objectivity. ISA(UK&I)620(9)			
3	Obtain a sufficient understanding of the field of experience of the auditor's expert to determine the nature, scope and objectives of that expert's work for the auditor's purposes and to evaluate the adequacy of that work. ISA(UK&I)620(10)			
4	Agree in writing with the auditor's expert the nature, scope and objectives of that expert's work, the respective roles and responsibilities of that auditor and that expert, the nature, timing and extent of communication between the auditor and that expert including the form of any report to be provided by that expert and the need for the auditor's expert to observe confidentiality requirements. ISA(UK&I)620(11)			

---

[5] Source: Procedures for Quality Audit 2010 (© Chartered Accountants Ireland, 2010).

	Audit Programme	Schedule/ Comment	Initials	Date
5	Include copies of agreements with auditor's experts and their subsequent reports in the audit documentation.			
6	Evaluate the adequacy of the auditor's expert's work including the relevance and reasonableness of the auditor's expert's conclusions, the assumptions and methods adopted and the relevance, completeness and accuracy of any source data used. ISA(UK&I)620(12)			
7	If it is determined that the work of the auditor's expert is not adequate agree with the expert on the nature, timing and extent of further work to be performed or perform additional procedures appropriate to the circumstances. ISA(UK&I)620(13)			
8	The auditor shall not refer to the work of an auditor's expert in an auditor's report containing an unmodified opinion unless required by law to do so. ISA(UK&I)620(14)			
9	If the auditor makes reference to the work of an auditor's expert in the auditor's report because such reference is relevant to an understanding of a modification to the auditor's opinion, the auditor shall indicate in the auditor's report that such reference does not reduce the auditor's responsibility for that opinion. ISA(UK&I)620(15)			

Conclusion

Subject to the matters noted for the reviewer, in my opinion sufficient audit assurance has been obtained to enable us to conclude that the work of an auditor's expert may be relied upon for inclusion in the financial statements.

	Signed
	Date
	Reviewed
	Date

7

COMPLETION PROCEDURES

LEARNING OBJECTIVES

In reading and studying this chapter, your objectives are to be able to:
- evaluate audit evidence and justify the appropriate report;
- action the auditor's responsibilities to consider uncorrected misstatements and their impact on internal control;
- execute completion procedures required to be performed by the auditor to conclude if the financial statements are free from material misstatement; and
- be able to communicate with those charged with governance at the completion of an audit as required by the auditing standards.

7.1 INTRODUCTION

As noted in **Chapter 1**, once the audit team has completed the audit testing, there are a number of steps involved in the completion stage prior to forming an opinion on the financial statements:

1. Review working papers and evaluate whether or not sufficient audit evidence has been obtained;
2. Evaluate misstatements noted during the audit;
3. Perform analytical procedures;
4. Perform a subsequent events review;
5. Consider the ability of the entity to continue as a going concern;
6. Obtain representations from those charged with governance;
7. Report to those charged with governance; and
8. Form an opinion on the financial statements (dealt with in **Chapter 8**).

Each of these steps is examined in turn below.

7.2 REVIEW OF WORKING PAPERS

A key step in the audit process at both the fieldwork and the completion stages is the review of the audit working papers. The audit team's responsibilities could be delegated as follows:

Audit Assistant	Performing audit procedures as directed by the audit senior
Audit Senior	Review of audit assistant's working papers and performing audit procedures in line with the audit strategy and plan
Audit Manager	Detailed planning of audit tasks in line with audit strategy and plan; review of audit team's working papers

Ultimately, the review responsibilities of team members must be determined on the basis that the work of less experienced team members is reviewed by more experienced team members. The Engagement Partner, however, has ultimate responsibility for the direction, supervision and performance of the audit engagement, including reviews being performed in accordance with the firm's review policies and procedures. The engagement partner's responsibilities can be summarised as follows:

Engagement Partner	• Set audit strategy and plan; • Review of audit working papers; and • Be satisfied that sufficient appropriate audit evidence has been obtained to support the conclusions reached and for the auditor's report to be issued

When reviewing working papers, the auditor should be conscious of:

- the **sufficiency and appropriateness of audit evidence** obtained based on the requirements of ISA 500 (UK and Ireland) *Audit Evidence* ('ISA 500') (as discussed below in **Section 7.3**); and
- the **quality of the audit working papers** in communicating the audit evidence (as discussed below in this section).

ISA 230 (UK and Ireland) *Audit Documentation* ('ISA 230') requires that audit documentation should be sufficient to enable an experienced auditor, having no previous connection with the audit, to understand:

- the nature, timing and extent of the audit procedures performed to comply with the ISAs and applicable legal and regulatory requirements;
- the results of audit procedures performed, and the audit evidence obtained; and
- significant matters arising during the audit, the conclusions reached thereon and significant professional judgements made in reaching those conclusions.

Therefore, when reviewing audit working papers, the audit team member must ensure that the documentation meets ISA 230, as well as being sufficient and appropriate to support the conclusions reached. If not, it is the responsibility of the reviewer to direct the audit team to carry out further audit procedures, and update the audit working papers until they meet the requirements of ISA 230, ISA 500 and ISA 320 (UK and Ireland) *Materiality in Planning and Performing an Audit.*

A review of the quality of audit working papers can be illustrated by referring to a past Chartered Accountants exam paper. In the 2010 FAE Paper, Simulation 2, the following working paper was included in the case study. One of the requirements was for the auditor to provide review points on the working paper.

EXAMPLE 7.1: AUDIT WORKING PAPER

Client name:	Diamond Dublin Hotel Ltd	**Prepared by:**	Team member
		Date:	4 February 2010
Year ended:	31 December 2009		
		Reviewed by:	
Subject:	Intercompany transactions	**Date:**	
Financial statement areas and assertions to be addressed			
Balance Sheet:	Intercompany debtors/creditors (rights and obligations).		
Income Statement:	Sales (completeness, accuracy); cost of sales (completeness, accuracy).		

Process narrative

Advertising fees – invoices are raised on an *ad hoc* basis by either the national parent company (Diamond Hotels Ireland Ltd.) or the global parent company (Diamond Hotels International Inc.). On receipt they are debited to the advertising code in the profit and loss account and credited to the appropriate Diamond Hotels Ireland or Diamond Hotels International account on the creditors' ledger. Diamond Hotels Dublin does not maintain its own records of advertising activity.

Loyalty point fees – when a Diamond Hotels' frequent guest card is presented at check-in or on check-out the receptionist logs the card number on the room account. On a monthly basis the accounts manager prints a report showing frequent guest numbers and the total charges paid by each guest on check-out. The number of points awarded is determined based on the guest's total bill. This is then faxed to the global frequent guest accounts department which updates customer frequent guest accounts and issues an invoice to the hotel representing its cost for the month. This process generally takes around two to three weeks after each month end.

The global frequent guest accounts department reconciles the total points issued each month to the total charges invoiced back to all participating hotels as a check to ensure that frequent guest balances are updated accurately.

When a guest uses their frequent guest points to book a reward stay, the room charges are invoiced back to the global frequent guest accounts department as each guest checks out. The hotel has access to a database of frequent guest account card numbers and balances and uses this to ensure that a guest has sufficient points for their reward stay. The reward stay transaction is credited to revenue in the Diamond Dublin Hotel's accounts and debited against the Diamond Hotels International account on the creditors' ledger. Additional charges (e.g. meals, minibar, in-room movies etc.) are settled by cash/credit card and booked as a normal sale. The receptionist manually allocates the room charge to intercompany and the extras to the alternative form of payment provided by the guest.

Reservation fees – when an on-line reservation is made the Diamond Hotels International system records a transaction charge against the hotel owner. These charges are billed via annual invoice and credits are given for reservations subsequently cancelled. Diamond Hotels Dublin books the cost on receipt of the invoice.

Intercompany accounts with both Diamond Hotels Ireland and Diamond Hotels International are settled by bank transfer on a quarterly basis. On each occasion the hotel accountant remits the balance owing as shown on the creditors' ledger. Annually, each July, the group treasurer at Diamond Hotels International reconciles the remittances against balances held by Diamond Hotels International and any differences are adjusted in the books of Diamond Hotels Dublin and the balance settled by bank transfer.

Substantive testing performed

Translation of foreign currency balances.

Intercompany balances as shown on the creditors' ledger have been extracted and detailed below:

Account	Invoice Type	Invoice Date	Amount in original currency	€/£ Balance in ledger	Comments
Diamond Hotels International	Advertising	23/11/09	$105,500	68,506	Correctly translated at average rate for November of $1.54 = €/£1
	Reservation	15/9/09	$42,590	26,290	Correctly translated at average rate for September of $1.62 = €/£1

Conclusion: Intercompany balances have been correctly translated and are valued appropriately at the balance sheet date.

Discussion of Solution

When carrying out a review of a working paper, either in answering an exam paper or in practice, the correct approach is to comment on the **quality** of the audit work documented on the working paper and **direct further work** to be completed if required.

The review points for the above working paper in **Example 7.1** are as follows:

- No testing of completeness and valuation of balance sheet values. Further work required as follows:
  - examine post-year-end intercompany invoices to ensure that all costs are included in correct period (completeness);
  - obtain intercompany confirmations for all balances (completeness);
  - review guest transactions to ensure that only room charges have been invoiced back to parent (valuation); and
  - for debtors' balances, request a copy of intercompany accounts to ensure that balances are recoverable and can be paid (valuation).

- There are good narratives regarding intercompany processes whereby the working paper highlights a number of weaknesses which should be provided in the management letter.
- The working paper included workings relating to the translation of foreign exchange balances. However, it failed to state that balances should be retranslated at year end. Therefore further work is required to re-compute the foreign exchange balances at the year-end rate and calculate the potential error. The projected error should be brought to the schedule of differences.

A reviewer has not completed a review of a working paper until all review points set have been dealt with satisfactorily by the audit team. Only then will the audit documentation meet the requirements of ISA 500 and ISA 230 and substantiate the final opinion in the audit report.

7.3 SUFFICIENT APPROPRIATE AUDIT EVIDENCE

'Audit evidence' is defined in ISA 500 (UK and Ireland) *Audit Evidence* ('ISA 500') as information used by the auditor in arriving at the conclusions on which the auditor's opinion is based. Audit evidence includes both information contained in the accounting records underlying the financial statements and other information.

The quality of audit evidence can vary significantly, but in all cases the auditor must consider both the sufficiency and appropriateness of audit evidence.

7.3.1 Sufficient and Appropriate Audit Evidence

Sufficiency is the measure of the quantity of audit evidence. Appropriateness is the measure of the quality of audit evidence, that is, its relevance and its reliability in providing support for, or detecting misstatements in, the classes of transactions, account balances, and disclosures and related assertions. The auditor should consider the sufficiency and appropriateness of audit evidence to be obtained when assessing risks and designing further audit procedures.

7.3.2 Sufficiency

The sufficiency, or quantity of audit evidence needed is affected by the risk of misstatement (the greater the risk, the more audit evidence is likely to be required) and also by the quality of such audit evidence (the higher the quality, the less the audit evidence that may be required). Accordingly, the sufficiency and appropriateness of audit evidence are interrelated. However, merely obtaining more audit evidence may not compensate if it is of a lower quality.

For example, in obtaining audit evidence in relation to existence of stock at the year end, the auditor may decide to obtain invoices for all stock items purchased during the year. While this may be a lot of audit evidence, it is not relevant to the existence of stock as it does not test whether the stock is in existence at the year end. It is therefore not appropriate audit evidence.

7.3.3 Relevance and Reliability of Audit Evidence

A given set of audit procedures may provide audit evidence that is *relevant* to certain assertions but not to others. For example, inspection of records and documents related to the collection of debtors after the period end may provide audit evidence regarding both existence and valuation, although not necessarily the appropriateness of period-end cut-offs. Therefore, the auditor needs to ensure that the audit evidence obtained is relevant to the assertion.

When planning procedures, the auditor must consider whether the evidence that will be obtained from carrying out that procedure is relevant to the audit. This can be illustrated as follows in **Figure 7.1**:

FIGURE 7.1: RELEVANCE OF AUDIT EVIDENCE

Assertion	Audit Evidence	
	Relevant	**Not Relevant**
Existence of creditors at year end	Payments made to creditors after the year end are audit evidence of the existence of creditors at the year-end	Payments made to creditors during the year are not audit evidence of the existence of creditors at the year-end
Valuation of debtors at year end	Receipts from debtors received after the year end are audit evidence of the valuation of that debtor at the year-end	Debtors' confirmations may not give the auditor evidence that the valuation of debtors is valid at the year end, because it does not test whether the customer is likely to pay the debt

The *reliability* of audit evidence is influenced by its source and by its nature and is dependent on the individual circumstances under which it is obtained. Generalisations about the reliability of various kinds of audit evidence can be made; however, such generalisations are subject to important exceptions. Even when audit evidence is obtained from sources external to the entity, circumstances may exist that could affect the reliability of the information obtained. For example, audit evidence obtained from an independent external source may not be reliable if the source is not knowledgeable.

While recognising that exceptions may exist, the following generalisations noted in **Figure 7.2** about the reliability of audit evidence are useful.

FIGURE 7.2: RELIABILITY OF AUDIT EVIDENCE

Evidence that is more reliable	Evidence that is less reliable
Direct evidence obtained through procedures such as inspection or recalculation, e.g. reviewing customer contracts to test revenue recognition	Indirect evidence obtained through inquiry, e.g. discussion with management regarding the terms of customer contracts
Evidence obtained from outside, independent sources, e.g. bank confirmation	Evidence obtained solely from management, e.g. bank statement
Documented evidence	Undocumented evidence
Evidence obtained from inspecting original documents	Evidence obtained from inspecting copies and faxes
Evidence obtained in the presence of an effective control environment	Evidence obtained in the context of an ineffective control environment

7.4 EVALUATE MISSTATEMENTS

ISA 450 (UK and Ireland) *Evaluation of Misstatements Identified During the Audit* ('ISA 450') defines a misstatement as a difference between the amount, classification, presentation or disclosure of a reported amount and that which is required by the applicable financial reporting framework.

In relation to misstatements, the standard states that the objective of auditors is to evaluate:
1. the effect of identified misstatements on the audit; and
2. the effect of uncorrected misstatements, if any, on the financial statements.

In addressing these objectives, we will discuss separately the auditor's responsibilities at the fieldwork stage and at the completion stage.

7.4.1 Fieldwork

When the auditor is carrying out the audit fieldwork, they must accumulate all audit adjustments over a 'clearly trivial' amount. 'Clearly trivial' is defined in ISA 450 as those matters that are clearly inconsequential, whether taken individually or in aggregate.

While the standard does not specify what constitutes 'clearly trivial', a good basis in practice is to apply a percentage, say 2-5%, to the same benchmark used for materiality (set at planning stage as discussed in **Chapter 3**). Therefore, all errors or misstatements detected throughout the audit which quantify as greater than, say, 2% of overall materiality value (as calculated in **Chapter 3**) should be accumulated on an Audit Adjustment Schedule.

An example of an Audit Adjustment Schedule, taken from Chartered Accountants Ireland's *Procedures for Quality Audit 2010*, is provided below in **Appendix 7.1**.

When identifying misstatements during the audit, the auditor should communicate them to management on a timely basis which, when practical, is as and when they arise. Management can then correct the errors as the audit progresses. If management refuses to correct a misstatement, the auditor still records the misstatement on the Audit Adjustment Schedule and it will form part of the evaluation of uncorrected misstatements which is discussed below in **Section 7.4.2**.

If the misstatements identified during the audit are either material or are not isolated occurrences, the auditor may request management to examine the class of transactions, account balance or disclosure in order for the auditor to perform further procedures. For example, if the auditor identifies misstatements in the valuation of some stock items, the auditor may ask management to review all stock items for valuation prior to the auditor carrying out further testing.

Furthermore, the auditor needs to consider if these adjusted errors indicate issues for other balances in the financial statements. For example, if there are numerous errors in the valuation stock, the auditor may conclude that this is a result of the weak controls surrounding the valuation of stock. This may then indicate that weak controls may exist in other areas, such as debtors or creditors and therefore the auditor may decide to carry out further substantive testing on those balances.

Furthermore, as the audit progresses and the audit team becomes aware of new information, this shall cause them to revise materiality from that which they first selected.

As discussed in **Chapter 3**, materiality is set at the planning stage and may be based on prior year results or draft results for the current year. The auditor should continually reassess this materiality based on actual results and any material adjustments that have been made. This may also result in a requirement for further substantive testing.

7.4.2 Completion

At the completion stage of the audit, the auditor should consider all the non-adjusted errors which have been accumulated by the audit team on the Audit Adjustment Schedule. The auditor should also reassess materiality, if they have not already done so.

With the revised materiality, the auditor then reviews the uncorrected misstatements to determine if, either individually or in aggregate, they exceed materiality. If the misstatements, either individually or in aggregate, exceed materiality, the auditor must request management to correct the misstatements so that the aggregate unadjusted misstatements are below materiality. If management does not adjust the records and financial statements accordingly, this will lead to a modification of the audit report. This can be illustrated in **Example 7.2** below:

EXAMPLE 7.2: ASSESSMENT OF UNADJUSTED ERRORS — → this found during audit, but not adjusted

Below is an extract from the Unadjusted Audit Adjustment Schedule for your client. You have just revised materiality to €/£100,000.

Details	Profit and Loss Impact DR/(CR) €/£	Balance Sheet Impact DR/(CR) €/£
DR Stock balance sheet		45,000
CR Stock – profit and loss	(45,000)	
Being error in stock valuation		
DR Bad debt provision	15,000	
CR Trade debtors		(15,000)
Being increase in bad debt provision		
DR Write down of investments	120,000	
CR Investments		(120,000)
Being correction of market value of investments		
DR Fixed assets		75,000
CR Repairs and maintenance	(75,000)	
Being assets incorrectly treated as repairs and maintenance		
Total Effect of Uncorrected Misstatements	**15,000**	**(15,000)**

In this case, whilst the aggregate error to the profit or loss of €/£15,000 is not material, there is one error that individually is above materiality. Therefore, the auditor would first request that the correction of market value of investments is adjusted.

If this was adjusted by management, the remaining aggregate errors amount to (€/£105,000) (this is the total of the remaining errors) which is also above materiality. The auditor should then request management to adjust one of the errors to bring the aggregate error below materiality. For example, if management correctly capitalised the fixed assets included in repairs and maintenance (adjustment of €75,000), the aggregate unadjusted error would be (€/£30,000) which is below materiality. Best practice is to request management to adjust all errors.

If management refuse to post the errors to bring the aggregate misstatement to below materiality, the auditor will have to modify the audit report because there is a material misstatement in the financial statements.

Furthermore, in assessing the unadjusted errors, unrecorded misstatements from prior periods that affect the current period should be accumulated and evaluated with misstatements discovered during the current period. For example, let's say the audited entity has not paid rates either in the prior year or current year due to their local council omitting to send invoices. The entity did not accrue for the rates in the prior year and therefore it was included on the unadjusted errors by the auditor but was not posted as it was below materiality. In the current year, the entity still has not received an invoice so the auditor proposes a further adjustment for the current year's rates cost. In reviewing the unadjusted errors in the current year, the auditor should consider if the aggregate of the unadjusted accrual in the prior and current year is material.

7.4.3 Communication

As noted above, the auditor should communicate misstatements to management and/or those charged with governance on a timely basis throughout the audit and request that they are adjusted.

The auditor should also communicate all unadjusted misstatements and request written representation from management and, where appropriate, those charged with governance that the uncorrected misstatements are not material to the financial statements. This is normally done by including a paragraph in the letter of representation as such, and attaching the schedule of unadjusted misstatements to the letter.

7.4.4 Documentation

The auditor should ensure that all misstatements other than the clearly trivial, both adjusted and unadjusted, are documented in the audit file. The auditor should express an opinion about the unadjusted misstatements as to whether or not they are material individually or in aggregate, and the basis for that conclusion.

7.5 FINAL ANALYTICAL REVIEW

Chapter 3 discussed analytical procedures carried out at the planning stage of the audit as required by ISA 315 (UK and Ireland) *Identifying and Assessing the Risks of Material Misstatement Through Understating the Entity and Its Environment* ('ISA 315'). In **Chapter 6** we also noted the use of analytical procedures as a substantive test.

In accordance with ISA 520 (UK and Ireland) *Analytical Procedures* ('ISA 520'), analytical procedures are required to be carried out at the concluding stage of the audit. The procedures used are often similar to the ones used as risk assessment procedures, but at this stage their objective is to assess whether:
1. there are significant fluctuations or unusual items in the audited financial statements that were not sufficiently explained; and
2. the financial statements and disclosures are consistent with the results of the audit procedures performed and the audit team's understanding of the entity and its environment.

For example, changes in cash, receivables, inventory and payables might have appeared reasonable when audited individually but, in combination, they result in a significant working capital fluctuation that is not in line with the auditor's expectation. Therefore, using analytical procedures can help identify such unexpected variances and allow the auditor to carry out further procedures to ensure that the financial statements give a true and fair view.

Analytical procedures as risk assessment procedures and as concluding procedures should probably include financial liquidity ratio analysis. Typical ratios used are:
• acid test ratio;
• current ratio;
• debt to equity ratio;
• interest coverage ratio; and
• other key performance indicators, as appropriate.

These can also be useful as indicators of going concern problems. For example, a very high debt to equity ratio may indicate that the entity does not have adequate resources to finance its liabilities.

In concluding the audit, the audit team reads the final financial statements (including disclosures) and considers:

- the adequacy of the audit evidence gathered with respect to unusual or unexpected balances identified in performing risk assessment procedures or during the course of the audit;
- unusual or unexpected balances or relationships that were not previously identified; and
- whether the current year's financial statements are comparable to the prior year, considering the auditor's understanding of the entity and its environment.

This final review integrates the results of all the audit work performed and gives added support that there is a low risk of the financial statements being materially misstated because of undetected misstatements.

7.6 SUBSEQUENT EVENTS REVIEW

A subsequent events review is carried out at the completion stage of the audit to ensure that no events have occurred since the balance sheet date that would impact upon the financial statements.

IAS 10 *Events after the Reporting Period* defines subsequent events and dictates how they should be accounted for. In summary there are two types of subsequent events: adjusting events and non-adjusting events. These are explained as follows:

1.**Adjusting Events**   Those events whose conditions existed at the balance sheet date are known as 'adjusting events'.

EXAMPLE 7.3: ADJUSTING EVENTS

The settlement of a court case after the balance sheet date which was provided for in the financial statements – the event existed at the year end and therefore any material difference should be adjusted.

A debtor going into liquidation after the year end where there was a debtor balance in the financial statements at the year-end – this should be provided for as the balance existed at the year end and it is likely the customer was in difficulty and therefore the balance should be written down to the recoverable amount.

2.**Non-adjusting Events**   Those events that are indicative of conditions arising subsequent to the balance sheet date are known as 'non-adjusting events'.

EXAMPLE 7.4: NON-ADJUSTING EVENTS

A significant decline in the market value of investments after the year-end: as the value had not declined at the year-end, no adjustment would be made.

Damage to the building due to a fire after the year-end: as the fire did not exist at the balance sheet date, no adjustment would be made.

ISA 560 (UK and Ireland) *Subsequent Events* ('ISA 560') details the auditor's responsibilities in relation to subsequent events and states that the auditor should obtain audit evidence of events occurring after the year end and ensure that they have been treated in accordance with the financial reporting framework, and consider any impact on the audit report.

The standard defines three distinct periods:

Period 1: Between the Date of the Financial Statements and the Date of the Auditor's Report

ISA 560 states that the auditor shall perform procedures designed to obtain sufficient appropriate audit evidence that all events occurring between the date of the financial statements and the date of the auditor's report that require adjustment of, or disclosures in, the financial statements have been identified.

The auditor will perform these procedures in two ways:
- by being alert during fieldwork. For example, review of post-year-end payments when auditing the completion of accruals may highlight an event that requires adjustment or disclosure.
- by performing additional procedures at the completion stage of the audit, i.e. the Subsequent Events Review. Examples of subsequent events review procedures are noted in *Nolan*,[1] Chapter 15 as follows:
  o read the minutes of management and/or shareholder meetings;
  o enquire of legal advisors;
  o enquire of management about the following:
    – any new commitments or borrowings entered into,
    – any major sale or acquisition planned,
    – any increase in capital or debt instruments, and
    – any assets appropriated or destroyed by fire, flood, etc.;
  o review the latest management accounts, budgets and cash flows for unusual trends; and
  o investigate any unusual transactions occurring shortly before or after the balance sheet date.

If these procedures indicate the existence of events that require adjustment or disclosure, the auditor must discuss with management/directors and request amendments to

[1] Martin Nolan, *External Auditing and Assurance: An Irish Textbook* (1st Edition, Chartered Accountants Ireland, 2010)

the financial statements. If they do not agree to make changes, the auditor must consider modifying the audit report.

The auditor will also request written representation from management/directors that they have included all events which occurred after the balance sheet date as required by the applicable financial reporting framework. This, as always, would be included in the letter of representation.

Period 2: Between the Date of the Audit Report and the Date the Financial Statements are Issued

This period is often short as best practice is to issue the financial statements as soon as possible after the audit report is signed. However, as per ISA 560, while the auditor has no obligation to perform audit procedures during this period, if a fact becomes known to the auditor that would have impacted upon the audit report if it had become known prior to the signing of the audit report, the auditor must discuss with management and inquire how management intends to amend the financial statements.

If management agrees to amend the financial statements, the auditor must audit those adjustments accordingly and issue a new audit report. If management do not agree to amend the financial statements, the auditor shall modify the audit report.

Period 3: After the Financial Statements have been Issued

The auditor has no obligation to perform procedures after the financial statements have been issued. However, if a fact becomes known to the auditor that would have impacted upon the audit report if it had become known prior to the signing of the audit report, the auditor must discuss with management and inquire how management intends to amend the financial statements.

If management intends to amend the financial statements, the auditor must audit those adjustments accordingly and issue a new audit report. When issuing a new audit report the auditor has regard to the regulations relating to reports on revised annual financial statements and directors' reports. In the UK, the detailed regulations governing revised financial statements and directors' reports, where the revision is voluntary, are set out in section 454 of the Companies Act 2006. There are no provisions in the Irish Companies Acts for revising financial statements.

If management fails to amend the financial statements, and does not take the necessary steps to ensure that anyone in receipt of the previously issued financial statements is informed of the situation, the auditor shall inform management and/or those charged with governance that they will seek to take appropriate action to prevent the future reliance on the auditor's report. In the UK and the ROI, this may be done, e.g. by a statement at the annual general meeting. Alternatively, the auditor may seek legal advice in this regard.

7.7 GOING CONCERN REVIEW

IAS 1 *Presentation of Financial Statements* requires management to make an assessment of an entity's ability to continue as a going concern.

ISA 570 (UK and Ireland) *Going Concern* ('ISA 570') states that it is the auditor's responsibility to obtain sufficient appropriate audit evidence regarding the appropriateness of management's going concern assumption. Management's going concern assessment should cover a period of one year from the intended signing date of the audit report.

During the audit fieldwork, the auditor should always be aware of risk indicators that may cast doubt over the going concern assumption. These are detailed in ISA 570, paragraph A2, and include financial indicators such as net liability position or inability to pay creditors, and operating indicators such as loss of key management or management's intentions to liquidate or cease operations. You should read these and be familiar with them as they could be occurring in an entity that you may be auditing, yet management maintains that the financial statements should be prepared on a going concern basis.

At the completion stage, bearing in mind any indicators noted throughout the fieldwork, the auditor should perform audit procedures on management's assessment of the company's ability to continue as a going concern. As discussed in **Chapter 6**, examples of these procedures are as follows:

- obtain management's cash flow projections and discuss the assumptions used:
  - compare the assumptions to actual events post-year end, and
  - compare the targets to the industry norm and the marketplace;
- review the prior year's cash flow projections and compare them to the entity's actual cash flows to assess the accuracy of management's assumptions;
- review loan agreements and banking facilities for any covenant breaches which may indicate there is a risk that facilities will not be renewed;
- read the minutes of management and/or board meetings which may indicate any financial difficulty during the year; and
- review events subsequent to the reporting date for any further indications of going concern difficulties.

The standard also requires the auditor to ensure that the financial statements contain adequate disclosures in relation to going concern. The entity is required to include in the notes to the financial statements the basis on which the entity can continue as a going concern. If there were uncertainties surrounding their ability to continue as a going concern, e.g. renewal of finance facilities, this would also be included in the disclosure.

In carrying out the going concern review, the auditor may come across some difficulties in obtaining information or, indeed, obtaining comfort over the going concern assumption. These are summarised below, along with actions that the auditor should take in each circumstance.

FIGURE 7.3: ACTIONS WHEN THERE ARE ISSUES OVER THE
GOING CONCERN ASSUMPTION

Difficulty/Conclusion	Action
Management has not prepared cash flow projections at all, or not for the full period of 12 months from the audit report signing date	• Request management to prepare cash flows and for the full 12-month period • If management disagree, the audit report should be qualified on the basis of limitation of scope; 'except for' opinion if management have prepared projections for some of the period; 'disclaimer' opinion if management have not prepared any projections. The difference in opinion is on the basis that, if the auditor has projections for some of the period, they will be able to conclude that the projected error is not pervasive
Going concern assumption is appropriate but uncertainties exist; the directors have not included adequate disclosure of the uncertainties in the notes to the financial statements	• Include emphasis of matter paragraph in the audit report as regards the uncertainties that exist in relation to going concern • Request management to include adequate disclosures in the notes regarding uncertainties that exist • If management disagree, the audit report should be qualified on the basis of disagreement, 'except for' opinion
Management has prepared the financial statements on a going concern basis, but the auditor has concluded that this is not appropriate and the financial statements should be prepared on a break-up basis	• Request management to prepare the financial statements on a break-up basis • If management disagrees, the audit report should be qualified on the basis of disagreement, 'adverse' opinion

Additional guidance in relation to going concern issues and their relevance for auditors can be found in:
• APB Bulletin 2008/01 *Audit issues when financial market conditions are difficult and credit facilities may be restricted*; and
• APB Bulletin 2008/10 *Going concern issues during the current economic conditions*.

7.8 WRITTEN REPRESENTATIONS

You will by now be familiar with the fact that, in a number of auditing standards, the auditor is required to obtain written representations from management and/or those charged with governance confirming that they have fulfilled their responsibilities with regard to the financial reporting framework in relation to certain balances and transactions. As a reminder, the following standards require receipt of written representations:

FIGURE 7.4: WRITTEN REPRESENTATIONS REQUIRED

Standard	Written Representations
ISA 240 (UK and Ireland) *The Auditor's Responsibilities Relating to Fraud in an Audit of Financial Statements* paragraph 39	Acknowledge responsibilities regarding prevention and detection of fraud and have disclosed all knowledge of fraud or suspected fraud
ISA 250 (Section A) (UK and Ireland) *Consideration of Laws and Regulations in an Audit of Financial Statements* paragraph 16	Have disclosed all known instances, or suspicion of, of non-compliance with laws and regulations affecting the preparation of financial statements
ISA 450 (UK and Ireland) *Evaluation of Misstatements Identified During the Audit* paragraph 14	That all uncorrected misstatements are not material, both individually and in aggregate
ISA 501 (UK and Ireland) *Audit Evidence – Specific Considerations for Selected Items* paragraph 12	All potential litigation and claims have been disclosed to the auditor
ISA 540 (UK and Ireland) *Auditing Accounting Estimates, Including Fair Value Accounting Estimates, and Related Disclosures* paragraph 22	That significant assumptions used in accounting estimates are reasonable
ISA 550 (UK and Ireland) *Related Parties* paragraph 26	That all related parties have been disclosed and correctly accounted for
ISA 560 (UK and Ireland) *Subsequent Events* paragraph 9	All events that occurred between balance sheet date and signing of audit report have been correctly accounted for in the financial statements
ISA 570 (UK and Ireland) *Going Concern* paragraph 16e	Details of their future plans and feasibility of these plans
ISA 710 (UK and Ireland) *Comparative Information – Corresponding Figures and Comparative Financial Statements* paragraph 9	Regarding any restatement made to comparative information

[handwritten note: compay to the prev. yr. statent.]

219

ISA 580 (UK and Ireland) *Written Representations* ('ISA 580') includes requirements and guidance on written representations. ISA 580 requires that the auditor request written representations from management. As well as representations for the matters noted above, ISA 580 also requires written representations to be requested from management acknowledging that:

- they have fulfilled their responsibilities for the preparation of the financial statements in accordance with the financial reporting framework – these responsibilities should mirror those that were agreed in the terms of engagement;
- they have provided the auditor with all relevant information and access as agreed in the terms of engagement;
- all transactions have been recorded and reflected in the financial statements; and
- any other areas that the auditor feels require additional confirmation from management.

The written representations should be received either on the audit report date, or as near to it as practical, but not after.

The written representations can all be presented together in the form of a letter of representation. An example of this letter is illustrated in ISA 580, Appendix 2, and has been reproduced below.[2] It should be noted that auditors may wish to add further representations to this letter as they see fit.

EXAMPLE 7.5: ILLUSTRATIVE REPRESENTATION LETTER

(Entity Letterhead)

(To Auditor)

(Date)

This representation letter is provided in connection with your audit of the financial statements of ABC Company for the year ended December 31, 20XX for the purpose of expressing an opinion as to whether the financial statements give a true and fair view in accordance with International Financial Reporting Standards.

We confirm that, to the best of our knowledge and belief, having made such inquiries as we considered necessary for the purpose of appropriately informing ourselves:

Financial Statements
- We have fulfilled our responsibilities, as set out in the terms of the audit engagement dated [insert date], for the preparation of the financial statements in accordance with International Financial Reporting Standards; in particular the financial statements give a true and fair view in accordance therewith.
- Significant assumptions used by us in making accounting estimates, including those measured at fair value, are reasonable (ISA 540).

---

[2] Please note that this has not been tailored for UK and Ireland, and is for illustrative purposes only.

- Related party relationships and transactions have been appropriately accounted for and disclosed in accordance with the requirements of International Financial Reporting Standards (ISA 550).
- All events subsequent to the date of the financial statements and for which International Financial Reporting Standards require adjustment or disclosure have been adjusted or disclosed (ISA 560).
- The effects of uncorrected misstatements are immaterial, both individually and in the aggregate, to the financial statements as a whole. A list of the uncorrected misstatements is attached to the representation letter (ISA 450).
- *Any other matters that the auditor may consider appropriate.*

Information Provided

We have provided you with:
  - access to all information of which we are aware that is relevant to the preparation of the financial statements such as records, documentation and other matters;
  - additional information that you have requested from us for the purpose of the audit; and
  - unrestricted access to persons within the entity from whom you determined it necessary to obtain audit evidence.
- All transactions have been recorded in the accounting records and are reflected in the financial statements.
- We have disclosed to you the results of our assessment of the risk that the financial statements may be materially misstated as a result of fraud. (ISA 240)
- We have disclosed to you all information in relation to fraud or suspected fraud that we are aware of and that affects the entity and involves:
  - management;
  - employees who have significant roles in internal control; or
  - others where the fraud could have a material effect on the financial statements. (ISA 240)
- We have disclosed to you all information in relation to allegations of fraud, or suspected fraud, affecting the entity's financial statements communicated by employees, former employees, analysts, regulators or others. (ISA 240)
- We have disclosed to you all known instances of non-compliance or suspected non-compliance with laws and regulations whose effects should be considered when preparing financial statements. (ISA 250)
- We have disclosed to you the identity of the entity's related parties and all the related party relationships and transactions of which we are aware. (ISA 550)
- *Any other matters that the auditor may consider appropriate.*

Management

Failure by management to provide written representations will lead to the auditor modifying the audit report.

221

7.9 REPORT TO THOSE CHARGED WITH GOVERNANCE

ISA 260 (UK and Ireland) *Communication With Those Charged With Governance* ('ISA 260') requires the auditor to agree communication lines with those charged with governance at various stages of the audit. In **Chapter 2** above we discussed the communication at the planning stage as required by paragraphs 14 and 15 of the standard.

ISA 260, paragraph 16, requires that the auditor communicate significant findings from the audit to those charged with governance and/or management:

- The auditor's views about significant qualitative aspects of the entity's accounting practices, including accounting policies, accounting estimates and financial statement disclosures. For example, the impact of a particular accounting policy chosen by management.
- Significant difficulties, if any, encountered during the audit. For example, delays in receiving information or unavailability of selected information.
- Significant matters, if any, discussed with management during the audit process. For example, business plans affecting the entity or concerns about technical accounting matters.
- Written representations requested by the auditor.
- Other matters which, in the auditor's opinion, are significant to the overall financial reporting process.

The manner in which the auditor communicates to management and/or those charged with governance will depend on the size of the entity and the significance of the issues. Communication will be either oral, written or a combination of both:

- For smaller owner-managed entities, communication is largely oral and on a relatively informal basis. This may take the form of a close out meeting or close out call where all issues are discussed and dealt with.
- For large, listed companies, the communication will be more formal, and may take the form of a presentation to an audit committee, as well as a written report detailing the audit process, assumptions and findings.
- If the findings are considered to be significant to the auditor and, in their professional judgement, oral communication would not be adequate, the auditor may elect to communicate significant findings in writing.

While auditors should communicate with management and/or those charged with governance on a timely basis, the communication of findings as explained above takes place at the end of the audit, just prior to the auditor finalising all issues and signing the audit report. However, it is important to remember that ISA 265 (UK and Ireland) *Communicating Deficiencies in Internal Control to Those Charged With Governance and Management* ('ISA 265') requires certain communications to be made in writing, particularly with regard to significant deficiencies in internal control.

SUMMARY OF LEARNING OBJECTIVES

Learning Objective 1 To evaluate audit evidence and justify the appropriate report

An auditor must review the audit working papers for sufficiency, relevance and reliability of the audit evidence. The auditor must then decide if the audit evidence accumulated is appropriate to conclude that the financial statements are free from material misstatement or, alternatively, that there will be a negative impact on the audit report.

Learning Objective 2 To action the auditor's responsibilities to consider uncorrected misstatements and their impact on internal control

At the completion stage of the audit, the auditor assesses the level of uncorrected misstatements and considers the impact of the errors on the audit opinion, as well as the quality of the control environment.

Learning Objective 3 To execute completion procedures required to be performed by the auditor to conclude if the financial statements are free from material misstatement

At the completion stage of the audit, the auditor must conclude if the financial statements are free from material misstatement. In order to form their opinion, the auditor will carry out various reviews to comply with the auditing standards.

Learning Objective 4 To be able to communicate with those charged with governance at the completion of an audit as required by the auditing standards

The auditing standards require the auditor to communicate significant matters to those charged with governance at the completion of an audit and issue of the audit report. The manner of this communication will depend on the size of the entity and the significance of the issues.

QUESTIONS

In each of the scenarios presented in the questions below, there is an issue/(s) which needs to be addressed by the auditor (an indicator) in relation to completion procedures. You should read the questions and attempt to address the issues relating to completion procedures.

(See **Appendix One** of this text for Suggested Solutions to Review Questions.)

Review Questions

Question 7.1 (Based on Chartered Accountants Ireland, FAE Autumn 2011, Simulation 1)

Executive Motors Limited

You are an Audit Senior with the firm of Bentley Ferguson, Chartered Accountants. It is 18 January 2011 and the firm's Senior Partner, James Bentley, calls you into his office to discuss a non-audit engagement carried out recently by Shauna O'Donnell, an Audit Junior in your firm. He has just received a phone call requesting him to attend an important client meeting in London which means that he will be away from the office for the next few days.

He hands you one of the many files from his desk and explains that he has not yet had time to review the contents but that the client, Chevhall, would like the associated report to be issued on the day he returns. He indicates that he has reviewed and is satisfied with the planning for this engagement but has yet to review the execution and documentation of the work performed by Shauna (reproduced at Appendix 1). The drafting of the report is also outstanding and he asks you to take care of these tasks while he is away and drop him a note of the results of your review and a draft report to Chevhall.

He explains the background to the piece of work as follows: "Executive Motors Ltd (Executive Motors) is a small local motor dealership and holds the area franchise for Chevhall, a manufacturer of luxury, executive motor vehicles. As part of its franchise agreement Executive Motors is responsible for all warranty repairs and servicing for Chevhall customers in the local area. Chevhall supplies the parts for the repairs and servicing on a consignment stock basis and requires Executive Motors to hold a minimum level of each part, to ensure that repairs can be performed on demand, without the need to wait for additional parts to be delivered. The franchise agreement contains a clause which allows Chevhall to request a report from independent accountants detailing whether the stock levels held by Executive Motors agree with the records maintained by Chevhall and also comply with the minimum stockholding requirements. Chevhall has engaged Bentley Ferguson to carry out this work at Executive Motors as at 31 December 2010, which was the date upon which Shauna visited Executive Motors' premises and conducted the testing described in her working paper."

APPENDIX 1

Bentley Ferguson, Chartered Accountants
Client: Chevhall (Executive Motors Ltd franchise)
Subject: Working paper on consignment inventory

Prepared by: Shauna O'Donnell   **Date:** 15 January 2011

Reviewed by: **Date:**

Note: the first four columns are a copy of Executive Motors' total consignment stock listing, the remaining four columns have been added by Bentley Ferguson to note work performed.

Chevhall faxed through its records of Executive Motors' stock on 31 December 2010.

Item code	Description	Location	Quantity	Existence agreed	Quantity per Chevhall's records at 31 December 2010	Minimum quantity per Chevhall	Comments
CM01-472	Alternator fan	A-01	3	Y			
		A-02	3	Y			
		A-03	1	Y			Appears damaged
		Total	7		7	5	OK
CM02-361	Temperature sensor	B-03	4	Y	4	4	OK
CM10-987	Brake pad	B-09	20	Y			
		B-10	18	Y			
		Total	38		38	35	OK
CM10-989	Brake pressure differential valve	C-01	4	Y	4	4	OK
CM12-056	Cylinder head gasket	D-08	2	Y	2	1	OK
CM12-061	Drive belt	D-09	5	Y	5	3	OK
CM12-087	Distributor	D-11	2	Y	2	2	OK
CM12-109	Piston ring	E-01	4	Y	4	3	OK
CM12-112	Piston valve	E-02	8	Y			
		E-03	4	Y			
		Total	12		12	10	OK
CM12-114	Starter motor	E-05	4	Y	4	2	OK
CM15-001	Fan blade	F-12	10	Y	10	8	OK
CM16-098	Radiator gasket	F-13	7	Y	7	6	OK
CM18-104	Oil filter	G-01	8	Y			
		G-02	8	Y			
		G-03	7	Y			
		Total	23		23	20	OK
CM19-032	Carburettor	H-01	2	Y	2	2	OK
CM20-074	Fuel injection nozzle	H-03	4	Y	4	5	OK

Conclusion: No issues arising.

Question 7.2 (Based on Chartered Accountants Ireland, FAE Autumn 2010)

RX Pharma

Refer to the scenario presented in **Question 3.2**.

Question 7.3 (Based on Chartered Accountants Ireland, FAE Autumn 2010, Simulation 3)

Castleford Credit Union

Refer to the scenario presented in **Question 4.2**.

APPENDIX 7.1: EXAMPLE OF AN AUDIT ADJUSTMENT SCHEDULE[3]

Insert Client Name on Frontsheet
31 December 2010

A 9.1

Audit Materiality	0
Performance Materiality	0

	Initials	Date
Prepared by:		
Reviewed by:		
Return to Index		

SUMMARY OF ERRORS

Nature of and Reason for Error or Deviation	Sch Ref.	Actual Error	Projected Error	Unadjusted Profit Effect	Unadjusted B/S Effect	Potential Adjusting Journals
		€	€	€	€	€
Total:						
For example:						
Tangible Fixed Assets						
Investments						

---

[3] Source: Procedures for Quality Audit 2010 (©Chartered Accountants Ireland, 2010).

All errors and deviations must be recorded and comments noted as to the consequences of the error. If adjustments are made then this should be noted accordingly. Unadjusted errors brought forward from the previous period which do not reverse (i.e. have a cumulative effect) should also be included on this schedule.

Record the reference and an actual (that is an established) or known amount. Where an error has been found as a result of sampling techniques, the error will need extrapolating (projecting) in order to impute sample findings to the whole population.

RESULTS

The audit Materiality level set at planning and updated as appropriate is as noted below:

Audit materiality:

| 0 |

Performance materiality:

| 0 |

Specific materiality (see definition on B3):

Audit balance A | 0 |

Audit balance B | 0 |

The aggregate of uncorrected misstatements is/is not considered to be material. (Delete as appropriate)

Materiality for the audit should/should not be reassessed as a result of errors found. (Delete as appropriate)

8

AUDIT REPORTS

8.1 Introduction
8.2 Forming an Opinion
8.3 Uncertainties
8.4 Modified Audit Reports
8.5 Other Reporting Considerations
8.6 Approaching Audit Report Exam Questions
8.7 Conclusion

LEARNING OBJECTIVE

In reading and studying this chapter, your objective is to be able to:
• draft the appropriate audit report, in line with relevant standards and legislation.

8.1 INTRODUCTION

Audit reports are covered in detail in **Nolan**,[1] Chapter 16, and by now you should be very familiar with audit reports and their format. The purpose of this chapter is to remind you of the key issues and offer further practical examples to assist in your understanding of the topic. There are three key reporting standards issued by the IAASB:
• ISA 700 (UK and Ireland) *The Auditor's Report on Financial Statements* (Revised) (issued October 2012) ('ISA 700');
• ISA 705 (UK and Ireland) *Modifications to Opinions in the Independent Auditor's Report* (Revised) (issued October 2012) ('ISA 705'); and
• ISA 706 (UK and Ireland) *Emphasis of Matter Paragraphs and Other Matter Paragraphs in the Independent Auditor's Report* (Revised) (issued October 2012) ('ISA 706').

---

[1] Martin Nolan, *External Auditing and Assurance: An Irish Textbook* (1st Edition, Chartered Accountants Ireland, 2010)

Prior to October 2012, for Irish audits, the new ISA 700, ISA 705 and 706 had yet to be adopted in the Republic of Ireland. However, the revisions mean that, for periods commencing on or after 1 October 2012, the same version of ISA (UK and Ireland) 700 (revised) *The Auditor's Report on Financial Statements* is now applicable in both Ireland and the UK. The revisions also mean that ISA (UK and Ireland) 705 (revised) *Modifications to the Opinion in the Independent Auditor's Report* and ISA (UK and Ireland) 706 (revised) *Emphasis of Matter Paragraphs and Other Matter Paragraphs in the Independent Auditor's Report* are now also applicable in Ireland for the first time.

Based on these auditing standards, we can split audit reporting into three distinct areas:
1. forming an opinion;
2. uncertainties; and
3. modified audit reports.

Each of these three areas is discussed below.

8.2 FORMING AN OPINION

In accordance with ISA 700 (October 2012), an unmodified opinion is given when the auditor obtains sufficient appropriate audit evidence to conclude that the financial statements are prepared, in all material respects, in accordance with the (applicable) financial reporting standards.

As well as forming an opinion required by ISA 700, according to company law, in both the UK and in the Republic of Ireland, the auditor of a company is obliged to give an opinion as to whether the accounts have been prepared in accordance with the requirements of company law.

The auditor is also required by law to report on a number of other legal and regulatory matters, as detailed in **Figure 8.1** below:

FIGURE 8.1: COMPANY LAW REPORTING REQUIREMENTS FOR AUDITORS

NORTHERN IRELAND

Under the Companies Act 2006 (UK) the auditor is required to report on:
- Whether adequate accounting records have been kept
- If the financial statements are not in agreement with the accounting records
- If certain disclosures of directors' remuneration specified by law are not made; or
- If we have not received all the information and explanations we require for our audit.

REPUBLIC OF IRELAND

Under the Companies Act 1963-2012 the auditor is required to report on:
- If we have obtained all the information and explanations which we consider necessary for the purposes of our audit
- If proper books of account have been kept by the company
- If the financial statements are in agreement with the books of account
- If the information in the directors' report is consistent with the financial statements
- If, at the balance sheet date, there exists a financial situation requiring the convening of an extraordinary general meeting
- If disclosures of directors' remuneration and transactions specified by law are not made.

These matters do not form part of the opinion; rather, they are included in the audit report as a positive statement and/or reported on by exception. That is, if one of the requirements is not complied with, the auditor will state this separately in the audit report, usually in an 'other matters' paragraph.

The following Auditing Practices Board (APB) Bulletins set out the format and layout of audit reports:
- Republic of Ireland Audit Reports – FRC Bulletin 1(1): *Compendium of Illustrative Auditor's Reports on Irish Financial Statements,* Appendix 1–3
- UK/Northern Ireland Audit Reports – APB Bulletin 2010/2 (Revised), *Compendium of Illustrative Auditor's Reports on United Kingdom Private Sector Financial Statements for periods ended on or after 15 December 2010 (Revised),* Appendix 1–4

8.3 UNCERTAINTIES

In forming an opinion, the auditor may be aware of a significant matter/(s) the outcome of which is/(are) uncertain. In such a circumstance, the auditor should draw the users' attention to the significant uncertainty in the audit report. Examples of such uncertainties are as follows:
- Uncertainty in relation to the outcome of a legal case – the client may be in the middle of a legal case where no provision has been made in the financial statements for potential payment as it is not quantifiable and therefore cannot be recognised as per IAS 34 *Interim Financial Reporting.* The potential payment should be disclosed as a contingent liability. Due to the significance of this uncertainty, the auditor should draw attention to this uncertainty by referring to it in the audit report.
- Uncertainty in relation to the agreement of an additional finance facility – the company has commenced discussions with its bankers about an additional finance facility that may prove to be necessary should the sale of a substantial property not proceed. It is likely that these discussions will not be completed until six months after the signing of the audit report. Due to the significance of this uncertainty, the auditor should draw attention to this uncertainty by referring to it in the audit report.

In the circumstances outlined above, the auditor will summarise the uncertainty/(ies) in an '**Emphasis of Matter**' paragraph. The Emphasis of Matter paragraph is included immediately after the opinion paragraph in the audit report.

If a material uncertainty exists, but the auditor concludes that the use of the going concern assumption is still appropriate, then ISA 570 (UK and Ireland) *Going Concern* requires the auditor to ensure that the directors have appropriately disclosed the material uncertainty in the financial statements. The auditor is then required to make reference to that disclosure in the emphasis of matter paragraph. If the directors refuse to include appropriate disclosures of the matter, they would not be complying with financial reporting standards. In such a situation, the auditor would have to qualify their opinion because management has not complied with the financial reporting standards in this regard.

8.3.1 Examples of Emphasis of Matter Paragraphs

When including an emphasis of matter paragraph, the only amendment to the audit report is to include the emphasis of matter paragraph at the end of the audit report.

EXAMPLE 8.1: WHERE THE COMPANY HAS UNCERTAINTIES
SURROUNDING GOING CONCERN

Emphasis of Matter – Going Concern In forming our opinion, we have considered the adequacy of the disclosures made in Note 1 to the financial statements concerning the company's ability to continue as a going concern. The Company incurred a net loss of €XXXX during the year ended 31 December 2012 and, at that date, the company's current liabilities exceeded its total assets by €XXXX. These conditions, along with the other matters explained in Note 1 to the financial statements, indicate the existence of a material uncertainty which may cast significant doubt on the company's ability to continue as a going concern. The financial statements do not include the adjustments that would result if the company were unable to continue as a going concern.

EXAMPLE 8.2: DEVELOPMENT COMPANY WHERE THERE ARE UNCERTAINTIES
SURROUNDING THE VALUATION OF DEVELOPMENT LAND INCLUDED IN STOCK

Emphasis of Matter – Carrying Value of Development Lands In forming our opinion we have considered the adequacy of the disclosures made in Note 11 to the financial statements concerning the uncertainty surrounding the carrying value of development land. The uncertainty arises as a result of uncertain economic circumstances that currently prevail within the residential property market. The directors have written down, where necessary, the carrying value of developments lands to the lower of cost and estimated net realisable value.

You will note that both these paragraphs refer to the disclosure in the notes to the financial statements – the directors must have adequate disclosures for an auditor to include an emphasis of matter. As discussed above, if the disclosure is not adequate, the auditor may have to qualify the audit report on the basis of disagreement.

To review further audit reports with emphasis of matter paragraphs, please refer to:
• Republic of Ireland Audit Reports – FRC Bulletin 1(1): *Compendium of Illustrative Auditor's Reports on Irish Financial Statements*, Appendix 4, Examples 24 and 25
• UK/Northern Ireland Audit Reports – APB Bulletin 2010/2 (Revised), *Compendium of Illustrative Auditor's Reports on United Kingdom Private Sector Financial Statements for periods ended on or after 15 December 2010 (Revised)*, Appendix 5, Examples 12 and 13

8.4 MODIFIED AUDIT REPORTS

The modification of audit reports arises when, in forming an opinion on the financial statements, the auditor concludes that a modification to the opinion is necessary. Under ISA 700, possible modifications are summarised in **Figure 8.2** as follows:

FIGURE 8.2: MODIFICATIONS TO AUDIT REPORT

Nature of Matter Giving Rise to the Modification	Auditor's Judgment about the Pervasiveness of the Effects or Possible Effects on the Financial Statements	
	Material but Not Pervasive	*Material and Pervasive*
Financial statements are materially misstated (also referred to as disagreement)	Qualified opinion	Adverse opinion
Inability to obtain sufficient appropriate audit evidence (also referred to as limitation of scope)	Qualified opinion	Disclaimer opinion

8.4.1 Limitation on Scope

Limitation on scope occurs when the auditor cannot obtain sufficient audit evidence to form an opinion. Limitation on scope can be differentiated between limitations:
• imposed by timing or circumstance; and
• imposed by management.

8.4.1.1 Limitation on Scope Imposed by Timing or Circumstance

Limitation on scope imposed by timing or circumstance is when the auditor is unable to obtain the relevant information due to circumstances that are independent of management.

EXAMPLE 8.3: LIMITATION ON SCOPE IMPOSED BY TIMING OR CIRCUMSTANCE

Example A

The auditor was unable to attend the stocktake at the year-end as they were only appointed auditors after the year-end. Therefore, the reason for the limitation is due to timing. In this case, if the auditor could not perform additional procedures to verify the existence of stock at the year end, they would qualify the audit report on the basis of limitation of scope.

Example B

The auditor was unable to obtain sufficient audit evidence as the client's books and records were destroyed in a fire. This is a limitation imposed by circumstances and beyond the control of management. In this case, the auditor would also qualify on the basis of limitation of scope.

In such circumstances where there is a limitation of scope imposed by timing or circumstances the auditor will either qualify the opinion (described in the report as "except for") or disclaim the opinion. The deciding factor as to whether the auditor qualifies an opinion or disclaims an opinion depends on how pervasive the material misstatement might be. The standard defines 'pervasive' as being material to more than one conclusion, or confined to one conclusion but representing a substantial portion of the financial statements. This can be illustrated by applying this to the previous examples:

EXAMPLE 8.4: LIMITATION ON SCOPE – EXCEPT FOR AND DISCLAIMER OPINION

Example A

The inability to substantiate the existence of stock only affects one conclusion and therefore would be limitation of scope, 'except for' opinion. However, if the stock balance represented the majority of the value of the balance sheet, it is likely the auditor would consider this to be pervasive and disclaim an opinion.

Example B

The inability to obtain any audit evidence due to lack of books and records would affect more than one conclusion and therefore would be considered pervasive. The auditor would, therefore, disclaim an opinion.

8.4.1.2 Limitation on Scope Imposed by Management

A limitation on scope imposed by management is where management refuses to give the auditor the information required to form an opinion.

EXAMPLE 8.5: LIMITATION ON SCOPE IMPOSED BY MANAGEMENT

Example A

The auditor identifies a risk of material misstatement regarding a material litigation, but management refuses to give the auditor permission to communicate or meet with the company's legal counsel and the auditor is unable to obtain audit evidence by performing alternative procedures.

Example B

The auditor is unable to perform audit procedures on the existence of debtors as management refuses to allow the auditor to execute a debtors' circularisation.

In both circumstances in **Example A** and **B** above, management has imposed the limitation. Similar to the circumstances when there is an imposed limitation on scope, the auditor assesses whether the potential misstatement is material resulting in an 'except for' opinion, or pervasive, resulting in the auditor disclaiming an opinion.

However, in addition, if the auditor concludes that the limitation on scope imposed by management results in disclaiming an opinion, ISA 705 states that the auditor should consider withdrawing from the engagement.

8.4.1.3 Examples of Audit Report Modifications

When modifying the audit report as a result of a limitation of scope, there are three main sections of the audit report that are amended – the basis of opinion, opinion paragraph and matters required to be reported by the relevant Companies Act. Furthermore, when the limitation of scope results in a disclaimer opinion, the respective responsibilities paragraph is also amended. Two examples are illustrated below with the amendments to the audit report in italics.

EXAMPLE 8.6: AUDIT REPORT MODIFICATIONS

Example 1: The auditor was not appointed at the time of the stocktake

ROI

Basis for qualified opinion on financial statements

With respect to stock having a carrying amount of €X the audit evidence available to us was limited because we did not observe the counting of the physical stock as at 31 December 20X1, since that date was prior to our appointment as auditor of the company. Owing to the nature of the company's records, we were unable to obtain sufficient appropriate audit evidence regarding the stock quantities by using other audit procedures.

Qualified opinion on financial statements

In our opinion, *except for the possible effects of the matters described in the 'basis for qualified opinion' paragraph*, the financial statements:

- give a true and fair view, in accordance with Generally Accepted Accounting Practice in Ireland, of the state of the company's affairs as at 31 December 20X1 and of its profit/loss for the year then ended; and
- have been properly prepared in accordance with the requirements of the Companies Acts 1963–2012.

Matters on which we are required to report by the Companies Acts 1963–2012

- *In respect solely of the limitation on our work relating to stock, described above:*
  - we have *not* obtained all the information and explanations that we consider necessary for the purpose of our audit; and
  - *we were unable to determine whether proper books of account have been kept.*
- The financial statements are in agreement with the books of account.
- In our opinion the information given in the directors' report is consistent with the financial statements.
- The net assets of the company, as stated in the balance sheet, are more than half of the amount of its called-up share capital and, in our opinion, on that basis there did not exist at ... a financial situation which under section 40 (1) of the Companies (Amendment) Act, 1983 would require the convening of an extraordinary general meeting of the company.

Matters on which we are required to report by exception

We have nothing to report in respect of the provisions in the Companies Acts 1963–2012 which require us to report to you if, in our opinion, the disclosures of directors' remuneration and transactions specified by law are not made.

UK

Basis for qualified opinion on financial statements

With respect to stock having a carrying amount of £X the audit evidence available to us was limited because we did not observe the counting of the physical stock as at 31 December 20X1, since that date was prior to our appointment as auditor of the company. Owing to the nature of the company's records, we were unable to obtain sufficient appropriate audit evidence regarding the stock quantities by using other audit procedures.

Qualified opinion on financial statements

In our opinion, *except for the possible effects of the matters described in the Basis for Qualified Opinion paragraph*, the financial statements:

- give a true and fair view of the state of the company's affairs as at 31 December 20X1 and of its profit [loss]for the year then ended;
- have been properly prepared in accordance with United Kingdom Generally Accepted Accounting Practice; and
- have been prepared in accordance with the requirements of the Companies Act 2006.

Opinion on other matter prescribed by the Companies Act 2006

In our opinion the information given in the Directors' Report for the financial year for which the financial statements are prepared is consistent with the financial statements.

Matters on which we are required to report by exception

In respect solely of the limitation on our work relating to stock, described above:
- *we have not obtained all the information and explanations that we considered necessary for the purpose of our audit; and*
- *we were unable to determine whether adequate accounting records had been kept.*

We have nothing to report in respect of the following matters where the Companies Act 2006 requires us to report to you if, in our opinion:

- returns adequate for our audit have not been received from branches not visited by us; or
- the financial statements are not in agreement with the accounting records and returns; or
- certain disclosures of directors' remuneration specified by law are not made.

Example 2: Unable to observe all physical stock and confirm trade debtors

ROI

Respective responsibilities of the directors and the auditor

As explained more fully in the Directors' Responsibilities Statement [set out [on page ...]], the directors are responsible for the preparation of the financial statements giving a true and fair view. Our responsibility is to audit and express an opinion on the financial statements in accordance with law and International Standards on Auditing (UK and Ireland). Those standards require us to comply with the Auditing Practices Board's (APB's) Ethical Standards for Auditors. *Because of the matter described in the Basis for Disclaimer of Opinion paragraph, however, we were not able to obtain sufficient appropriate audit evidence to provide a basis for an audit opinion.*

Scope of the audit of the financial statements

An audit involves obtaining evidence about the amounts and disclosures in the financial statements sufficient to give reasonable assurance that the financial statements are free from material misstatement, whether caused by fraud or error. This includes an assessment of: whether the accounting policies are appropriate to the company's circumstances and have been consistently applied and adequately disclosed; the reasonableness of significant accounting estimates made by the directors; and the overall presentation of the financial statements. In addition, we read all the financial and non-financial information in the [describe the annual report] to identify material inconsistencies with the audited financial statements. If we become aware of any apparent material misstatements or inconsistencies we consider the implications for our report.

Basis for disclaimer of opinion on financial statements

The audit evidence available to us was limited because we were unable to observe the counting of physical stock having a carrying amount of €X and send confirmation letters to trade debtors having a carrying amount of €Y due to limitations placed on the scope of our work by the directors of the company. As a result of this we have been unable to obtain sufficient appropriate audit evidence concerning both stock and trade debtors.

Disclaimer of opinion on financial statements

Because of the significance of the matter described in the Basis for Disclaimer of Opinion paragraph, we have not been able to obtain sufficient appropriate audit evidence to provide a basis for an audit opinion. Accordingly we do not express an opinion on the financial statements.

Matters on which we are required to report by the Companies Acts 1963–2012

Arising from the limitation of our work referred to above:
- *we have not obtained all the information and explanations that we consider necessary for the purpose of our audit;*
- *we were unable to determine whether proper books of account have been kept;*
- *we have been unable to form an opinion as to whether there did or did not exist at ... a financial situation which under section 40 (1) of the Companies (Amendment) Act, 1983 would require the convening of an extraordinary general meeting of the company.*

Notwithstanding our disclaimer of an opinion on the financial statements:
- the financial statements are in agreement with the books of account; and
- in our opinion the information given in the directors' report is consistent with the financial statements.

Matters on which we are required to report by exception

We have nothing to report in respect of the provisions in the Companies Acts 1963–2012 which require us to report to you if, in our opinion, the disclosures of directors' remuneration and transactions specified by law are not made.

UK

Respective responsibilities of the directors and the auditor

As explained more fully in the Directors' Responsibilities Statement [set out [on page ...]], the directors are responsible for the preparation of the financial statements and for being satisfied that they give a true and fair view. Our responsibility is to audit and express an opinion on the financial statements in accordance with applicable law and International Standards on Auditing (UK and Ireland). Those standards require us to comply with the Auditing Practices Board's (APB's) Ethical Standards for Auditors. *Because of the matter described in the Basis for Disclaimer of Opinion paragraph, however, we were not able to obtain sufficient appropriate audit evidence to provide a basis for an audit opinion.*

Scope of the audit of the financial statements

An audit involves obtaining evidence about the amounts and disclosures in the financial statements sufficient to give reasonable assurance that the financial statements are free from material misstatement, whether caused by fraud or error. This includes an assessment of: whether the accounting policies are appropriate to the company's circumstances and have been consistently applied and adequately disclosed; the reasonableness of significant accounting estimates made by the directors; and the overall presentation of the financial statements. In addition, we read all the financial and non-financial information in the [*describe the annual report*] to identify material inconsistencies with the audited financial statements. If we become aware of any apparent material misstatements or inconsistencies we consider the implications for our report.

Basis for disclaimer of opinion on financial statements

The audit evidence available to us was limited because we were unable to observe the counting of physical stock having a carrying amount of £X and send confirmation letters to trade debtors having a carrying amount of £Y due to limitations placed on the scope of our work by the directors of the company. As a result of this we have been unable to obtain sufficient appropriate audit evidence concerning both stock and trade debtors.

Disclaimer of opinion on financial statements

Because of the significance of the matter described in the Basis for Disclaimer of Opinion on Financial Statements paragraph, we have not been able to obtain sufficient appropriate audit evidence to provide a basis for an audit opinion. Accordingly we do not express an opinion on the financial statements.

Opinion on other matter prescribed by the Companies Act 2006

Notwithstanding our disclaimer of an opinion on the financial statements, in our opinion the information given in the Directors' Report for the financial year for which the financial statements are prepared is consistent with the financial statements.

Matters on which we are required to report by exception

Arising from the limitation of our work referred to above:
- *we have not obtained all the information and explanations that we considered necessary for the purpose of our audit; and*
- *we were unable to determine whether adequate accounting records have been kept.*

We have nothing to report in respect of the following matters where the Companies Act 2006 requires us to report to you if, in our opinion:

- returns adequate for our audit have not been received from branches not visited by us; or
- the financial statements are not in agreement with the accounting records and returns; or
- certain disclosures of directors' remuneration specified by law are not made.

For further review of modified audit reports, refer to:

- Republic of Ireland Audit Reports – FRC Bulletin 1(1): *Compendium of Illustrative Auditor's Reports on Irish Financial Statements,* Appendix 5, Examples 29 and 30; Appendix 7, Example 33
- UK/Northern Ireland Audit Reports – APB Bulletin 2010/2 (Revised), *Compendium of Illustrative Auditor's Reports on United Kingdom Private Sector Financial Statements for periods ended on or after 15 December 2010 (Revised),* Appendix 13, Examples 40 and 41

8.4.2 Disagreement with Management

In ISA 705, when the auditor is qualifying the audit report on the basis of disagreement with management, the modification in the audit report is described as "financial statements are materially misstated". The auditor has concluded, based on the audit evidence obtained, that the financial statements as a whole are not free from material misstatement. The most common example is when the auditor believes there is a material misstatement because management's accounting treatment of a particular transaction or balance is not in compliance with accounting standards and/or company law. Examples of this are presented below:

EXAMPLE 8.7: QUALIFICATION – THE FINANCIAL STATEMENTS ARE MATERIALLY MISSTATED/DISAGREEMENT

Debtors are not valued at recoverable amount Included in the debtors listing is an outstanding debt which has not been paid in over two years. As accounting standards require current assets to be valued at their recoverable amount, in the auditor's opinion the non-payment of the debt should be provided for. Management are refusing to adjust the provision, and the balance is material.

Inadequate disclosures for related-party disclosures During the fieldwork the audit team obtained evidence that the company had made material payments to related parties and those payments had not been disclosed in the financial statements. Accounting standards require related party transactions to be disclosed. Management tells the audit team that they will not make the disclosures due to 'commercial' reasons.

In both circumstances, management has not complied with the accounting standards and therefore there is a material misstatement in the financial statements. Based on **Figure 8.1**, when a disagreement with management such as this occurs the auditor would use his or her professional judgement to determine whether the impact on the financial statements is material or pervasive and qualifies or gives an adverse opinion respectively. As noted earlier, it would be pervasive if the matter impacted on numerous balances, or individually related to one of the most material balances in the financial statements.

Taking the two situations above in **Example 8.7**, these would likely to be 'except for' qualifications as the valuation of debtors impacts a limited number of balances, and the related party transaction is in relation to a disclosure. As numerous transactions or balances are not impacted upon, the potential error would not be considered to be pervasive.

An example of when a disagreement may be pervasive, and therefore lead to an adverse opinion, is given below:

EXAMPLE 8.8: ADVERSE OPINION

Acme Ltd is a property development company where the largest balance in the financial statements is development land and work in progress. The directors purchased the land three years ago and the market, having significantly declined since then, would indicate that the cost of the development land and work in progress should be written down to the recoverable amount. If management refuses to make this adjustment, the materiality of this balance would be so pervasive as to result in an adverse opinion.

8.4.2.1 Examples of Audit Report Modifications

When modifying the audit report as a result of a disagreement/material misstatement, only the basis opinion and opinion paragraphs are amended. Two examples are illustrated below with the amendments to the audit report in italics.

EXAMPLE 8.9: AUDIT REPORT MODIFICATIONS RESULTING FROM DISAGREEMENT/
MATERIAL MISSTATEMENT

Example 1: Inappropriate accounting treatment of debtors

ROI

Basis for qualified opinion on financial statements

Included in the debtors shown on the balance sheet is an amount of €Y due from a company which has ceased trading. XYZ Limited has no security for this debt. In our opinion the company is unlikely to receive any payment and full allowance of €Y should have been made.

Accordingly, debtors should be reduced by €Y, the deferred tax liability should be reduced by €X and profit for the year and retained earnings should be reduced by €Z.

Qualified opinion on financial statements

In our opinion, *except for the effects of the matter described in the Basis for Qualified Opinion paragraph*, the financial statements:

- give a true and fair view, in accordance with Generally Accepted Accounting Practice in Ireland, of the state of the company's affairs as at ... and of its profit/loss for the year then ended; and
- have been properly prepared in accordance with the requirements of the Companies Acts 1963–2012.

Matters on which we are required to report by the Companies Acts 1963–2012

- We have obtained all the information and explanations which we consider necessary for the purposes of our audit.
- In our opinion proper books of account have been kept by the company.
- The financial statements are in agreement with the books of account.
- In our opinion the information given in the directors' report is consistent with the financial statements.
- The net assets of the company, as stated in the balance sheet, are more than half of the amount of its called-up share capital and, in our opinion, on that basis there did not exist at ... a financial situation which under section 40(1) of the Companies (Amendment) Act, 1983 would require the convening of an extraordinary general meeting of the company.

Matters on which we are required to report by exception

We have nothing to report in respect of the provisions in the Companies Acts 1963–2012 which require us to report to you if, in our opinion, the disclosures of directors' remuneration and transactions specified by law are not made.

UK

Basis for qualified opinion on financial statements

Included in the debtors shown on the balance sheet is an amount of £Y due from a company which has ceased trading. XYZ Limited has no security for this debt. In our opinion the company is unlikely to receive any payment and full provision of £Y should have been made. Accordingly, debtors should be reduced by £Y, the deferred tax liability should be reduced by £X and profit for the year and retained earnings should be reduced by £Z.

Qualified opinion on financial statements

In our opinion, *except for the effects of the matter described in the Basis for Qualified Opinion paragraph*, the financial statements:

- give a true and fair view of the state of the company's affairs as at ... and of its profit [loss] for the year then ended;

- have been properly prepared in accordance with United Kingdom Generally Accepted Accounting Practice; and
- have been prepared in accordance with the requirements of the Companies Act 2006.

Opinion on other matters prescribed by the Companies Act 2006

In our opinion the information given in the Directors' Report for the financial year for which the financial statements are prepared is consistent with the financial statements.

Matters on which we are required to report by exception

We have nothing to report in respect of the following matters where the Companies Act 2006 requires us to report to you if, in our opinion:

- adequate accounting records have not been kept, or returns adequate for our audit have not been received from branches not visited by us; or
- the financial statements are not in agreement with the accounting records and returns; or
- certain disclosures of directors' remuneration specified by law are not made; or
- we have not received all the information and explanations we require for our audit.

Example 2: No provision for losses expected to arise on contracts which is considered pervasive due to impact on profit for the year, work in progress and deferred taxes

ROI

Basis for adverse opinion on financial statements

As more fully explained in note [x] to the financial statements no provision has been made for losses expected to arise on certain long-term contracts currently in progress, as the directors consider that such losses should be offset against amounts recoverable on other long-term contracts. In our opinion, provision should be made for foreseeable losses on individual contracts as required by Statement of Standard Accounting Practice 9: Stocks and long-term contracts. If losses had been so recognised the effect would have been to reduce the carrying amount of contract work in progress by €X, the deferred tax liability by €Y and the profit for the year and retained earnings at 31 December 20X1 by €Z.

Adverse opinion on financial statements

In our opinion, *because of the significance of the matter described in the Basis for adverse opinion paragraph*, the financial statements do *not* give a true and fair view, in accordance with Generally Accepted Accounting Practice in Ireland, of the state of the company's affairs as at 31 December 20X1 and of its profit/loss for the year then ended.

In all other respects, in our opinion the financial statements have been properly prepared in accordance with the requirements of the Companies Acts 1963–2012.

Matters on which we are required to report by the Companies Acts 1963–2012

Notwithstanding our adverse opinion on the financial statements:

- we have obtained all the information and explanations which we consider necessary for the purposes of our audit;

- in our opinion proper books of account have been kept by the company;
- the financial statements are in agreement with the books of account;
- in our opinion the information given in the directors' report is consistent with the financial statements; and
- the net assets of the company, as stated in the balance sheet are more than half of the amount of its called-up share capital and, in our opinion, on that basis there did not exist at .... a financial situation which under section 40(1) of the Companies (Amendment) Act, 1983 would require the convening of an extraordinary general meeting of the company.

Matters on which we are required to report by exception

We have nothing to report in respect of the provisions in the Companies Acts 1963–2012 which require us to report to you if, in our opinion, the disclosures of directors' remuneration and transactions specified by law are not made.

UK

Basis for adverse opinion on financial statements

As more fully explained in note [x] to the financial statements no provision has been made for losses expected to arise on certain long-term contracts currently in progress, as the directors consider that such losses should be off-set against amounts recoverable on other long-term contracts. In our opinion, provision should be made for foreseeable losses on individual contracts as required by Statement of Standard Accounting Practice 9: Stocks and long-term contracts. If losses had been so recognised the effect would have been to reduce the carrying amount of contract work in progress by £X, the deferred tax liability by £Y and the profit for the year and retained earnings at 31 December 20X1 by £Z.

Adverse opinion on financial statements

In our opinion, *because of the significance of the matter described in the Basis for Adverse Opinion paragraph*, the financial statements:
- do *not* give a true and fair view of the state of the company's affairs as at 31 December 20X1 and of its profit [loss] for the year then ended; and
- have *not* been properly prepared in accordance with United Kingdom Generally Accepted Accounting Practice.

In all other respects, in our opinion the financial statements have been prepared in accordance with the requirements of the Companies Act 2006.

Opinion on other matter prescribed by the Companies Act 2006

Notwithstanding our adverse opinion on the financial statements, in our opinion the information given in the Directors' Report for the financial year for which the financial statements are prepared is consistent with the financial statements.

Matters on which we are required to report by exception

We have nothing to report in respect of the following matters where the Companies Act 2006 requires us to report to you if, in our opinion:

- adequate accounting records have not been kept, or returns adequate for our audit have not been received from branches not visited by us; or
- the financial statements are not in agreement with the accounting records and returns; or
- certain disclosures of directors' remuneration specified by law are not made; or
- we have not received all the information and explanations we require for our audit.

For further review of modifications, refer to:

- Republic of Ireland Audit Reports – FRC Bulletin 1(1): *Compendium of Illustrative Auditor's Reports on Irish Financial Statements*, Appendix 5, Examples 26, 27 and 28; Appendix 6, Example 31 and 32
- UK/Northern Ireland Audit Reports – APB Bulletin 2010/2 (Revised), *Compendium of Illustrative Auditor's Reports on United Kingdom Private Sector Financial Statements for periods ended on or after 15 December 2010 (Revised)*, Appendix 13, Examples 37, 38 and 39; Appendix 14, Examples 42 and 43.

8.4.3 Multiple Uncertainties

It might be necessary to modify the audit report due to multiple uncertainties when the auditor concludes that, notwithstanding having obtained sufficient appropriate audit evidence regarding each of the individual uncertainties, it is not possible to form an opinion on the financial statements due to the potential interaction of the uncertainties and their possible cumulative effect on the financial statements.

Examples of when it might be necessary to modify the audit report due to multiple uncertainties could include:

- uncertainty regarding the outcome of a significant claim – this would impact upon the income statement and balance sheet;
- uncertainty regarding the going concern status which relies upon the timing of the renewal of finance facilities from the bank; and
- uncertainty regarding the value of an investment in a subsidiary which is making net losses and relies on the support of the parent.

While individually these uncertainties may not lead to a qualification, in aggregate they result in significant uncertainty as to the true and fair view required to be expressed in the auditor's opinion. As a result, the auditor would disclaim an opinion in the audit report.

8.4.3.1 *Examples of Audit Report Modifications*

When modifying the audit report as a result of a multiple uncertainties, amendments to the audit report are in the respective responsibilities paragraph, basis of opinion and opinion paragraphs and matters required to report by Companies Act. An example is illustrated below with the amendments to the audit report in italics.

EXAMPLE 8.10: AUDIT REPORT MODIFICATIONS RESULTING FROM
MULTIPLE UNCERTAINTIES

ROI

Respective responsibilities of directors and auditor

As explained more fully in the Directors' Responsibilities Statement [set out [on page ...]], the directors are responsible for the preparation of the financial statements and for being satisfied that they give a true and fair view. Our responsibility is to audit and express an opinion on the financial statements in accordance with Irish law and International Standards on Auditing (UK and Ireland). Those standards require us to comply with the Auditing Practices Board's (APB's) Ethical Standards for Auditors. *Because of the matters described in the Basis for Disclaimer of Opinion paragraph, however, we were not able to obtain sufficient appropriate audit evidence to provide a basis for an audit opinion.*

Scope of the audit of the financial statements

An audit involves obtaining evidence about the amounts and disclosures in the financial statements sufficient to give reasonable assurance that the financial statements are free from material misstatement, whether caused by fraud or error. This includes an assessment of: whether the accounting policies are appropriate to the company's circumstances and have been consistently applied and adequately disclosed; the reasonableness of significant accounting estimates made by the directors; and the overall presentation of the financial statements. In addition, we read all the financial and non-financial information in the [describe the annual report] to identify material inconsistencies with the audited financial statements. If we become aware of any apparent material misstatements or inconsistencies we consider the implications for our report.

Basis for disclaimer of opinion on financial statements

In seeking to form an opinion on the financial statements we considered the implications of the significant uncertainties disclosed in the financial statements concerning the following matters:
- *[Describe uncertainty 1]*
- *[Describe uncertainty 2]*

There is potential for the uncertainties to interact with one another such that we have been unable to obtain sufficient appropriate audit evidence regarding the possible effect of the uncertainties taken together.

Disclaimer of opinion on financial statements

Because of the significance of the possible impact of the uncertainties, described in the Basis for Disclaimer of Opinion on Financial Statements paragraph, to the financial statements, we have not been able to obtain sufficient appropriate audit evidence to provide a basis for an audit opinion. Accordingly we do not express an opinion on the financial statements.

Matters on which we are required to report by the Companies Acts 1963 to 2012

We have been unable to form an opinion as to whether there did or did not exist at ... a financial situation which under section 40(1) of the Companies (Amendment) Act, 1983 would require the convening of an extraordinary general meeting of the company.

Notwithstanding our disclaimer of an opinion on the financial statements:

- we have obtained all the information and explanations which we consider necessary for the purposes of our audit;
- in our opinion proper books of account have been kept by the company;
- the financial statements are in agreement with the books of account;
- in our opinion the information given in the directors' report is consistent with the financial statements; and
- the net assets of the company, as stated in the balance sheet are more than half of the amount of its called-up share capital and, in our opinion, on that basis there did not exist at ... a financial situation which under section 40(1) of the Companies (Amendment) Act, 1983 would require the convening of an extraordinary general meeting of the company.

Matters on which we are required to report by exception

We have nothing to report in respect of the provisions in the Companies Acts 1963 to 2012 which require us to report to you if, in our opinion, the disclosures of directors' remuneration and transactions specified by law are not made.

UK

Respective responsibilities of directors and auditor

As explained more fully in the Directors' Responsibilities Statement [set out [on page ...]], the directors are responsible for the preparation of the financial statements and for being satisfied that they give a true and fair view. Our responsibility is to audit and express an opinion on the financial statements in accordance with applicable law and International Standards on Auditing (UK and Ireland). Those standards require us to comply with the Auditing Practices Board's [(APB's)] Ethical Standards for Auditors. *Because of the matters described in the Basis for Disclaimer of Opinion paragraph, however, we were not able to obtain sufficient appropriate audit evidence to provide a basis for an audit opinion.*

Scope of the audit of the financial statements

An audit involves obtaining evidence about the amounts and disclosures in the financial statements sufficient to give reasonable assurance that the financial statements are free from material misstatement, whether caused by fraud or error. This includes an assessment of: whether the accounting policies are appropriate to the company's circumstances and have been consistently applied and adequately disclosed; the reasonableness of significant accounting estimates made by the directors; and the overall presentation of the financial statements. In addition, we read all the financial and non-financial information in the [*describe the annual report*] to identify material inconsistencies with the audited financial statements. If we become aware of any apparent material misstatements or inconsistencies we consider the implications for our report.

Basis for disclaimer of opinion on financial statements

In seeking to form an opinion on the financial statements we considered the implications of the significant uncertainties disclosed in the financial statements concerning the following matters:
- *[Describe uncertainty 1]*
- *[Describe uncertainty 2]*

There is potential for the uncertainties to interact with one another such that we have been unable to obtain sufficient appropriate audit evidence regarding the possible effect of the uncertainties taken together.

Disclaimer of opinion on financial statements

Because of the significance of the possible impact of the uncertainties, described in the Basis for Disclaimer of Opinion on Financial Statements paragraph, to the financial statements, we have not been able to obtain sufficient appropriate audit evidence to provide a basis for an audit opinion. Accordingly we do not express an opinion on the financial statements.

Opinion on other matter prescribed by the Companies Act 2006

Notwithstanding our disclaimer of an opinion on the financial statements, in our opinion the information given in the Directors' Report for the financial year for which the financial statements are prepared is consistent with the financial statements.

Matters on which we are required to report by exception

We have nothing to report in respect of the following matters where the Companies Act 2006 requires us to report to you if, in our opinion:
- adequate accounting records have not been kept, or returns adequate for our audit have not been received from branches not visited by us; or
- the financial statements are not in agreement with the accounting records and returns; or
- certain disclosures of directors' remuneration specified by law are not made; or
- we have not received all the information and explanations we require for our audit.

For further review of modifications, refer to:
- Republic of Ireland Audit Reports – FRC Bulletin 1(1): *Compendium of Illustrative Auditor's Reports on Irish Financial Statements,* Appendix 7, Example 34
- UK/Northern Ireland Audit Reports – APB Bulletin 2010/2 (Revised), *Compendium of Illustrative Auditor's Reports on United Kingdom Private Sector Financial Statements for periods ended on or after 15 December 2010 (Revised),* Appendix 15, Example 45.

8.5 OTHER REPORTING CONSIDERATIONS

In discussing audit reports, there are a number of other factors that should be high-lighted as follows:
- 'Other matters' paragraph;
- Auditor's responsibilities relating to other documents in the financial statements;
- Corresponding figures; and
- Listed company requirements.

8.5.1 'Other Matters' Paragraph

An 'other matters' paragraph is used when the auditor feels it is necessary to draw the users' attention to a matter which is relevant to the users' understanding of the audit, the auditor's responsibilities or the auditor's report. Examples of 'other matters' can be:
- an outline of the circumstances preventing the auditor from withdrawing from the engagement, even though there is a management imposed limitation on scope;
- an elaboration of the auditor's responsibilities, e.g. that the comparative figures have not been audited as it is the first year that the company qualifies for audit.

8.5.2 Auditor's Responsibilities Relating to Other Documents in the Financial Statements

In forming an opinion, the auditor is only responsible for forming an opinion on the primary financial statements which include the following:
- income statement;
- statement of other comprehensive income;
- balance sheet/statement of financial position;
- statement of changes in equity;
- cash flow statement; and
- notes to the financial statements.

Any other information included in financial statements or annual reports is referred to as 'other information' and includes, for example:
- Chairman's Report;
- Financial and Operating Review;
- Corporate Governance Statement;
- Directors' Remuneration Report; and
- Audit Committee Report.

It is advisable to familiarise yourself with the format and layout of annual reports. These can be downloaded from the websites of any Irish or UK Plc, e.g. Kingspan Plc, CRH Plc, etc.

ISA 720 (UK and Ireland) Section A – *The Auditor's Responsibilities Relating to Other Information in Documents Containing Audited Financial Statements* requires the auditor to read the other information and identify material inconsistencies, if any, with the audited financial statements. It is important to clarify that, when the auditor reads the other information, the auditor does so in the light of the knowledge acquired during the audit. The auditor is not expected to verify any of the other information.

If the auditor notes inconsistencies between other information and the audited financial statements, and management refuses to make any changes, the auditor considers the implications for the audit report. This may be inserted into the audit report as an 'other matter' paragraph.

ISA 720 (UK and Ireland) Section B – *The Auditor's Statutory Responsibility in Relation to Directors' Reports* specifically requires the auditor to review the directors' report and assess whether it is consistent with the financial statements. An example of an inconsistency may be differences between the amounts or narrative appearing in the financial statements and directors' report.

If the auditor does detect inconsistencies, they should seek to resolve them. If they are unable to resolve the differences and conclude that the directors' report is materially inconsistent with the financial statements, the auditor shall state that opinion and describe the inconsistency in the auditor's report.

8.5.3 Corresponding Figures

ISA 710 (UK and Ireland) *Comparative Information – Corresponding Figures and Comparative Financial Statements* defines '*corresponding figures*' as comparative information where amounts and other disclosures for the prior period are included as an integral part of the current period financial statements, and are intended to be read only in relation to the amounts and other disclosures relating to the current period. Whilst the standard also refers to comparative financial statements, in NI and ROI the corresponding figures presentation is usually required.

In summary, therefore, when an auditor is forming an opinion on the financial statements, it is on the current year financial statements as a whole, including the corresponding figures. Whilst the auditor does not refer to the corresponding figures in the audit report, unless there is a modification required, the opinion is interpreted as including both current and prior-year figures.

The audit report may include a modification in relation to the corresponding figures in the following circumstances:
• Where the prior-year audit report was qualified and the issue is not resolved, e.g. if the client has not received a professional valuation for a revalued property, the qualification paragraph would refer to the potential misstatement in the prior year and current year figures.

- Where the auditor discovers a material misstatement during audit fieldwork that relates to the corresponding figures, e.g. research and development costs were incorrectly capitalised in the prior year. If management will not make the necessary adjustment the auditor would qualify the audit report referring to both prior-year and current-year figures.
- Where, in the example used in the immediately preceding bullet point above, management do make the necessary restatement adjustments to the prior-year figures, the auditor may consider it necessary to include an 'emphasis of matter' paragraph describing the circumstances and referring to the relevant disclosures in the notes to the accounts that fully describe the matter.
- Where the corresponding figures were not audited due to the client being audit exempt in the prior year, the auditor does not have an obligation to audit the prior year figures, but must carry out required audit work on the opening balances as per ISA 510. If sufficient appropriate audit evidence is obtained on the opening balances, the auditor inserts an 'other matter' paragraph in the audit report stating the fact that the corresponding figures are unaudited.

8.5.4 Listed Companies

The audit report for a listed company has additional reporting requirements for the auditor to report on; under listing rules the auditor is required to state that:
- the company has complied with certain provisions of the UK Corporate Governance Code;[2] and
- the directors have reviewed the internal control environment and have included a statement of this review in the financial statements.

If the company has not complied with these requirements, the auditor would include this as an 'other matter' paragraph.

8.6 APPROACHING AUDIT REPORT EXAM QUESTIONS

The best way to understand audit reports is to practise answering questions which will enable you to grow in confidence in coming to a decision as to whether or not an issue will result in a qualification. A few useful questions for this purpose have been included as review questions at the end of this chapter. The purpose of including these questions is to assist your thought process when faced with an audit report issue in an exam.

The solutions provided in **Appendix One** are outlines only and represent a structured thought process to assist you in dealing with audit report issues as follows:
- What is the issue?
- What accounting standard or company law regulation is it in disagreement with, if applicable?

---

[2] See www.frc.org.uk/corporate/ukcgcode.cfm

- Is it material? (If not, the issue has no impact on the audit report.)
- Will the directors make the adjustment? (If so, there is no impact on the audit report.)
- Is it 'disagreement' or 'except for'?
- Is it material or pervasive?

By documenting this thought process for audit report issues, you should easily find a solution and, even if the qualification you decide upon is incorrect, you should pick up some level of competency from noting your thought process as you will be highlighting why the issue results in qualification.

8.7 CONCLUSION

The auditor qualifies the audit report if they conclude that the financial statements are not free from material misstatement. The materiality of the potential error determines the type of qualification included on the audit report. Furthermore, the audit report can also be used to draw the readers' attention to a significant uncertainty, even though the auditor is not qualifying on that basis.

SUMMARY OF LEARNING OBJECTIVE

Learning Objective To be able to draft the appropriate audit report, in line with relevant standards and legislation

The auditor forms an opinion on the financial statements that they are free from material misstatement. When the auditor qualifies the report on this basis, there are numerous considerations to be taken into account when deciding on the type of qualification. Furthermore, the auditor should also be aware of the other reporting considerations that need to be taken into account when completing the audit report.

QUESTIONS

In each of the scenarios presented in the questions below, there is an issue/(s) which needs to be addressed by the auditor (an indicator) in relation to audit reports. You should read the questions and attempt to address the issues relating to audit reports based on the guidance in **Section 8.6**.

Review Questions

Question 8.1 (Based on Chartered Accountants Ireland, FAE Autumn 2006, Paper 1, Question 2)

Crystal

Your firm is the auditor of Crystal Ltd ('Crystal'). The principal business of Crystal comprises the design, supply and installation of home entertainment systems. The company has recently introduced the new Media Centre PC to its product range. The diversification of the business into a new product range is the company's strategic response to the market conditions prevailing within the core business and an opportunity to lever existing skills into the PC market. Crystal regards the Media Centre PC to be the next generation of computing and home entertainment that will deliver the complete computing experience and enable Crystal to regain market share as none of its competitors have launched a similar product. The company has been actively developing its new product. However, by December 2005 only one machine type has been designed although the product development plan anticipates that a range of machines will be available for sale by June 2007.

You are the audit senior responsible for the audit of Crystal and are aware of the company's recent poor trading performance. It is evident that the future viability of the business is dependent on the successful implementation of the new product range. During the course of the audit for the year ended 31 December 2005, the following matters have come to your attention.

1. Crystal is currently underperforming and incurred a loss of €/£1,560k for the year to December 2005. This is primarily due to a general decline in revenues in the standard home entertainment systems division. However, following a comprehensive discussion with the Financial Director, you identify the following additional factors contributing to the poor trading performance:
    (a) Introduction of a rebate policy as an incentive to large corporate customers.
    (b) Significant expenditure in developing the new product – the Media Centre PC.
    (c) Substantial marketing spend on a television advertising campaign to promote the new product.
    (d) Rent increase on the company's prime high street retail outlet from €/£210k to €/£390k per annum.
    (e) Recognition of a redundancy provision of €/£120k following a formal announcement in November 2005.

There are no audit issues arising in relation to the accounting treatment of the above areas.

2. In May 2005 Crystal entered into a number of leasing arrangements all of which have been accounted for as operating leases. However, it has come to light through your fieldwork that these agreements are actually finance leases. The total cost of the assets acquired is €/£1,760,000 and the monthly rentals are €/£37,000. You communicate these findings to the Financial Accountant who does not wish to adjust Crystal's financial statements at this late stage.

After further investigation into the planned restructuring, you understand that management propose to enter into a sale and leaseback arrangement on their manufacturing plant in order to raise finance to complete the development of the new product. Crystal has existing bank borrowings of €/£2 million and the bank is not prepared to extend this facility. In addition, the bank has suggested that it is considering calling in €/£1 million of the existing borrowing, subject to discussions with management scheduled in one month's time. Management have indicated that they are confident that the existing debt will not be called in and, as a result, do not refer to this matter in the financial statements. Approval of the financial statements is scheduled for three weeks' time.

Question 8.2 (Based on Chartered Accountants Ireland, FAE Autumn 2007, Paper 1, Question 3)

Build

You are the audit senior in charge of the audit of Build Ltd ('Build'), a building contracting company based in Ireland. Build has on-going contracts throughout Ireland and the UK. Three years ago the Board of the company established a wholly owned subsidiary company in Hong Kong, Build HK Ltd ('BHK'), in response to the growing amount of large contracting work in mainland China. For the year ended 31 December 2006 the group has consolidated turnover of €/£50 million and net assets of €/£22 million.

BHK is audited by your firm's overseas office in Hong Kong. In reviewing the group clearance documents received from BHK's auditors, you note that the auditors have expressed concern over trade debtors of €/£5,287,000 which represent an estimate of the amounts expected to be recovered from contracted works currently being undertaken on a particular contract in China. The main issue noted relates to the recoverability of additional costs, amounting to €/£3,500,000 included in the above amount. These additional costs were submitted to the customer just prior to the company's year-end.

You have discussed all of the components of the amount of €/£5,287,000 with the Finance Director and he has provided you with all information available to him in this regard, including relevant legal correspondence. The ultimate recovery of the additional costs of €/£3,500,000 is dependent upon the input of experts employed by the Hong Kong customer, Build has also employed experts to assist in reaching a mutually satisfactory agreement on this issue. It has been agreed that the joint findings of these experts will be mutually binding on the company and the customer.

In February 2006, the Board of Build agreed to dispose of its investment in an associate company, ABBA Ltd ('ABBA') to the majority shareholder. ABBA is an electrical and mechanical contracting firm based in London, which has been consistently profitable and has shown strong growth over the past five years. ABBA had been accounted for by Build under the equity method of accounting. The group's gross investment in ABBA at the time of sale was €/£3,575,000 made up of a share of results totalling €/£1,575,000, and loans of €/£2 million.

Under the sale agreement, the proceeds of the sale of the investment are to be based on the audited profits (if earned) of ABBA for the two years ending on 31 December 2007 and

31 December 2008, subject to an upper ceiling on the sales proceeds of €/£2 million. The loans due from ABBA to Build of €/£2 million are to be met out of the proceeds of a contractual claim that is being pursued by ABBA. The Financial Director of Build has reviewed this situation and believes that the full amount of the claim, in excess of €/£2 million, will be received by ABBA.

You have carried out further audit work on this issue which confirms to you that the full amount of the claim will not be recovered by ABBA; the legal correspondence supports this view. You have discussed your workings with the audit engagement partner and he has agreed with your assessment that the full amount of the claim will not be recovered and that a provision of €/£1 million is required as a result. You have discussed this matter with the Finance Director who is not in a position to disagree with the conclusions you have reached in this regard. However, as indicated to you, he does not propose to amend the financial statements for the year ended 31 December 2006 in this respect, as his experience is that these matters are usually settled in full.

Question 8.3 (Based on Chartered Accountants Ireland, FAE Autumn 2008, Paper 1, Question 2)

Tex

Tex Ltd ('Tex') is a company that specialises in the dyeing and printing of fabric. It is a well-established company with an excellent reputation throughout the UK and Ireland for quality. Customers' greige cloth is supplied by customers to Tex which then dyes the cloth to the required colour. Although the greige cloth does not actually belong to Tex, it is recorded on the inventory system in order to track the cloth through the dyeing process. Tex also has its own inventory of greige cloth which it dyes for selling through its three factory stores and also for sale to customers who do not supply their own greige cloth.

The company has been facing increasing pressures from overseas competitors and has been finding that margins have been in gradual decline. To address this risk, Tex established a wholly owned subsidiary, East Ltd ('East'), in China which has been trading successfully for the past two years.

You are the audit senior responsible for the audit of Tex for the year ended 31 December 2007 and you have been asked by the engagement partner to prepare a summary of the issues that have arisen to date during the audit fieldwork. Below is the extract from the audit summary memorandum you prepared.

1. A deficiency of €/£147,000 has arisen between the physical inventory count and the book value of inventory held on the accounting system. The Stock Controller of Tex has undertaken an extensive reconciliation between the results of the physical inventory count and the book inventory. From this exercise, the Stock Controller believes that either the greige cloth of some customers may have been recorded on the system as 'Tex's own cloth' rather than 'customer greige cloth' or vice versa. However, due to inventory movements since the year end, the Stock Controller has been unable to identify a list of incorrectly coded cloth to reconcile the difference. Based on these facts, the Financial Director has written the full difference of €/£147,000 off to the income statement thereby reducing profit for the year to €/£294,271.

2. Discussions are currently taking place with the Revenue authorities concerning the basis of certain inter-company transactions between Tex and East. From discussions with the Financial Director, you have ascertained that, until the outcome of this matter has been resolved, he does not believe that it is possible to determine the effect, if any, that it might have on the company's tax position. Given the facts, he does not believe that it is necessary to make any provision or disclosure in the financial statements for the year ended 31 December 2007. He has not disclosed this matter in the financial statements as he believes it will prejudice Tex's case with the Revenue authorities. Our audit work suggests that, if the company is not successful in its discussions with the Revenue authorities, the resulting cost to the company will be €/£360,000.

3. A public announcement was made during December 2007 by the Directors of Tex that, in order to drive efficiencies, the factory store in Galway would be closed from March 2008. The Financial Director has made full provision in the financial statements at 31 December 2007 for all costs arising from the closure.

9

GROUP AUDITS

Learning Objectives

- To understand the responsibilities of the group auditor prior to the acceptance of the engagement
- To be able to execute the risk assessment process to be employed by the group auditor in relation to the component audits
- To be able to execute the group auditor's responsibilities in developing audit procedures for the components' auditors
- To understand the involvement of the group auditor at the completion stage, including components
- To understand the group auditor's responsibilities in relation to auditing the consolidation process

9.1 INTRODUCTION

As defined by both Irish and UK company law, a group is a parent company and all its subsidiaries. This can be illustrated by the simple group structure below:

FIGURE 9.1: SIMPLE GROUP STRUCTURE

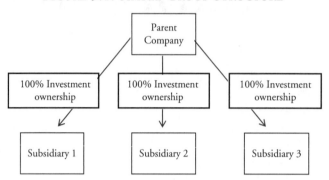

In the UK and the ROI, groups over a certain size (medium and large companies in the UK, large companies in the ROI) must prepare consolidated accounts. As you will be aware, this means that, for the group illustrated in **Figure 9.1**, there would be one set of financial statements for the parent company which will incorporate the consolidated results of the entire group, including the three subsidiaries. If the reporting framework was IFRS, these consolidated financial statements would be prepared in accordance with IFRS 3 *Business Combinations.*

Company law also requires group companies to be audited if they exceed audit thresholds (noted in **Chapter 1**). This means that the consolidated financial statements of the group must be audited.

When auditing a group entity, the auditor will need access to audit evidence that supports the assertions in the consolidated financial statements, i.e. the auditor will need access to the financial information of the subsidiary companies and supporting evidence.

Auditing a parent company and subsidiaries is generally less complex to plan if the auditor is responsible for both the parent and subsidiary companies' audits. However, it is often the case that the auditor of the parent company is not the auditor of the subsidiary companies and the subsidiaries may also be based in different countries. In such cases, the role of the parent company's auditor differs slightly from the role of auditor of the entire group, and they have to develop policies and procedures to comply with ISA 600 (UK and Ireland) *Special Considerations – Audits of Group Financial Statements (Including the Work of Component Auditors)* ('ISA 600').

ISA 600 does not refer to subsidiaries; instead it refers to components. A component is defined as an entity or business activity for which group or component management prepares financial information which should be included in the group financial statements. You will note that, based on this definition, a component is not necessarily a subsidiary but can also be, e.g. a branch or division of the parent company.

ISA 600 defines the objectives of the auditor in group audits as follows:
- to determine whether to act as the auditor of the group financial statements; and
- if acting as auditor of the group financial statements:
  - to communicate clearly with component auditors about the scope and timing of their work on financial information related to components and their findings; and
  - to obtain sufficient appropriate audit evidence regarding the financial information of the components and the consolidation process to express an opinion on whether the group financial statements are prepared, in all material respects, in accordance with the applicable financial reporting framework.

The level of involvement of a group auditor in the audit of the components will depend on the size of those components. ISA 600 defines a significant component as a component identified by the group engagement team which:
1. is of individual financial significance to the group; or
2. due to its specific nature or circumstances, is likely to include significant risks of material misstatement of the group financial statements.

In determining the financial significance of a component, the group engagement team may apply a chosen benchmark as an aid, e.g. the group engagement team may consider that components exceeding 15% of the assets or profit of the entire group are significant components. **Note**: identification of significant components is an important step as the group auditor's involvement in significant components is significantly different to their involvement in other components. This will become clearer as you work through this chapter.

This chapter explains the objectives of the auditor of the parent company when auditing a consolidation and the requirements of ISA 600 in this regard. It is split into the stages of an audit in order to assist you to understand the responsibilities of the group auditor at each stage:
- Pre-audit activities (**Section 9.2**)
- Risk assessment (**Section 9.3**)
- Responses to assessed risks (**Section 9.4**)
- Concluding activities (**Section 9.5**)
- Consolidation process (**Section 9.6**)
- Communication and documentation (**Section 9.7**)

9.2 PRE-AUDIT ACTIVITIES

The auditor of the parent company is responsible for the direction, supervision and performance of the group audit engagement and for signing off on the audit opinion for that group. Therefore, prior to accepting the engagement, the auditor needs to:

- Consider if any components are significant and, if so, will the group auditor be able to get sufficient access to the component's financial information, e.g. will the component and component's auditors allow the group auditor sufficient appropriate audit evidence? If the auditor concludes that this will not be the case and that the inability to obtain this information will result in disclaiming an opinion, the auditor should not accept the engagement.
- Understand the component's auditors, e.g. if they comply with ethical requirements, are competent to carry out the work and if they operate in a strong regulatory environment.

These requirements, along with how the group auditor would meet these requirements, can be summarised as follows in **Figure 9.2**:

FIGURE 9.2: PRE-AUDIT ACTIVITIES

Requirement	Action
Determine whether the component auditors will comply with the ethical requirements of the audit, particularly independence	• Obtain written confirmation from the component auditors • Consider the requirements of their recognised accountancy body and request copies of any inspection reports
Determine the professional competence, of the component auditors i.e. do they have the correct skills, sufficient resources and understanding of auditing and financial reporting standards	• Obtain written confirmation from the component auditors • Consider the requirements of their recognised accountancy body and request copies of any inspection reports • Obtain confirmations of membership and professional competence from the professional body to which the auditors of the components belong
Determine whether a group engagement team will be able to be involved in the work of the component auditors	• Discuss with the component auditors and receive confirmation in writing
Determine whether the component auditors operate in an environment in which there is regulatory oversight of auditors	• Discuss with the component auditors or obtain confirmation from the regulatory oversight bodies in the relevant jurisdiction

If the group auditor is not satisfied that the component auditors can meet the conditions above, the group engagement team will be required to obtain audit evidence relating to that component without the assistance of the component auditors, i.e. they will have to carry out the audit procedures themselves. This requires agreement from group and component management.

9.3 RISK ASSESSMENT

At the risk assessment stage, the group auditor must do the following:
- set the group audit strategy and audit plan;
- understand the group, its components and their environments; and
- set materiality levels.

9.3.1 Set Group Audit Strategy and Audit Plan

In **Chapter 3**, we discussed the auditor's responsibility to set an audit plan and strategy at the commencement of the engagement. Similarly, at the commencement of a group audit, the auditor is required to set the audit plan and strategy for the **overall group.** This is to satisfy the requirement of ISA 600 and ISA 200 whereby the engagement partner is responsible for the direction of the group audit and solely responsible for the group audit opinion.

(At this point, you should refer back to **Chapter 3** to refresh your understanding of the elements included in an audit plan and strategy.)

9.3.2 Understand the Group, its Components and their Environments

In **Chapter 3**, we discussed the requirements of ISA 315 (UK and Ireland) *Identifying and Assessing the Risks of Material Misstatement Through Understanding of the Entity and Its Environment* ('ISA 315') and ISA 240 (UK and Ireland) *The Auditor's Responsibilities Relating to Fraud in an Audit of Financial Statements* ('ISA 240') whereby the auditor must obtain an understanding of the entity, its environment and its internal controls in order to identify the risks of material misstatement. ISA 600 requires the group auditor to:
- Obtain an understanding of the group, its components and their environments, including group-wide controls. This is done in a similar way identified in ISA 315, i.e. by discussion with management, analytical procedures and observation of controls.
- Obtain an understanding of the consolidation process, for example:
  o What is the reporting package used by management?
  o Do components feed individual management packs to the parent entity on a monthly basis?

o Are all accounting policies consistent throughout the group?
o Are there group instructions sent to all components?

Such a detailed understanding is required if the auditor is to carry out substantive testing on the consolidation process as required by ISA 600.

Identify and assess the risk of material misstatement of the financial statements due to fraud as required by ISA 240. In a group audit these discussions will involve the component auditors as they will be able to share knowledge regarding the risk of fraud in the components and therefore the group as a whole. These discussions may take the form of a conference call, face-to-face meeting or video conference, and provide an opportunity for the group auditor and component auditors to:
o share knowledge about the components, their environments and controls;
o exchange ideas as to how the group financial statements may be susceptible to fraud;
o consider risk of over-ride of controls by group or component management; and
o discuss fraud that has been identified in components.

9.3.3 Set Materiality

At the risk assessment stage ISA 600 has a number of requirements for the group auditor in relation to materiality for both the group and the components. The group auditor must set the following materiality:
- Materiality for the group financial statements as a whole, which is based on the requirements of ISA 320 (as discussed in **Chapter 3**).
- Performance materiality for the group financial statements to be applied to specific transactions or balances, as required, based on the requirements of ISA 320 (again, as discussed in **Chapter 3**).
- Component materiality, which should be set at a level lower than group materiality for the financial statements as a whole, to reduce the risk of aggregate uncorrected or undetected misstatements in the group financial statements. Though the standard does not specify what component materiality should be in practice, it is calculated as a percentage, e.g. 60%, of group materiality. This materiality level is communicated to, and used by, the component auditors in risk assessment and performance of audit tests.
- Performance materiality for components (see **Chapter 3**) – this may be calculated as, say, 60% of component materiality. Again, this should be communicated to the component auditors.
- Clearly trivial amounts for the group financial statements. As discussed in **Chapter 3**, this could be calculated as, say, 2% of group materiality. Similarly, this should be communicated to the component auditors.

It should be noted that in some cases the component may have to be audited for local statutory purposes and the component auditors would therefore set their own materiality for these purposes. The group auditor can only rely on the audit work of the component's auditors if it is carried out using materiality either the same as, or lower than, component materiality set by the group auditor. If the component auditors continue to use their own statutory materiality, which is higher than component materiality set by the group auditors, the group auditors must obtain their own sufficient appropriate audit evidence based on component materiality.

9.4 RESPONSES TO ASSESSED RISKS

In line with ISA 330, once the auditor has completed the risk assessment process, the auditor is required to design and implement appropriate audit tests to address the assessed risks of material misstatement in the financial statements. The group engagement team determines the audit work to be performed by the group audit team, or the component's auditor on its behalf.

The level of audit work to be performed at a component level will depend on the size or significance of that component, which is discussed below.

9.4.1 Significant Components

For significant components (as defined in **Section 9.1**), the group auditor will require the following:
- a full audit to be performed by the group auditor, or a component auditor on their behalf, using component materiality based on the agreed risk assessment; or
- if the component is considered significant due to the fact that its nature or circumstances may result in a risk of material misstatement to the group financial statements, it may be possible to carry out an audit of the specific transactions or account balances using component materiality.

See **Example 9.1** below as an example of considerations of audit approach for components.

9.4.2 Components that are not Significant Components

For components that are not considered to be significant, the group auditor is required to carry out analytical procedures at group level to ensure that the components do not contain any risk of material misstatement.

See **Example 9.1** as an example of considerations of audit approach for components.

EXAMPLE 9.1: AUDITOR CONSIDERATIONS OF COMPONENTS

Example Client Component Evaluation 2011 Year End

Components	Current Assets	Total Assets	Current Liabilities	Total Liabilities	Equity	Revenues	Earnings Before Taxes	Significant Components	Response	Rationale
			Evaluate Benchmarks							
A	75%	82%	74%	73%	76%	78%	82%	Yes	Comprehensive	
B	12%	10%	14%	13%	12%	11%	10%	Yes	Targeted	Revenue is assessed as a significant risk for the group financial statements
C	13%	8%	12%	14%	12%	11%	8%	No	Analytical	
Total Group	100%	100%	100%	100%	100%	100%	100%			

9.4.3 Additional work

If the group auditor does not consider that appropriate audit evidence will be obtained from work on significant components and non-significant components as noted above, they will carry out additional procedures by selecting non-significant components and perform:
- an audit using component materiality; or
- audit procedures on one or more account balances or transactions; or
- a review of the component using component materiality; or
- specified procedures targeted at the significant components and areas that are considered a significant risk to the group.

9.5 CONCLUDING ACTIVITIES

For non-significant components, the analytical reviews of the components form part of the group audit work and are performed in accordance with those requirements.

However, for significant components, there are a number of additional considerations in relation to the involvement of the group auditors in the fieldwork and completion activities of the component auditor's work.

As noted above, the group auditor requires the component auditor to carry out a full audit using component materiality set by the group auditor. The group auditor is, therefore, highly involved in the risk assessment process in order to determine this. Once the group auditor has set the responses to the assessed risks, i.e. a full audit, the component auditor then performs the work.

As the group auditor is forming an opinion of the group financial statements as whole, it is important that the group auditor maintains a close involvement in the work of the component auditor. This will involve reviewing the component auditor's work at the end of the audit to conclude that the component auditor has obtained sufficient appropriate audit evidence that the component's financial statements are free from material misstatement.

In practical terms, this will work in one of two ways:
1. if the component auditor is within the same network of firms as the group's firm of auditors, files may be transferred electronically for review; or
2. if the component auditor is not within the same network, the group auditor will have to arrange an on-site visit to the component auditor to review the working papers.

If the group auditor concludes that the work of the component auditor is insufficient, the group engagement team shall determine additional work to be performed by the component auditor or the group engagement team.

Furthermore, when the group auditor is communicating with those charged with governance regarding significant deficiencies or significant audit issues as required by ISA 260 and ISA 265, these should include any significant items arising from the component audits.

Therefore, as part of the concluding procedures, the group engagement team shall request the component auditor to communicate matters relevant to the group engagement team's conclusion with regard to the group audit. Such communication shall include:

- whether the component auditor has complied with all ethical and independence requirements;
- whether the component auditor has complied with the group engagement team's requirements;
- identification of the financial information of the component on which the component auditor is reporting;
- information on instances of non-compliance with laws or regulations that could give rise to a risk of material misstatement of the group financial statements;
- a list of uncorrected misstatements above the group clearly trivial amount;
- indicators of possible management bias;
- description of any identified significant deficiencies in internal control at a component level;
- any other significant matters that the component auditor communicated to component management;
- any other matters that may be relevant to the group audit; and
- the component auditor's overall findings, conclusions or opinion.

This information, along with the knowledge obtained by the group auditor in risk assessment and review of the audit work, will allow the group auditor to draw a conclusion as to whether the group financial statements give a true and fair view.

9.6 CONSOLIDATION PROCESS

As noted at the beginning of this chapter, ISA 600 requires the group auditor to obtain an understanding of the group-wide controls and consolidation process. This is to enable the group auditor to then either test the operating effectiveness of the controls, or perform substantive procedures on the consolidation process.

Substantive testing on the consolidation process would include tests such as the following:

- ensure all components have been included in the consolidation;
- test appropriateness of consolidation adjustments and if they have be adequately supported and documented;

- check that accounting policies are consistent between parent and components and, if not, ensure that the necessary adjustments have been made; and
- obtain reconciliations of intragroup balances and ensure that they have all been eliminated in the consolidation.

The group auditor is required to conclude that they are satisfied that the consolidation process is not materially misstated.

9.7 COMMUNICATION AND DOCUMENTATION

For significant components, you should now understand that there is a very high level of group audit involvement in the work of the component auditor's work. In summary, the group audit is involved in:
- the risk assessment process of the component auditor to ensure that the significant risks of the group are addressed at the component level;
- setting materiality for the component auditor at a lower level than that of group materiality to ensure that any aggregate undetected errors in the component would not result in the financial statements of the group being materially misstated;
- reviewing the sufficiency and appropriateness of audit evidence obtained by the component auditor to ensure that the group auditor can form an opinion on the group financial statements;
- discussing significant deficiencies and audit issues with the component auditor so that the group auditor can discuss these deficiencies with those charged with governance in the parent company;
- obtaining all uncorrected misstatements to ensure that the aggregate of the uncorrected misstatements of all components is not above group materiality; and
- obtaining confirmation of compliance with the group engagement team's requirements from the component auditor, to ensure that the component auditor complies with the necessary ethical and independence requirements.

This communication will be a combination of the following:
- **Written Communication** For example, issuing group instructions to the component auditor at the beginning of the audit setting out requirements and requests for confirmation of ethical and independence requirements.
- **Face-to-face Meetings** For example, to review the audit work.
- **Conference Calls or Video Conferencing** For example, to discuss risk assessment or completion issues.

The group auditor must also ensure that all this communication is documented on the audit file, along with any written communication sent or received from the component auditor.

9.8 CONCLUSION

The group's firm of auditors has significant obligations in relation to the components in a group, even when it does not audit those components. These obligations lead to a requirement for the group auditor to plan the audit, and the involvement of the group's auditors, efficiently and effectively.

SUMMARY OF LEARNING OBJECTIVES

Learning Objective 1 To understand the responsibilities of the group auditor prior to the acceptance of the engagement

Prior to accepting an engagement as group auditor, the auditor must ensure that: there are no restrictions on their work, they will be able to access work of component auditors, and they are satisfied with the competence of the audit firms auditing the components to carry out the required audit work.

Learning Objective 2 To be able to execute the risk assessment process to be employed by the group auditor in relation to the component audits

The group auditor is required to be involved in the risk assessment process of the components to ensure that the significant risks of the group are addressed at the component level. This will mean communication with the component auditors during the risk assessment stage.

Learning Objective 3 To be able to execute the group auditor's responsibilities in developing audit procedures for the components' auditors

The group auditor is required to work closely with the component auditors to ensure they respond to the group's risks, either by carrying out a full audit or targeted audit procedures provided by the group auditor.

Learning Objective 4 To understand the involvement of the group auditor at the completion stage, including components

The group auditor is responsible for forming an opinion on the group financial statements. Therefore, in order to be satisfied that the components are not materially misstated, they are required to review the work of the component auditors and develop further audit procedures if necessary.

Learning Objective 5 To understand the group auditor's responsibilities in relation to auditing the consolidation process

The group auditor has a responsibility to obtain an understanding of the group-wide controls and consolidation process. This is to enable the group auditor to perform audit procedures to conclude that the consolidation is free from material misstatements.

QUESTIONS

In the scenario presented in the question below, there is an issue/(s) which needs to be addressed by the auditor (an indicator) in relation to group audits. You should read the question and attempt to address the issue/(s) relating to group audits.

(See **Appendix One** of this text for Suggested Solutions to Questions.)

Review Questions

Question 9.1 (Based on Chartered Accountants Ireland, FAE 2011 Mock Paper, Simulation 3)

Pybex Limited

Refer to the scenario presented in ***Question 2.2***.

10

OTHER REPORTS TO THIRD PARTIES

LEARNING OBJECTIVES

In reading and studying this chapter, your objectives are to be able to:
- understand the principles underpinning reporting engagements to third parties;
- execute an engagement to prepare a report for a third party, including drafting these reports; and
- apply the necessary safeguards to minimise the risk implications of providing reports to third parties.

10.1 INTRODUCTION – REPORTS OTHER THAN AUDIT REPORTS

The focus of this book has been on the audit process including audit reporting. There are, however, many other types of '**reporting engagements**' which practitioners regularly undertake for clients, resulting in different types of reports. Clients may request reports from practitioners for internal use in their company or because a third party requires the client to do so, e.g. regulators, tax authorities, trade bodies, grant agencies, lenders, etc. Although reporting engagements are many and varied they can be categorised into the following engagement types, depending on the form of report that is to be provided:

- review engagements – reviews of financial statements and of interim financial information;
- assurance engagements, other than audits or reviews of historical information (e.g. reporting on the effectiveness of internal control);
- examination of prospective financial information;
- agreed upon procedures; and
- engagements to compile financial information (preparing financial information on behalf of clients).

These other types of reporting engagements are the subject of this chapter.

As discussed throughout this text, the ISAs (UK and Ireland) are the professional standards governing the conduct of audit work in Northern Ireland and in the Republic of Ireland. As outlined in **Chapter 1**, there are additional pronouncements that are issued by the IAASB which can be applied to other types of engagements. These are:

- International Standards on Review Engagements (ISREs),
- International Standards on Assurance Engagements (ISAEs); and
- International Standards on Related Services (ISRSs).

The engagements discussed in this chapter require knowledge of the relevant ISAEs, ISREs and ISRSs.

To date, the APB has adopted only one of these pronouncements: ISRE 2410 (UK and Ireland) *Review of Interim Financial Information Performed by the Independent Auditor of the Entity* (ISRE 2410). However, accountants are not prohibited from using the other pronouncements issued by the IAASB and, indeed, are encouraged by Chartered Accountants Ireland and other recognised accountancy bodies to have a thorough understanding of the other pronouncements.

Miscellaneous Technical Statement *M39 Reporting to Third Parties* (M39), from Chartered Accountants Ireland, also provides guidance to accountants in the Republic of Ireland and Northern Ireland in relation to managing the risks involved in undertaking engagements to report to third parties and will be referred to in this chapter.

10.2 ASSURANCE AND NON-ASSURANCE ENGAGEMENTS

Reporting engagements undertaken by practitioners are either assurance engagements or non-assurance engagements, and the distinction is important.

An **assurance engagement** is defined in the IAASB's *International Framework for Assurance Engagements*. Essentially an assurance engagement is one in which a practitioner obtains evidence in order to express a conclusion. The conclusion expressed is designed to enhance the degree of confidence of the user about the outcome of the measurement or evaluation of an underlying subject matter against given criteria. This is explained more fully below.

The most common example of an assurance engagement is an audit of financial statements. Here the auditor obtains sufficient appropriate evidence in order to express an opinion on the financial statements. The financial statements (outcome or subject matter information) are prepared by applying the financial reporting framework (the criteria) to the underlying subject matter, e.g. inventories (subject matter) are measured (valued in accordance with IAS 2) at the lower of cost and net realisable value. The auditor's opinion is designed to give users of the financial statements more confidence in the financial statements.

Accordingly, the **objective** of an assurance engagement might be to improve the confidence of a third party in relation to information or a process assessed against an agreed criterion through the expression of a written opinion.

Assurance engagements include:
- audits of financial statements;
- assurance engagements to report on the effectiveness of an internal control system;
- reporting on the reliability and adequacy of IT systems;
- due diligence engagements;
- review of financial statements;
- grant claims reported on in accordance with Miscellaneous Technical Statement *M45 Grant Claims* (M45);
- engagements to provide assurance in relation to non-financial information, such as corporate social responsibility reports or environmental reports; and
- assurance engagements in relation to compliance with specified legal requirements (e.g. at the request of a regulator).

Practitioners also perform engagements that do not meet the definition of an assurance engagement as outlined above. Such engagements are described as **non-assurance engagements** and include, among others:
- engagements covered by the ISRS, such as agreed-upon procedures engagements and compilations of financial or other information;
- the preparation of tax returns where no conclusion conveying assurance is expressed; and
- consulting (or advisory) engagements, such as management or tax consulting. Such engagements may involve objective-setting, fact-finding, definition of problems or opportunities, evaluation of alternatives, development of recommendations including actions, communication of results and sometimes implementation and follow-up. Reports on consulting engagements are often written in a narrative style.

It is not the objective of non-assurance engagements to enhance the confidence of users about the subject matter information.

10.3 ASSURANCE ENGAGEMENTS

The IAASB's *International Framework for Assurance Engagements* and ISAE 3000 *Assurance Engagements Other than Audits or Reviews of Historical Financial Information* provide guidance in relation to assurance engagements. This guidance is discussed below.

10.3.1 The Elements of an Assurance Engagement

There are some elements that are common to all assurance engagements. The essential elements of an assurance engagement are:
- a three-party relationship;
- an appropriate subject matter;
- suitable criteria;
- sufficient appropriate evidence; and
- a written assurance report.

10.3.1.1 A Three-party Relationship

All assurance engagements involve three parties. These consist of:
1. an accounting/auditing practitioner;
2. a responsible party (usually the company or entity responsible for the preparation and maintenance of the information or processes which are the subject matter of the engagement); and
3. the intended users of the assurance report.

The party responsible for the information or process which is the subject matter of the assurance report can be in the same organisation as those who are intended to use the assurance report, or the intended user could be external to the responsible party's organisation. For example, the responsible party could be the senior management in a company and the intended users could be the board of directors where the board wants to be able to rely on specific information prepared by senior management. In another case, the responsible party could be a company's board of directors and the intended user could be the company's shareholders, a bank or an industry regulator.

It is possible for the responsible party to be **one** of the intended users of the assurance report but **not the only one**.

It is common for the responsible party also to be the engaging party, i.e. the client.

The intended users are the people, or groups of people, for whom the assurance report is prepared. Miscellaneous Technical Statement *M39 Reporting to Third Parties* emphasises the importance of identifying third parties who will rely on the accountant's report and understanding the reason why they need a practitioner to report on the information or process. The practitioner should always clearly identify the intended users at the commencement of the engagement and will sometimes need to limit the use of the report to defined users. This restriction would be set out in the terms of the engagement and in the text of the assurance report. See discussion at **Section 10.3.3** below.

10.3.1.2 Appropriate Subject Matter

The subject matter of an assurance engagement can take many forms:
- financial performance or conditions (e.g. historical financial information as in the financial statements of an entity);
- non-financial performance or conditions which might be represented as an entity's key performance indicators of efficiency and effectiveness;
- physical characteristics (such as the capacity of a plant which may be expressed through a specifications document);
- systems and processes (such as a company's internal controls system); or
- behaviour (such as compliance with regulations or corporate governance).

To be appropriate as the subject matter of an assurance engagement it is important that:
1. the subject matter is identifiable, and capable of consistent evaluation or measurement against the criteria identified for the engagement; and
2. information about the subject matter can be subjected to procedures for gathering sufficient appropriate evidence to support the appropriate assurance conclusion.

10.3.1.3 Suitable Criteria

Criteria are the objective benchmarks or standards used to evaluate or measure the subject matter. It is important that a clearly identifiable set of criteria for the evaluation and measurement of the subject matter can be pointed to as the basis for the practitioner's conclusion. The chosen criteria must be appropriate to the engagement circumstances and free from bias.

The criteria for the preparation of financial statements might be, e.g. IFRS, or the criteria for assessing human resource practices in an organisation could be the company's (or its group's) prepared human resources policy or some agreed external framework.

10.3.1.4 Sufficient Appropriate Evidence

The practitioner must be able to obtain evidence as to whether the subject matter information is free from material misstatement. The amount (sufficiency) of evidence gathered and its quality (appropriateness) is assessed as to whether it is adequate to form an opinion. In an assurance engagement the procedures for gathering evidence are determined by the practitioner in accordance with professional standards and professional judgement.

The level of evidence required varies depending on whether the engagement is a reasonable assurance engagement or a limited assurance engagement as described at **Section 10.3.2** below.

10.3.1.5 Assurance Report

The practitioner provides a written report containing a conclusion that conveys the assurance obtained by the practitioner about the subject matter information. The form of the wording of the report depends on the level of assurance being provided (see the discussion of reasonable assurance and limited assurance at **Section 10.3.2** below).

The practitioner's conclusion will either be unqualified or qualified, as appropriate, based on the evidence obtained.

10.3.2 Reasonable Assurance and Limited Assurance

The level of assurance obtained by the practitioner is not always the same. Specifically, the IAASB's *International Framework for Assurance Engagements* focuses on two types of assurance that a practitioner can obtain. These are:

1. **Reasonable Assurance** (Reasonable Assurance Engagement)

   In a reasonable assurance engagement, the practitioner performs procedures to reduce the engagement risk to an acceptably low level such that the report can include a positive form of expression of the practitioner's conclusion. For example, the financial statements "**give a true and fair view**, in accordance with international financial reporting standards", or "In our opinion internal control **is effective,** in all material respects, based on XYZ criteria." You can see that in both examples the conclusion is expressed in a positive way.

   Reasonable assurance is, of course, not absolute assurance. It is usually not possible, or cost beneficial, to reduce the engagement risk to zero.

2. **Limited Assurance** (Limited Assurance Engagement)

   In a limited assurance engagement, the work is designed to enable the practitioner to express the conclusion in a negative form. For example, in a limited assurance engagement to evaluate the effectiveness of internal controls the practitioner may report that "**nothing has come to our attention** that indicates significant internal control deficiencies".

   The acceptable engagement risk is higher for a limited assurance engagement than for a reasonable assurance engagement and the procedures performed are consequently more limited relative to a reasonable assurance engagement.

It is of course essential to agree at the outset of the engagement on the level of assurance required by the engaging party.

Table 10.1 below summarises the differences between a reasonable assurance engagement and a limited assurance engagement.

TABLE 10.1: REASONABLE ASSURANCE ENGAGEMENT
vs. LIMITED ASSURANCE ENGAGEMENT[1]

Type of Assurance Engagement	Objective	Evidence-gathering Procedures	The Assurance Report

Reasonable assurance engagement	A reduction in engagement risk to an acceptably low level in the circumstances of the engagement*, as the basis for a positive form of expression of the practitioner's conclusion.	Sufficient appropriate evidence is obtained as part of a systematic engagement process that includes:
		• obtaining an understanding of the engagement circumstances;
		• assessing risks;
		• responding to risks;
		• performing further procedures using a combination of:
		  ○ inspection,
		  ○ observation,
		  ○ confirmation,
		  ○ re-calculation,
		  ○ re-performance,
		  ○ analytical procedures; and
		  ○ inquiry.
		Such further procedures involve substantive procedures including, where applicable, obtaining corroborating information, and, depending on the nature of the subject matter, tests of the operating controls; and
		• evaluating the evidence obtained.
			Description of the engagement circumstances* and a positive form of expression of the conclusion.

---

[1] IAASB International Framework for Assurance Engagements.

276

| Limited assurance engagement | A reduction in assurance engagement risk to a level that is acceptable in the circumstances of the engagement* but where that risk is greater than for a reasonable assurance engagement, as the basis for a negative form of expression of the practitioner's conclusion. | Sufficient appropriate evidence is obtained as part of a systematic engagement process that includes obtaining an understanding of the subject matter and other engagement circumstances, but in which procedures are deliberately limited relative to a reasonable assurance engagement. | Description of the engagement circumstances*, and a negative form of expression of the conclusion. |

* Engagement circumstances include: the terms of the engagement as set out in the engagement letter; the characteristics of the subject matter and subject matter information; the criteria to be used; the needs of the intended users; relevant characteristics of the party responsible for the information and its environment; and other matters such as events, transactions, conditions and practices, that may have a significant effect on the engagement.

10.3.3 The Process of an Assurance Engagement

Regardless of the type of assurance engagement the following stages are involved:
1. Engagement acceptance and/or continuance;
2. Agreeing the terms of the engagement;
3. Planning and performing the engagement; and
4. Reporting.

10.3.3.1 Engagement Acceptance and/or Continuance

There are a number of pre-acceptance considerations for the practitioner:

Will acceptance of this engagement have any ethical consequences? Before accepting an assurance engagement (or agreeing to continue an engagement) the practitioner must consider whether the requirements of Chartered Accountants Ireland's *Standards of Professional Conduct,* including the *Code of Ethics* or, where relevant, the APB *Ethical Standards for Auditors,* have been complied with in relation to the engagement.

Is an assurance engagement appropriate? It is important to gain sufficient knowledge of the client and the requirements of the client in the particular circumstances before accepting an engagement. The practitioner considers whether:

- the necessary elements of an assurance engagement apply;
- the subject matter is appropriate;
- the criteria are suitable;
- there is access to sufficient appropriate evidence; and
- a written assurance report is to be provided.

It is important to determine whether an assurance engagement is the appropriate type of engagement in the circumstances. Following appropriate enquiry, the accountant may consider that it is not possible to provide the level of assurance desired by the client due to the nature of the subject matter or the information available, or within the time frame that the client requires, or indeed, for the level of fees which the client is willing to pay for the work. Generally, the higher the level of assurance sought in a report, the more work is necessary and the greater the cost to the client. The practitioner should not accept an engagement if the client is not willing to pay sufficient fees for the scope of work requested. It may be possible to agree on a different type of assurance engagement, e.g. a limited assurance engagement may be sufficient to meet the needs of both the client and the intended user.

Does the responsible party acknowledge appropriate responsibility? It is important to get acknowledgement from the responsible party that they understand their responsibilities and their relationship with the intended user. This would usually be set out in the engagement letter, an example of which is set out below.

EXAMPLE 10.1: SAMPLE PARAGRAPH FROM AN ENGAGEMENT LETTER
IN RELATION TO MANAGEMENT RESPONSIBILITY

> Responsibility for the financial statements which comply with [IFRS] and company law, including adequate disclosure, is that of the management of the company. This includes the maintenance of adequate accounting records and internal controls and the selection and application of accounting policies.

Will there be third parties relying on the report? Miscellaneous Technical Statement *M39 Reporting to Third Parties* emphasises the importance of determining who will rely on the practitioner's work and for what purpose before accepting any reporting engagement, as discussed in **Section 10.8** below.

When practitioners know that their report has been requested by a third party and that the third party will rely on the report, there is a risk that the accountants may owe a duty of care to the third party in preparing and providing the report. It is therefore vital to understand:

- who the third party is;

- why the third party requires the work to be undertaken; and
- the extent of loss which the third party could suffer in relying on the work the practitioner has undertaken.

The practitioner needs to assess the risk involved and consider appropriate action before deciding to accept the engagement. Such actions could include:
- entering into a contract with the third party as well as the client;
- limitation of liability;
- asking the third party to acknowledge in writing that they are owed no duty of care by the practitioner; and
- including similar disclaimers in the practitioner's report.

Managing the duty of care owed to third parties is discussed in further detail at **Section 10.8** below.

Can the practitioner competently perform the work? Of course an assurance engagement should only be accepted if the practitioner is confident that he can assign an engagement team with the appropriate professional competencies. Since the subject matter of assurance engagements can vary, the expertise required will vary and so it is important to make sure that any specialised skill requirements can be met.

10.3.3.2 Agreeing the Terms of the Engagement

To avoid any misunderstanding, the agreed terms of the engagement are recorded in an engagement letter. The engagement terms will vary depending on a number of factors including:
- the level of assurance to be provided;
- the nature of the relationship between the responsible party and the intended users;
- the nature of the relationship between the responsible party and the engaging party (if not the same people);
- whether the engagement letter is agreed only between the engaging party/the client and the accountant (bipartite) or whether the third party, who will rely on the report, is also party to the engagement letter (tripartite);
- the nature of the subject matter;
- the nature of the criteria; and
- whether or not there is a legal mandate for the engagement.

It is, therefore, important that all relevant engagement details are set out clearly in the engagement letter agreed between the parties.

The engagement letter should at least include:
- the responsibilities of the parties involved;
- a clear identification of the subject matter;
- a clear identification of the criteria;
- an identification of the intended users and, where appropriate, of the use for which the report is intended including any limits on the use and distribution of the report;

- the type of assurance report which will be given at the conclusion of the engagement; and
- an agreement of fees and a timetable for the performance of the engagement.

10.3.3.3 *Planning and Performing the Engagement*

Planning involves developing an overall engagement strategy and a detailed engagement plan which includes procedures to be performed to gather evidence. Planning is not a discrete exercise to be done at the start of the engagement; rather it is an ongoing process which continues throughout the engagement with the plan being revised as a result of evidence obtained in the course of the work or some unexpected events that may change the outcome of the report.

Planning and performing the assurance engagement involves the following:

1. **Understanding** Obtaining and documenting an understanding of the subject matter and other engagement circumstances.

2. **Risk Assessment** The practitioner assesses engagement risk. Risk assessment procedures include enquiry, observation of controls and reference to the practitioner's understanding of the subject matter and the environment. Acceptable materiality levels should be determined at this stage.

3. **Responding to the Assessed Risks and Gathering Evidence** Responding to engagement risk includes determining the nature, timing and extent of further procedures to be performed to gather sufficient appropriate evidence. The practitioner performs further procedures clearly linked to the identified risks. Procedures may include tests of controls, substantive testing including analytical procedures, seeking representations, and considering the use of the work of experts. Evidence gathered through procedures performed is documented.

   For example, if the practitioner in a grant claim engagement has identified a risk that payroll expenditure may be overstated due to weak internal controls in that area he will design procedures which test payroll expenditure substantively in greater detail than he would do in an environment where he assesses the internal controls to be strong. In this case the practitioner might, e.g. select quite large sample sizes for examining employment contracts of the personnel named in the grant claim and for tracing payments from payroll records to bank records evidencing payment.

4. **Evaluating the Sufficiency and Appropriateness of Evidence** The practitioner evaluates the evidence gathered through the procedures performed to conclude whether it is adequate in terms of both quantity and quality to enable him/her to reach an opinion. Additional procedures to gather further information may be required.

10.3.3.4 *Reporting*

The assurance report should be in writing. It should include a clear expression of the practitioner's conclusion.

Assurance reports are tailored to the specific engagement circumstances. The assurance report should, however, include the following basic elements:

- a title – clearly identifying the report as an **independent** assurance report;
- an addressee;
- a description of the subject matter information;
- identification of the criteria;
- where appropriate, any limitation on the evaluation or measurement of the subject matter against the criteria;
- where appropriate, a statement restricting the use of the assurance report to specific intended users or for a specific purpose;
- identification of the responsible party and a description of their responsibilities and those of the practitioner;
- a summary of the work performed;
- a statement that the engagement was performed in accordance with ISAEs;
- the practitioner's conclusion;
- the assurance report date; and
- identification of the practitioner (name, firm, firm address).

The assurance report will either be unqualified or qualified depending on the findings of the practitioner. A qualified opinion can be expressed as 'qualified', 'adverse' or 'a disclaimer opinion'.

Examples of circumstances which would lead to a qualified opinion are set out below:

EXAMPLE 10.2: CIRCUMSTANCES THAT WOULD LEAD
TO A QUALIFIED OPINION

Nature of Matter	Effect on Report Conclusion
Where there is a limitation on the scope of the practitioner's work either due to circumstances or imposed by one of the parties	A qualified opinion is given or a disclaimer opinion, depending on the pervasive nature of the material misstatement
Where the practitioner concludes that the responsible party's assertion is not fairly stated in all material respects	A qualified or adverse opinion, depending on the pervasive nature of the material misstatement
Where the practitioner has found that the subject matter information is materially misstated	A qualified or adverse opinion, depending on the pervasive nature of the material misstatement
Where the practitioner has discovered, in the course of the work, that the criteria are unsuitable or the subject matter is inappropriate	A qualified, adverse or disclaimer opinion depending on how pervasive the material misstatement is

When expressing a qualified opinion, the practitioner should set out the circumstances which give rise to the qualification. For example, where the scope of the engagement has been limited the practitioner must explain in the report the way in which the scope was limited (what kind of information was unavailable which the practitioner considered necessary), the impact of the limitation (whether the limitation was pervasive to the whole engagement and therefore an opinion could not be formed – disclaimer; or whether the limitation applied only to a particular part of the subject matter information) and also whether the limitation was imposed by circumstances or by the responsible or engaging party specifically.

10.4 REVIEWS OF FINANCIAL STATEMENTS AND OF INTERIM FINANCIAL INFORMATION

A review of financial statements and a review of interim financial information are examples of limited assurance engagements. The objective of a review of financial statements or of a review of interim financial statements is to carry out procedures which enable practitioners to conclude **that nothing has come to their attention which causes them to believe that the financial statements/interim financial statements are not prepared, in all material respects,** in accordance with the applicable financial reporting framework (e.g. IFRS). The procedures performed are usually limited to inquiry and analytical procedures.

These provision of these reviews are governed by ISRE 2400 (UK and Ireland) *Engagements to Review Financial Statements* and ISRE 2410 (UK and Ireland) *Review of Interim Financial Information Performed by the Independent Auditor of the Entity* which include requirements and guidance on the performance of these types of engagements.

10.4.1 Review Engagement Acceptance

An engagement to review financial statements should only be accepted after the practitioner has considered the relevant ethical requirements and has concluded that there are no reasons (which cannot be managed through safeguards) why the engagement should not be accepted. Information gained at the acceptance phase of the engagement can, of course, be used to inform the practitioner's knowledge of the client and the engagement circumstances which are important in the planning and performance phase.

10.4.2 Agreeing the Terms of the Review Engagement

It is important to spend time agreeing the terms of the engagement with the client, to ensure that there are no misunderstandings in relation to matters such as the objective and scope of the engagement, and the responsibilities of the client, the practitioner and the form of report. It is especially important to clarify that the engagement is a limited assurance engagement and **not an audit.** It is not possible to overestimate the value of time spent ensuring that the client fully understands the scope of the engagement.

The engagement letter would typically include the following:
- the objective of the service being performed;
- the scope of the review;
- management's responsibility for the financial statements, the internal control environment and all financial records and supporting information;
- management's agreement to provide written representations when requested;
- unrestricted access to whatever records, documentation and other information requested by the practitioner in connection with the review;
- an example of the practitioner's report;
- the fact that the engagement cannot be relied upon to disclose errors, illegal acts or other irregularities, e.g. fraud or defalcations that may exist;
- a statement that **an audit is not being performed and that an audit opinion will not be expressed** (to emphasise this point and to avoid confusion, the practitioner may consider pointing out that a review engagement will not satisfy any statutory or third party requirements for an audit); and
- an agreement of fees and a timetable for the performance of the engagement.

10.4.3 Planning and Performing the Review Engagement

As with all assurance engagements an engagement strategy and detailed plan should be prepared and referred to throughout the engagement. An attitude of professional scepticism should always be maintained.

10.4.3.1 Obtaining an Appropriate Understanding and Assessing Risk

The practitioner uses judgement to plan the procedures to be performed to reduce the engagement risk to an acceptable level. Although the engagement risk in a limited assurance engagement is higher than in a reasonable assurance engagement the practitioner must still assess areas of risk and consider the objective of reducing risk in planning the review procedures. In determining the appropriate procedures the practitioner should consider the following:
- knowledge of the business and the industry and of the accounting and control systems in place at the entity. The practitioner is often also the auditor of the entity and therefore can refer to the knowledge gained in the course of previous audit work; such knowledge should of course be updated before it is relied upon;
- the extent to which management judgement is involved in arriving at particular account balances, transactions and disclosures; and
- materiality.

The **same materiality should be applied in a review engagement as in an audit engagement.** Although there is a greater risk that material misstatements will not be detected in a review engagement than in an audit engagement, the judgement as to what is material is made by reference to the information on which the practitioner is reporting and the needs of the users of that information. Materiality is discussed in greater detail in **Chapter 3**.

10.4.3.2 *Performing Procedures and Gathering Evidence*

Procedures to be performed in a review engagement are typically limited to inquiry and analytical procedures and would ordinarily include:

- obtaining an understanding of the entity's business and the industry in which it operates;
- inquiries of persons having responsibility for financial and accounting matters concerning, for example:
  - o whether all transactions have been properly recorded, classified and summarised;
  - o whether information is properly accumulated for disclosure in the financial statements;
  - o whether the financial statements have been prepared in accordance with the bases of accounting indicated;
  - o the nature of and a statement of the occurrence of any changes in the entity's business activities and accounting principles and practices; and
  - o significant assumptions made in relation to balances which are subject to management judgement;
- inquiries concerning actions taken at meetings of shareholders, the board of directors, committees of the board and other meetings that may affect the financial statements;
- analytical procedures designed to identify relationships and individual items that appear unusual. Such procedures include:
  - o comparison of the financial statements with statements from prior periods;
  - o comparison of the financial statements with anticipated results and financial position;
  - o study of the relationships of the elements of the financial statements that would be expected to conform to a predictable pattern based on the entity's experience or industry norm; and
  - o consideration of the types of matters which required accounting adjustments in prior periods;
- reading the financial statements/interim financial information to consider whether they appear to conform with the basis of accounting indicated;
- obtaining reports from other accountants, if any and if considered necessary, who have been engaged to audit or review the financial statements/interim financial information of the components of the entity; and
- obtaining written representations from management when considered appropriate.

The example below details the procedures a practitioner may carry out during a review engagement of a receivables balance.

EXAMPLE 10.3 PROCEDURES FOR REVIEW ENGAGEMENT
OF RECEIVABLES BALANCE

The procedures a practitioner might plan to carry out in relation to the receivables balance in the course of a review engagement could include:
- inquiring about the accounting policies for initially recording trade receivables;
- obtaining a schedule of receivables and determine whether the total agrees with the trial balance;
- obtaining and considering explanations of significant variations in account balances from previous periods;
- obtaining an aged analysis of the trade receivables. Inquiring about the reason for unusually large amounts, credit balances on accounts or any other unusual balances and inquire about the collectability of receivables;
- discussing with management the classification of receivables, including non-current balances, net credit balances and amounts due from shareholders, directors and other related parties in the financial statements;
- inquiring about the method for identifying 'slow payment' accounts and setting allowances for doubtful accounts and consider it for reasonableness;
- inquiring whether receivables have been pledged, factored or discounted; and
- inquiring about procedures applied to ensure that a proper cut-off of sales transactions and sales returns has been achieved.

The practitioner should document the procedures performed and the evidence gathered by the performance of those procedures.

10.4.3.3 Evaluation of Evidence

The practitioner evaluates the evidence gathered and assesses whether the evidence obtained is sufficient for the practitioner to draw a conclusion.

10.4.4 Reporting on the Review Engagement

The review report should include the following:
- title;
- addressee;
- a clear identification of the financial statements/interim financial information which are the subject of the review;
- a statement setting out the relative responsibilities of the entity's management and of the practitioner respectively;
- a statement that a review is limited primarily to inquiries and analytical procedures;

- a statement that the review has been carried out in accordance with ISRE 2410 (UK and Ireland) *Review of Interim Financial Information Performed by the Independent Auditor of the Entity* if appropriate;
- a statement that an audit has not been performed, that the procedures undertaken provide less assurance than an audit and that an audit opinion is not expressed;
- the practitioner's conclusion set out in a negative form, e.g.:
  "Based on our review, nothing has come to our attention that causes us to believe that the accompanying financial statements are not prepared, in all material respects, in accordance with IFRS";
- the report date; and
- the identification of the practitioner (name, firm, firm address).

The conclusion may be modified to express a qualified or adverse conclusion where a matter has come to the practitioner's attention which causes the practitioner to believe that a material adjustment should be made to the financial statements/interim financial information. The matters may have the following effects on the practitioner's conclusion:

FIGURE 10.1: IMPACT OF MATTERS ON A REVIEW
ENGAGEMENT CONCLUSION

Nature of Matter	Effect on Review Engagement Conclusion
Material impact (see sample wording below)	Express a qualified opinion that a particular aspect of the financial statements is not prepared in accordance with the applicable financial reporting framework
Pervasive impact	Express an adverse opinion that the financial statements are not prepared in accordance with the applicable financial reporting framework
Limitation of scope which is material to one area	Express a qualified opinion stating the limitation in one particular area (e.g. did not have evidence to support stock movements)
Limitation of scope which is pervasive to the financial statements	Do not express an opinion

When the conclusion is modified, the report should give details of the required adjustments. For example, a qualified conclusion where a matter has a material impact on the financial statements may be worded as follows:

EXAMPLE 10.4: EXTRACT FROM A REVIEW ENGAGEMENT REPORT WHERE MATTER HAS MATERIAL IMPACT

"Basis for Qualified Conclusion:

Based on information provided to us by management, ABC Ltd has excluded from property and long-term debt certain lease obligations that we believe should be capitalised to conform with IFRS. This information indicates that if these lease obligations were capitalised at 31 March 20XX property would be increased by €XXX, long-term debt by €XXX, and net income would be increased/decreased by €XXX for the three-month period then ended.

Qualified Conclusion:

Based on our review, with the exception of the matter described in the preceding paragraph, nothing has come to our attention that causes us to believe that the accompanying interim financial information is not prepared, in all material respects, in accordance with IFRS."[2]

10.5 EXAMINATION OF PROSPECTIVE INFORMATION

Prospective financial information is financial information based on assumptions about events that may occur in the future and the possible actions by an entity. It can be in the form of a forecast, a projection or a combination of both. It is highly subjective in nature and its preparation requires the exercise of considerable judgement. ISAE 3400 *The Examination of Prospective Financial Information* provides guidance on engagements of this type.

A forecast is prepared on the basis of assumptions as to future events which management expects to take place and the actions management expects to take (best-estimate assumptions). A projection is prepared on the basis of hypothetical assumptions about future events and management actions which are not necessarily expected to take place (e.g. when a company is considering a major change in the nature of its operations management would look at 'what-if' scenarios). A projection can also be based on a mixture of hypothetical and best-estimate assumptions.

Prospective financial information may be prepared by a company for:
- internal purposes – to inform management decision-making in a specified area such as whether to recruit additional salesmen in the coming season; or

---

[2] ISRE (UK and Ireland) 2410 *Review of Interim Financial Information Performed by the Independent Auditor of the Entity.*

- external purposes – for distribution to third parties in, for example:
  - a prospectus to provide potential investors with information about future expectations; or
  - a document for the information of lenders which may include, e.g. cash-flow forecasts.

Practitioners are often engaged to examine and report on prospective financial information to enhance the credibility of the forecasts or projections for the intended users. Because of the high degree of subjectivity involved in the generation of assumptions about the future, it is not surprising that most engagements of this type provide only a limited level of assurance and so are limited assurance engagements.

10.5.1 Accepting an Engagement to Examine Prospective Financial Information

Before accepting an engagement to examine prospective financial information, the practitioner should consider, among other things:
- the intended use of the information;
- whether the information will be for general or limited distribution;
- the nature of the assumptions, i.e. best-estimate or hypothetical assumptions;
- the elements to be included in the information (such as cash flow statements, profit and loss account etc.); and
- the period covered by the information and how well the assumptions are matched to the time period. (As the length of the period covered increases, assumptions become more speculative, and the ability of management to make best-estimate assumptions decreases.)

The engagement should not be accepted if the practitioner has reason to believe that the assumptions are clearly unrealistic or the prospective information will be inappropriate for its intended use.

10.5.2 Agreeing the Engagement Terms

It is important that the engagement terms are agreed and documented in an engagement letter at the start of the engagement to avoid any potential misunderstandings. The engagement letter in relation to an examination of prospective financial information should include:
- the responsibility of management for the assumptions and for providing the practitioner with all relevant information and source data used in developing the assumptions;
- the nature of the assumptions (best-estimate or hypothetical assumptions);
- the responsibility of the practitioner;

- a sample of the report to be given;
- the intended use of the information and any limitations/restrictions thereon;
- the intended distribution of the information and any limitations/restrictions thereon;
- the elements to be included in the information;
- the period covered by the information; and
- an agreement of fees and a timetable for the performance of the engagement.

10.5.3 Planning and Performing an Examination of Prospective Financial Information

When planning the procedures to be undertaken, the practitioner will need to obtain an understanding of the company and its business environment and of management's process for preparing the prospective information and developing relevant assumptions. It will be important to understand:
- the internal controls over the system used to prepare the prospective financial information;
- the expertise and experience of the people preparing the forecasts and/or projections;
- the methods used to develop and apply assumptions;
- the nature of the documentation prepared to support management's assumptions;
- the extent to which statistical, mathematical and computer-assisted techniques are used; and
- the accuracy of prospective financial information prepared by the company in previous periods and the reasons for significant variances.

This understanding assists the practitioner's assessment of engagement risk and the design of examination procedures. Procedures can include:
- Assessing the reliability of information underlying best-estimate assumptions. Evidence supporting the assumptions should be sought from external and internal sources.
- When hypothetical assumptions are used supporting evidence does not need to be obtained but the practitioner should satisfy him/herself that there is no reason to believe that they are clearly unrealistic. The accountant also considers whether all the implications of the hypothetical assumptions have been included in the projections (e.g. if sales are assumed to grow beyond the current manufacturing capacity the prospective financial information would need to include the necessary investment in additional plant capacity).
- Performance of clerical checks such as re-computation to be satisfied that the prospective financial information is properly prepared from the assumptions.
- Review of internal consistency in the prospective financial information. It is useful to consider whether different forecast actions are compatible with each other. The practitioner may also check that there are no inconsistencies in the use of common variables such as interest rates.

- Procedures will vary depending on the period covered by the prospective financial information as more reliable information is likely to be available to support short-term assumptions than long-term ones. Also, in some cases a portion of the period covered by the prospective financial information may already have elapsed and in this event the practitioner may consider the extent to which parts of the prospective financial information have proven to be accurate and the reasons for variances.
- Assess the presentation and disclosure of the prospective financial information to be satisfied that:
  o the presentation of the prospective financial information is not misleading or biased;
  o the accounting policies are clearly disclosed in the notes to the prospective financial information;
  o the assumptions are adequately disclosed in the notes to the prospective financial information. It must be clear whether assumptions are best-estimates or hypothetical; and
  o the date of preparation of the prospective financial information is disclosed.

10.5.4 Reporting on an Examination of Prospective Information

A written report should be provided. Key elements of a report on an examination of prospective information include:
- a clear identification of the prospective financial information being examined;
- a statement that management is responsible for the prospective financial information including the assumptions on which it is based;
- the practitioner's conclusion which consists of:
  o a statement of whether or not the assumptions provide a reasonable basis for the prospective financial information; and
  o an opinion as to whether the prospective financial information is properly prepared on the basis of the assumptions and is presented in accordance with the relevant financial reporting framework.

EXAMPLE 10.5: UNMODIFIED CONCLUSION

"Based on the examination of the evidence supporting the assumptions, nothing has come to our attention which causes us to believe that the assumptions do not provide a reasonable basis for the prospective financial information. In our opinion the prospective financial information is properly prepared on the basis of the assumptions and is presented in accordance with IFRS."[3]

- Appropriate caveats concerning the achievability of the results indicated by the prospective financial information.

---

[3] ISAE 3400 *The Examination of Prospective Financial Information.*

EXAMPLE 10.6: CAVEATS

Caveats could include statements such as:

"Actual results are likely to be different from the prospective financial information since anticipated events frequently do no occur as expected and the variation could be material."[4]

Or

"there can be no assurance that actual results will fall within the range"[4] (when the prospective financial information is expressed as a range).

Or

In the case of a projection: "the prospective financial information has been prepared for (state purpose) using a set of assumptions that include hypothetical assumptions about future events and management's actions that are not necessarily expected to occur. Consequently readers are cautioned that the prospective financial information is not used for purposes other than that described."[4]

Of course, there may be circumstances where an unmodified report cannot be given. The possible matters arising and impact on the accountant's report are set out in **Figure 10.2** below:

FIGURE 10.2: MATTERS WHICH MAY MODIFY THE REPORT

Nature of matter	Impact on the accountant's report on prospective financial information
Presentation and disclosure of the prospective financial information is not adequate	Express a qualified or adverse opinion or withdraw from the engagement
One or more significant assumptions do not provide a reasonable basis for the prospective financial information	Express an adverse opinion or withdraw from the engagement
Limitation on scope – conditions preclude the application of one or more procedures considered necessary	Disclaim an opinion or withdraw from the engagement

---

4 ISAE 3400 *The Examination of Prospective Financial Information.*

10.6 AGREED-UPON PROCEDURES REGARDING FINANCIAL INFORMATION

In an agreed-upon procedures engagement, the practitioner carries out procedures that have been agreed between the practitioner, the client and any third parties as appropriate, and reports factual findings as a result of the performance of those specified procedures.

The characteristics of an agreed-upon procedures engagement differ distinctly from an assurance engagement as summarised in **Figure 10.3** below.

FIGURE 10.3: DIFFERENCES BETWEEN AN AGREED-UPON PROCEDURES ENGAGEMENT AND AN ASSURANCE ENGAGEMENT

	Agreed-upon Procedures Engagement	**Assurance Engagement**
Procedures	Procedures are agreed in advance between the practitioner, the client and any appropriate third parties.	Procedures are determined by the practitioner in the exercise of professional judgement in response to assessed engagement risk.
Findings	Factual findings as a result of the agreed procedures. No further procedures evolve in the course of the engagement as a result of information gained in the course of the work.	The practitioner is required to pursue matters that may cause a material modification to be made to the subject matter information.
Report	Factual findings only – no opinion or assurance expressed.	Reasonable or limited assurance expressed.
Restriction of Use of the Report	Report is restricted to those parties that have agreed to the procedures since others, unaware of the reasons for the procedures, may misinterpret the results.	The report may be restricted to specific identified intended users but this is not always the case.

ISRS 4400 *Engagements to Perform Agreed-upon Procedures regarding Financial Information* provides requirements and guidance on the practitioner's responsibilities when performing this kind of engagement.

An example of an agreed-upon procedures engagement would be a due diligence engagement where only factual findings are reported.

10.6.1 Engagement Acceptance

Before accepting an agreed-upon procedures engagement practitioners must ensure they comply with the appropriate ethical principles of their membership body in relation to this type of engagement.

The practitioner needs to carefully consider the description of the procedures requested by the client, and third party as appropriate. Sometimes the description of the procedure(s) is not appropriate. For example, 'review the recoverability of debtors', would not be appropriate as it is not specific enough. In such cases the practitioner should suggest more specific procedures, e.g. "We will compare the (attached) debtors' listing of major debtors and amounts owed to us at (date) to the related names and amounts in the trial balance" and "We will request debtors to confirm balances owed at (date)".

Ultimately, the engagement should only be accepted if the practitioner can agree an acceptable (specific) description of the procedures. The practitioner also determines who will rely on the practitioner's report and for what purpose. M39 advises accountants not to allow their reports to be provided to a third party unless the basis and extent of their liability to the third party is clear and agreed.

10.6.2 Defining the Terms of the Engagement

When providing a report for the purposes of a third party, which is often the case with agreed-upon procedures engagements, the practitioner must manage the relationship with the third party as well as the client. This will sometimes result in a tripartite engagement letter where the terms of the engagement are signed up to by the practitioner, the client and the third party. In other cases the engagement letter will be a bipartite agreement between the practitioner and the client, but the practitioner may seek to disclaim liability to the third party in another way such as by specifying the restriction on the distribution and use of the report or by getting the third party to acknowledge separately that no duty of care is owed to them.

The engagement letter for an agreed-upon procedures engagement will include the following:
- nature of the engagement including the fact that the procedures performed will **not constitute an audit or a review** and that, accordingly, **no assurance will be expressed**;
- stated purpose of the engagement;
- identification of the financial information to which the agreed-upon procedures will be applied;
- nature, timing and extent of the specific procedures to be applied – this will constitute a listing of the procedures to be performed as agreed between the parties;

- anticipated form of the report of factual findings;
- limitations on the distribution of the report of factual findings to the specified parties who have agreed to the procedures to be performed; and
- an agreement of fees and a timetable for the performance of the engagement.

10.6.3 Planning and Performing the Engagement

The practitioner plans the engagement so that it is performed effectively. The practitioner carries out the procedures as agreed and uses the evidence obtained as the basis for the report of factual findings. The procedures can include:
- inquiry and analysis;
- computation, comparison and other clerical accuracy checks;
- observation;
- inspection; and
- obtaining confirmations.

10.6.4 Reporting

The report of factual findings should describe the purpose of the engagement and agreed-upon procedures in a way which enables the reader to understand the nature and extent of the work performed. The report should contain:
- title;
- addressee;
- identification of the specific information (financial or non-financial) to which the agreed-upon procedures have been applied;
- a statement that the procedures performed were those agreed upon with the recipient;
- a statement that the engagement was performed in accordance with ISRS 4400, which is applicable to agreed-upon procedures engagements, or relevant national standards;
- when relevant, a statement that the practitioner is not independent of the company;
- identification of the purpose for which the agreed-upon procedures were performed;
- a listing of the specific procedures performed;
- a description of the factual findings including sufficient details of errors and exceptions found;
- a statement that the procedures performed do not constitute either an audit or a review and, as such, no assurance is expressed;
- a statement that, had the practitioner performed additional procedures, an audit or a review, other matters might have come to light that would have been reported;
- a statement that the report is restricted to those parties that have agreed to the procedures to be performed;

- a statement (when applicable) that the report relates only to the elements, accounts, items or financial and non-financial information specified and that it does not extend to the entity's financial statements taken as a whole;
- date;
- practitioner's address; and
- practitioner's signature.

An illustrative Report of Factual Findings of an Agreed-upon Procedures Engagement, which is reproduced from ISRS 4400, is set out below in **Example 10.7**.

EXAMPLE 10.7: REPORT OF FACTUAL FINDINGS OF AN
AGREED-UPON PROCEDURES ENGAGEMENT[5]

Report of Factual Findings

To (those who engaged the practitioner)

We have performed the procedures agreed with you and enumerated below with respect to the accounts payable of ABC Company as at (date), set forth in the accompanying schedules (not shown in this example). Our engagement was undertaken in accordance with the International Standard on Related Services (or refer to relevant national standards or practices) applicable to agreed-upon procedures engagements. The procedures were performed solely to assist you in evaluating the validity of the accounts payable and are summarised as follows:

1. We obtained and checked the addition of the trial balance of accounts payable as at (date) prepared by ABC Company, and we compared the total to the balance in the related general ledger account.
2. We compared the attached list (not shown in this example) of major suppliers and the amounts owing at (date) to the related names and amounts in the trial balance.
3. We obtained suppliers' statements or requested suppliers to confirm balances owing at (date).
4. We compared such statements or confirmations to the amounts referred to in 2. For amounts which did not agree, we obtained reconciliations from ABC Company. For reconciliations obtained, we identified and listed outstanding invoices and credit notes subsequently received and cheques subsequently paid and we ascertained that they should in fact have been listed as outstanding on the reconciliations.

We report our findings below:

(a) With respect to item 1 we found the addition to be correct and the total amount to be in agreement.

(b) With respect to item 2 we found the amounts compared to be in agreement.

---

[5] ISRS 4400 *Engagements to Perform Agreed-upon Procedures regarding Financial Information.*

(c) With respect to item 3 we found there were suppliers' statements for all such suppliers.

(d) With respect to item 4 we found the amounts agreed, or with respect to amounts which did not agree, we found ABC Company had prepared reconciliations and that the credit notes, invoices and outstanding cheques over €/£xxx were appropriately listed as reconciling items with the following exceptions:

(Detail of the exceptions)

Because the above procedures do not constitute either an audit or a review made in accordance with International Standards on Auditing or International Standards on Review Engagements (or relevant national standards or practices), we do not express any assurance on the accounts payable as of (date).

Had we performed additional procedures or had we performed an audit or review of the financial statements in accordance with International Standards on Auditing or International Standards on Review Engagements (or relevant national standards or practices), other matters might have come to our attention that would have been reported to you.

Our report is solely for the purpose set forth in the first paragraph of this report and for your information and is not to be used for any other purpose or to be distributed to any other parties. The report relates only to the accounts and items specified above and does not extend to any financial statements of ABC Company, taken as a whole.

Practitioner

Date
Address

10.7 ENGAGEMENTS TO COMPILE FINANCIAL INFORMATION

In a compilation engagement the practitioner uses accounting expertise to collect, classify and present financial information from the sources made available by the client. This normally entails summarising the data to a manageable and understandable form. In a compilation engagement there is no requirement for the practitioners to test the assertions underlying the information and no assurance is expressed. A compilation engagement would usually include the preparation of financial statements though this is not always the case.

Useful guidance in this area is provided by:
• ISRS 4410 *Engagements to Compile Financial Information* ('ISRS 4410')
• Miscellaneous Technical Statement *M41 Chartered Accountants' Reports on the Compilation of Financial Statements of Incorporated Entities* (M41); and
• Miscellaneous Technical Statement *M48 Chartered Accountants' Reports on the Compilation of Historical Financial Information of Unincorporated Entities* (M48).

10.7.1 Accepting the Engagement

Before accepting the engagement the practitioner should ensure, as always, that appropriate ethical requirements are complied with.

The practitioner must understand the scope of the work requested by the client and the nature of information that will be made available to the practitioner. The basis of preparation for the information needs to be clearly defined in order that the practitioner can compile the information presented by the client.

For example, the client may require the preparation of financial statements which give a true and fair view and have been prepared in accordance with the applicable accounting framework and applicable law. Another client might agree that the basis to be used to compile the financial statements is one which provides sufficient and relevant information to enable the completion of a tax return.

10.7.2 Defining the Terms of the Engagement

Engagement terms should be agreed with the client in writing to avoid any misunderstandings as to the scope and objective of the engagement. The engagement letter in a compilation engagement should include:

- a statement outlining the nature of the engagement including the fact that neither an audit nor a review will be carried out and that, accordingly, no assurance will be expressed;
- the fact that the engagement cannot be relied upon to disclose errors, illegal acts or other irregularities, e.g. fraud;
- the nature of the information to be supplied by the client;
- the fact that the accountant will make enquiries of management and undertake any procedures that they judge appropriate but are under no obligation to perform procedures that may be required for assurance engagements such as audits or reviews;
- the fact that management is responsible for the accuracy and completeness of the information supplied to the accountant and for the completeness and accuracy of the compiled financial information;
- the basis of accounting on which the financial information is to be compiled and the fact that it, and any known departures therefrom, will be disclosed;
- the fact that it is the practitioner's obligation not to allow her name to be associated with misleading financial information;
- the fact that written management representations may be required;
- the fact that management will be expected to approve the financial information before the practitioner's report will be provided;
- the intended use and distribution of the information, once compiled;
- the form of the report to be rendered; and
- a statement of the agreed fees and a timetable for the performance of the engagement.

10.7.3 Planning and Performing a Compilation Engagement

The level of planning and the procedures applied will vary according to the complexity and completeness of the client's accounting records and systems and the practitioner's experience of the business.

The practitioner obtains a general understanding of the business and operations of the entity, considers the underlying financial records of the client, makes enquiries of management and undertakes other procedures deemed appropriate in the circumstances of the engagement. The practitioner considers whether the financial information is consistent with their understanding of the business, appropriate for the purpose for which it is required and whether it is misleading.

In compiling financial information, practitioners are normally reliant on management representations, particularly in relation to estimates and reliability, accuracy and completeness of the information provided. Written representations are sought in this case.

If, during the course of the engagement, matters come to light that appear to indicate that the financial information may be **misleading** (e.g. because of misclassifications in the financial information or mistakes in the application of the basis of preparation), the practitioner discusses the matter with the client with a view to agreeing appropriate adjustments and/or disclosures to be made in the financial information. If such an agreement cannot be reached and the practitioner considers that the financial information presented is misleading, the practitioner should withdraw from the engagement and should not permit her name to be associated with the financial information.

10.7.4 Reporting on Compilation Engagements

The practitioner's report helps users derive some comfort from the involvement of practitioners who are subject to ethical and other guidance in relation to the preparation of the financial information. It also helps prevent users from deriving any assurance from the financial information compiled where no audit or review has been performed and no opinion is being expressed by the practitioner. Key elements of a practitioner's report on a compilation engagement include:
* title;
* addressee;
* when relevant, a statement that the practitioner is not independent of the entity;
* identification of the financial information noting that it is based on information provided by management;
* a statement that management is responsible for the financial information compiled by the accountant;
* a statement that neither an audit nor a review has been carried out and that, accordingly, no assurance is expressed on the financial information;

- a paragraph, when considered necessary, drawing attention to the disclosure of material departures from the applicable financial reporting framework;
- date of the report;
- practitioner's address; and
- practitioner's signature.

10.8 MANAGING THE RISKS INVOLVED IN REPORTING TO THIRD PARTIES – M39

As we have seen, there are many different reports that practitioners are asked to prepare for their clients and often these reports have been requested by third parties such as regulators, trade bodies, lenders and others. Furthermore, it is important to give due care and attention to the decision to accept the engagement and the process of agreeing clear engagement terms with the client and sometimes with the third party as well.

M39 *Reporting to Third Parties* provides guidance on effectively managing the risks associated with reporting to third parties with a focus on highlighting risk issues at the acceptance phase of the engagement and ensuring that they are dealt with to the practitioner's satisfaction at that stage. If the practitioner cannot reduce engagement risk to an acceptable level then the engagement should not be accepted. The guidance in M39 is discussed below and should be borne in mind in the context of all the engagement types already outlined in this chapter when third parties are involved.

According to M39, the process to be followed in response to requests for reports from third parties is as follows:
1. determine who will rely on the practitioner's report and for what purpose;
2. consider the form and wording of the report requested by the client/third party;
3. agree the work to be performed and the form of report to be given;
4. agree appropriate terms of engagement;
5. plan and perform the work according to the engagement type (as set out in the earlier sections of this chapter); and
6. report (again refer to the applicable earlier sections of this chapter).

10.8.1 Determine who will rely on the Practitioner's Report and for what Purpose

When a practitioner knows that her report has been requested by a third party and that the third party will rely on the report, there is a risk, in the absence of an effective disclaimer, that the practitioner owes the third party a duty to take reasonable care in preparing and providing the report. If the practitioner does owe the third party such a duty, the practitioner could be liable to that third party if she were found to be negligent and the third party suffered loss. Practitioners seek to manage their exposure to this risk of liability.

The practitioner needs to identify the third party who will rely on the report and understand the purpose for which the third party seeks to rely on the report. Based on this information the practitioner can assess the risk involved. For example, if the third party runs a scheme for compensating the client's customers in the event of the client's insolvency the practitioner's risk is much greater than if, e.g. the third party's only role is to perform marketing for the client's particular service sector.

Depending on the risk identified, there are a number of courses of action available to the practitioner:

1. **Tripartite Agreement** The practitioner accepts that a duty of care is owed to the third party and enters into an engagement contract with the third party as well as the client, including provisions limiting liability if appropriate. A common example of a tripartite agreement is that in relation to the preparation of an accountant's report on a grant claim in accordance with the Miscellaneous Technical Statement *M45 Grant Claims* (M45), which includes model terms of engagement for an agreement between a grant claimant, its practitioners and the relevant agency in respect of an accountant's report on the grant claim. In this case the agencies mentioned in M45 have already agreed to be bound by the terms of engagement set out in M45.

Extract from a Tripartite Engagement Letter – Liability Provisions[6]

The accountant acknowledges that he will be liable to (insert name of client – in this case the grant claimant) and (insert name of third party – in this case the granting agency) for losses, damages, costs or expenses ('losses') caused by its breach of contract, negligence or wilful default, subject to the following paragraphs.

The accountant will not be so liable if such losses are due to the provision of false, misleading or incomplete information or documentation or due to the acts or omissions of any person other than the accountant, except where, on the basis of the enquiries normally undertaken by an accountant within the scope set out in these terms of engagement, it would have been reasonable for the accountant to discover such defects.

Any claims, whether in contract, negligence or otherwise, must be formally commenced within six years after the party bringing the claim becomes aware (or ought reasonably to have become aware) of the facts which give rise to the action.

This engagement is separate from and unrelated to the accountant's audit work on the financial statements of (insert name of client – in this case the grant claimant) for the purposes of the Companies Acts 1963–2009 or other legislation and nothing herein creates obligations or liabilities regarding the accountant's statutory audit work which would not otherwise exist.

---

[6] Miscellaneous Technical Statement *M45 Grant Claims* (Chartered Accountants Ireland CCAB-I 2006).

2. **Proceed with the engagement for their client but before allowing the third party access to their report, require the third party to acknowledge in writing that the practitioner owes no duty of care to the third party**. For example, an investigating accountant in a due diligence engagement might include the following in a release letter for their report to a prospective lender or investor:

> It is a condition of the receipt of our report by you as a prospective (lender)/(investor) that you accept that we have no responsibility or liability whatsoever to you in connection with our report.

> If you do lend to/invest in (name of client company), we agree to consider acceding to a request from you, if made in advance of your lending or investing, to recognise you as an addressee of the report, on the following conditions:
> • That you will be bound by and will accept all the provisions of our engagement letter;
> • (Any other conditions required by the investigating accountant).

3. **Proceed with an engagement for the client but disclaim or limit any liability or duty to the third party by notice in their report**. That is, the report states that it is made to the client only, with no responsibility for any other parties that may rely on the information.

Extract from a report where the practitioner is limiting any duty to a third party in the accountant's report for a compilation engagement:

"This report is made to you, in accordance with the terms of our engagement. Our work has been undertaken so that we might compile the (identify financial information) that we have been engaged to compile, report to you that we have done so, and state those matters that we have agreed to state to you in this report and for no other purpose. To the fullest extent permitted by law, we do not accept or assume responsibility to anyone other than the (insert addressee of the report), for our work, or for this report."

---

4. **Do not accept the engagement**. This is on the basis that they cannot implement appropriate safeguards included in the points above to limit potential liability.

10.8.2 Consider the Form of Report Requested by the Third Party

Often third parties will request a specific report wording. The practitioner does not have to accept the wording of a report proposed by a third party even where the third party argues that it is a 'standard' form of wording for their needs. Sometimes the third party asks the practitioner to sign statements concerning matters such as future solvency which cannot be supported by any amount of work performed by a practitioner. The practitioner should not undertake an engagement to provide a report if they cannot perform sufficient work and obtain sufficient evidence to support the statement they are asked to make in the report.

It may be necessary to agree a modified wording or a different engagement type with the client and the third party (e.g. an agreed-upon procedures engagement rather than an assurance engagement). Where this is not possible and the practitioner is not satisfied with the requested form of the report, the engagement should not be accepted.

In practice, e.g. it would not be unusual for a financial institution to ask a practitioner to sign a report confirming the future ability of a mutual client to repay a loan which the financial institution is considering making to the client. By signing such a report the practitioner may become equivalent to insurers or guarantors of the client's obligations to the financial institution. The practitioner should refuse to sign such a report. However the practitioner may be able to provide an alternative service which satisfies the bank's needs, e.g. a statement of factual information regarding the client's current situation based on information provided by the client. On behalf of practitioners, Chartered Accountants Ireland engages with financial institutions to encourage them to avoid issuing requests for reports containing wording which practitioners are not in a position to give.

Examples of unacceptable wording include:
- Wording giving an opinion on a matter as a statement of fact when that matter is, by its nature, inherently uncertain or a matter of judgement. Examples include:
  o 'we certify',
  o 'correct',
  o 'accurate', or
  o 'we have ensured'.

  These are avoided as they imply absolute certainty when it is not the objective of the report. Rather, the report is stating facts.
- Use of the term '**true and fair**' when financial information is not prepared under the framework of Financial Reporting Standards.
- 'Fair and reasonable' opinions. Practitioners generally avoid giving these as they are normally associated with investment banks or could be construed as valuations.
- Wording that might suggest that the third party is able to rely on the statutory audit of the client. Practitioners avoid any possibility of a link becoming established between the special report and the statutory audit report.
- Opinions that are open-ended or otherwise cannot be supported by the work carried out by the practitioner.
- Opinions which practitioners do not have the necessary competence to provide, e.g. an opinion of an actuarial nature or a property valuation without reference to the relevant expert.
- An engagement that is beyond the practitioner's knowledge and experience.
- Wording that is open to interpretation, e.g. 'review' and 'materiality'. These should be used in clearly defined circumstances where the meaning is well established and understood.
- Reports which do not specifically address the client, e.g. 'To whom it may concern'.

- Reports on financial information which is not explicitly approved by the client.
- The client must take responsibility for the financial information being provided.
- Qualifications in the covering letter only. Qualifications are included in the main body of the report so that they cannot be detached.
- Opinions which would impair the auditor's independence.

10.8.3 Agree the Work to be Performed and the Form of Report to be Given and Agree Appropriate Terms of Engagement

Having determined the third party and agreed on an appropriate course of action to limit third party risk and agreed the wording of the report, written terms of engagement should be prepared and agreed. The practitioner specifies the engagement type (e.g. reasonable or limited assurance, compilation, agreed-upon procedures) and the other engagement details and agrees these with the client. The engagement letter should agree the timetable for the engagement and the fees.

For non-statutory engagements, particularly where the risks associated therewith are unacceptably high, the practitioner can consider the need to negotiate a limitation on the monetary amount of any liability to the client. The purpose of such a clause in the engagement letter is to put a monetary limit on the claim that a client can make for the breach of the practitioner's contractual obligations and/or negligence. Any monetary limitation imposed under contract should be reasonable in amount and agreed by means of genuine negotiation with the client. This is usually agreed in the engagement letter with the client, as per the example below.

Example 10.8: Liability Cap in Engagement Letter

"We will perform the engagement with reasonable skill and care. The total aggregate liability to you, of whatever nature, whether in contract, tort or otherwise, of [insert name of practitioner's firm] for any losses whatsoever and howsoever caused arising from or in any way connected with this engagement shall not exceed [insert amount]."[7]

10.8.4 Plan and Perform the Work and Report

The engagement work should be properly planned and performed as discussed in **Sections 10.3–10.7** above and an appropriate report is subsequently provided, clean or modified in the particular circumstance.

10.8.5 Summary

The process of accepting an engagement to report to a third party as discussed in **Section 10.8** can be summarised diagrammatically below.

---

[7] Miscellaneous Technical Statement *M39 Reporting to Third Parties* (Chartered Accountants Ireland CCAB-I 2002).

FIGURE 10.4: FLOWCHART ILLUSTRATING THE PROCESS ACCOUNTANTS FOLLOW IN RESPONSE TO REQUESTS FOR REPORTS FROM THIRD PARTIES[8]

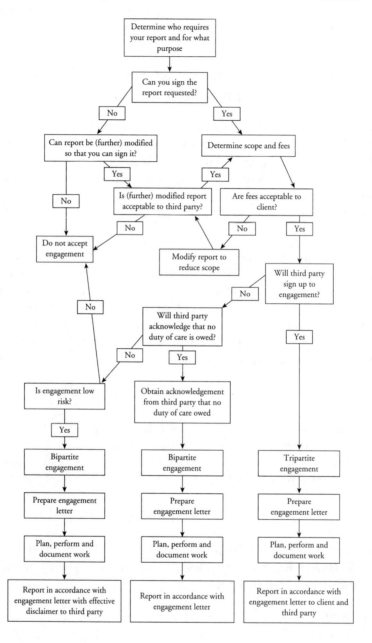

---

[8] Miscellaneous Technical Statement *M39 Reporting to Third Parties* (Chartered Accountants Ireland, CCAB-I 2002).

10.9 OTHER SPECIFIC ENGAGEMENTS

The principles outlined in this chapter can be applied by a practitioner to most requests by clients for an 'accountant's report'. The reports which clients can seek are too many and varied to be listed in their entirety, but some of the more common ones are listed and explained below:

10.9.1 Due Diligence Engagements

Due diligence can take many forms and often relates to enhancing the confidence of a potential purchaser in information provided by a vendor in a corporate acquisition. Financial due diligence is normally undertaken by a professional accountant in public practice. Financial due diligence can include review of historical financial information, examination of cash flows and projections of future performance and their underlying assumptions and valuation of assets and liabilities. A due diligence engagement can be an assurance engagement or a report of factual findings, depending on the agreement with the client.

10.9.2 Grant Claims

Grant Agencies in Ireland are responsible for determining the appropriate allocation of amounts of funding from the Irish Government and the EU. In so doing the Grant Agencies are required to ensure that those public funds are used in accordance with specific guidelines, applicable law and for approved purposes. The grant recipient is responsible for providing information to support any claim and on-going information regarding the application of those grant funds. This information is normally examined by a professional accountant (practitioner) the results of which are reported to the Grant Agencies. M45 sets out guidance in relation to this type of reporting engagement.

10.9.3 Reporting on Investment Circulars (Prospectuses, Listing Particulars or Circulars to Shareholders)

Accountants' Reports on Investment Circulars include reviews of historical financial information, including interim financial information, and examinations of prospective information. There are clear rules from the Irish Stock Exchange regarding the type of reports practitioners are required to deliver in relation to information made available by listed companies. APB Statements of Investment Reporting (SIRs) provide specific guidance on these reporting engagements. You will note that the principles outlined in this chapter include those referred to in the SIRs.

10.9.4 Accountants' Reports in accordance with the Solicitors' Accounts Regulations 2001

The Solicitors' Accounts Regulations 2001[9] set out the accounting and related record-keeping requirements with which solicitors should comply. There is a particular emphasis on the control of the handling of client monies by solicitors. In order that the Law Society of Ireland can satisfy itself that these Regulations are being adhered to, provision is made for the annual submission to it of a practitioner's report by each firm of solicitors. The engagement is an assurance engagement and a standard report format has been agreed with the Law Society of Ireland. Guidance in relation to performing an engagement to report in accordance with the Solicitors' Accounts Regulations 2001 and the standard report wording are available in Miscellaneous Technical Statement—*38 Solicitors' Accounts Regulations, 2001 – Republic of Ireland* (Chartered Accountants Ireland CCAB-I 2001).

10.10 CONCLUSION

In conclusion, an auditor can perform a wide variety of reports, either assurance or non-assurance. However, in accepting such engagements, the auditor should be very aware of third parties who may rely on the reports, and the auditor's related liability exposure. As a result, the auditor performs the necessary pre-engagement procedures, and applies the relevant report format to minimise the auditor's exposure to risk.

SUMMARY OF LEARNING OBJECTIVES

Learning Objective 1 To understand the principles underpinning reporting engagements to third parties.

Auditors can provide a range of reports to third parties, both assurance and non-assurance. These include:
- Review engagements
- Examination of prospective financial information
- Agreed-upon procedures
- Engagements to compile financial information.

Learning Objective 2 To be able to execute an engagement to prepare a report for a third party, including drafting these reports

In preparing a report to third parties, the practitioner should carry out engagement acceptance procedures, agree the terms of engagement, plan and perform the engagement and report to the third party. The format of the report will depend on the type of report being provided.

---

[9] S.I. No. 421 of 2001.

Learning Objective 3 To be able to apply the necessary safeguards to minimise the risk implications of providing reports to third parties.

The practitioner should always ensure that any risk exposure in carrying out an engagement to report to a third party is minimised. This may be done in a variety of ways such as a tripartite engagement letter or inclusion of a paragraph in the report disclaiming any liability to third parties other than those that the report is addressed to. If the practitioner cannot reduce the risk exposure to an acceptable level, they should not accept the assignment.

QUESTIONS

In each of the scenarios presented in the questions below, there is an issue/(s) which needs to be addressed by the auditor (an indicator) in relation to third party reporting. You should read the questions and attempt to address the issues relating to third party reporting.

(See **Appendix One** of this text for Suggested Solutions to the Review Questions.)

Review Questions

Question 10.1 (Based on Chartered Accountants Ireland, FAE Autumn 2010, Simulation 1)

Daniels Stores

Refer to the scenario presented in **Question 2.1.**

Question 10.2 (Based on Chartered Accountants Ireland, FAE Autumn 2011, Simulation 1)

Executive Motors Limited

Refer to the scenario presented in **Question 7.1.**

Appendix One

SUGGESTED SOLUTIONS TO REVIEW QUESTIONS

QUESTION 1.1

Guidance Notes – Raps Limited (Ethical Issues)

The ethical consideration is whether or not the engagement partner's continued involvement in the audit might be an issue.

It is clear that there are ethical considerations, given that Paul has been an engagement partner for 12 years, as the recommendation per ES 3 is a limit of 10 years or the implementation of appropriate safeguards if the 10-year limit is exceeded. The key to answering this question is to apply the technical requirements of ES 3 specifically to the question. You will not score highly if you simply regurgitate ES 3. Furthermore, as you are informing the partner about issues with this long association, you should also recommend a course of action, i.e. resignation or a second partner review.

ES 3 provides requirements and guidance on specific circumstances arising out of long association with the audit engagement which may create threats to the auditor's objectivity or perceived loss of independence.

In general the standard states that, where audit engagement partners, key partners involved in the audit, and partners and staff are involved in the audit for a long period of time, self-interest, self-review and familiarity threats to the auditor's independence may arise.

Suggested Solution – Raps Limited (Ethical Issues)

Paul has been audit engagement partner for 12 years, which exceeds the 10-year recommended limit set in ES 3. Due to this long association with the client, there may be a perceived risk to the objectivity and independence applied by Paul in carrying out the audit. This is mostly due to a familiarity threat.

The standard states that where audit engagement partners, key partners involved in the audit, and partners and staff in senior positions have a long association with the audit, the audit firm shall assess the threats to the auditor's objectivity and independence and shall apply safeguards to reduce the threats to an acceptable level. Where appropriate safeguards cannot be applied, the audit firm shall either resign as auditor or not stand for reappointment, as appropriate. Appropriate safeguards are detailed in the standard as removing ('rotating') the partners and the other senior members of the engagement team after a pre-determined number of years; involving an additional partner, who is not and has not recently been a member of the engagement team, to review the work done by the partners and the other senior members of the engagement team and to advise as necessary; or applying independent internal quality reviews to the engagement in question.

In reviewing the potential safeguards for RAPS Limited, it is clear that after 12 years Paul should be rotated off the assignment. However, since the audit has commenced, it would not be practical at this stage to remove the engagement partner from the assignment. Therefore, the firm should appoint an independent partner to review the work carried out by the team prior to the audit report being signed. In order to maintain independence, this partner should have had no association with the engagement previously. This will adequately reduce the familiarity threat to an acceptable level. However, the firm should ensure that Paul is removed from the engagement in 2011 and a new partner is appointed as audit engagement partner.

These ethical considerations, along with details of how the perceived independence threat was addressed should be documented on the audit file.

QUESTION 2.1

Guidance Notes – Daniels Stores (Client Acceptance Criteria)

The identified pre-audit activities are client acceptance criteria – the partner has asked you to identify and document all relevant matters that the firm must consider before accepting appointment as auditors.

The guidance for answering this question is found in ISQC 1, paragraphs 26–28, A18–A23 whereby in accepting the engagement the auditor must determine:
- Whether the firm is competent to carry out the engagement;
- The client's integrity and whether they are the type of client that the audit firm wants to be associated with; and
- That the firm can comply with relevant ethical requirements, particularly ES 1 re threats to our integrity, objectivity and independence and ES 2 re any relationships which would threaten our integrity, objectivity and independence.

As the majority of the answer can be extracted from the standards, the key point to remember is that you must ensure that you refer the technical requirements to the question where possible. That is, you must illustrate that you can apply technical knowledge to specific practical situations.

The question requires you to identify and document all relevant matters that the firm must consider before accepting appointment as auditors. In considering client acceptance we can assess the relevant matters by looking at, first, the client and their integrity, i.e. is it a client that we want to be associated with; and secondly our ability to perform the engagement, i.e. do we have adequate competencies, skills and resources to undertake the assignment, including compliance with ethical standards?

Suggested Solution – Daniels Stores (Client Acceptance Criteria)

Client Integrity

Before accepting the engagement, the firm should consider if the client has the type of reputation that the firm would like to be associated with. Points for consideration are as follows:
- The identity and business reputation of Simon and Caroline Daniels;
- The attitude of Simon and Caroline regarding aggressive interpretation of accounting standards and the internal control environment;
- If the client is aggressively concerned with maintaining the fee as low as possible as this may impact upon the ability of the firm to carry out the work;
- Indications of limitation in the scope of the work – this does not appear to be an issue at present;
- Full anti-money laundering procedures should be carried out on Simon and Caroline to ensure that they are not involved in any money-laundering activities; and
- Consideration of the reasons for change in auditors, though since the partner at the incumbent firm is retiring, there do not appear to be any issues underlying the change. Nevertheless, we should contact Mulligan and Aherne to ensure that there are no professional reasons why we cannot accept the engagement.

Firm Competence

Before accepting this client, the audit firm needs to consider if it has the competence, capabilities and resources to perform the audit of Daniels Stores. Such considerations include:
- Do firm personnel have knowledge of the retail industry, taking account of the potential future investment plans of Daniels Stores?
- Do the firm personnel have experience of the relevant regulatory or reporting requirements, or the ability to gain the necessary skills and knowledge effectively? For Daniels Stores this may require knowledge of Irish GAAP or IFRS.
- Does the firm have sufficient members of staff available who have the necessary competence and capabilities to carry out the assignment?

- Are experts available if needed?
- Does the firm have quality control reviewers available, if required?
- Is the firm able to meet any reporting deadlines that Simon and Caroline may require?
- Can the firm comply with all ethical requirements, e.g. are there any potential threats to the firm's independence should they accept the engagement?

QUESTION 2.2

Guidance Notes – Pybex Limited (Client Acceptance Procedures)

The pre-audit activities are client acceptance criteria – the client has asked for consideration of the client acceptance procedures.

Guidance for client acceptance procedures is found in ISQC 1, paragraphs 26–28, A18–A23 – in accepting the engagement the auditor must determine:
- Whether the firm is competent to carry out the engagement;
- The client's integrity and if they are the type of client that the audit firm wants to be associated with; and
- That the firm can comply with relevant ethical requirements, particularly ES 1 re threats to our integrity, objectivity and independence and ES 2 re any relationships which would threaten our integrity, objectivity and independence.

As the majority of the answer can be extracted from the standards, the key point to remember is that you must ensure that you refer the technical requirements to the question where possible. That is, you must illustrate that you can apply technical knowledge to specific practical situations.

The question requires you to identify and document client acceptance procedures. In considering client acceptance we can assess the relevant matters by looking at first, the client and their integrity, that is, is it a client that we want to be associated with; and secondly our ability to perform the engagement, that is, do we have adequate competencies, skills and resources to undertake the assignment, including compliance with ethical standards.

Suggested Solution – Pybex Limited (Client Acceptance Procedures)

Client Integrity

Before accepting the engagement, the firm should consider if the client has the type of reputation that the firm would like to be associated with. Points for consideration are as follows:
- The identity and business reputation of the client's principal owners, key management, and those charged with governance. The firm would want to understand why the former chief executive left Pybex to ensure there are no potential reputational issues.

- The attitude of the client's principal owners, key management, and those charged with governance regarding aggressive interpretation of accounting standards and internal control environment.
- If the client is aggressively concerned with maintaining the fee as low as possible, which may be the case as Tom Murray has already requested a low fee quote. The ability to carry out the work must be considered by the firm in that quality could be impaired if the firm agreed to carry out the work for an unrealistic fee.
- Indications of limitation in the scope of the work – the audits of the subsidiaries should be undertaken in line with ISA 600. The firm should consider if they will be able to get the required access to subsidiary audit files if the client is going to maintain the local auditors.
- Full anti-money laundering procedures should be carried out on the client and its principal owners to ensure that they are not involved in any money laundering activities.
- Consideration of the reasons for change in auditors – it appears that there may be underlying issues based on the comment received from Tom when the question was raised as to reasons for change in auditors.

Firm Competence

Before accepting this client, the audit firm needs to consider if it has the competence, capabilities and resources to perform the audit of Pybex Limited. Such considerations include:

- Do firm personnel have knowledge of the software industry?
- Do the firm personnel have experience of the relevant regulatory or reporting requirements, or the ability to gain the necessary skills and knowledge effectively? For example, this may require knowledge of Irish GAAP or IFRS. Furthermore, the firm should consider if the team have a detailed knowledge of ISA 600 requirements as there will be component auditors involved.
- Does the firm have sufficient members of staff available who have the necessary competence and capabilities to carry out the assignment?
- Are experts available if needed?
- Does the firm have available quality control reviewers, if required?
- Is the firm able to meet any reporting deadlines that Pybex Limited may require?
- Can the firm comply with all ethical requirements, e.g. are there any potential threats to the firm's independence should they accept the engagement?

QUESTION 3.1

Guidance Notes – Progressive Construction Limited (Planning Agenda)

The issue in relation to planning activities is a planning agenda that specifically includes significant risks for this year's audit as well as other general planning matters typically discussed at a planning meeting.

In documenting the significant risks, you are looking for issues in the information that was provided which may impact upon the financial statements and could lead to material misstatement. Significant risks are areas which you will want to address as part of your audit procedures.

In documenting the other planning items, good practical application will score well in this question.

Guidance on what should be included in a planning agenda can be found in ISA 260, paragraphs 15 and A11–A15, **Chapter 3** of this textbook and in any example audit programme. And, as always, remember, where possible, to link the generic requirements to the facts of the case.

In line with the question, the planning agenda can be split into three sections:
1. Significant Risks,
2. General Planning Matters, and
3. Further Information Required.

Suggested Solution – Progressive Construction Limited (Planning Agenda)
PROGRESSIVE CONSTRUCTION LIMITED

PLANNING AGENDA

Significant Risks
- Revenue recognition/work-in progress
- Recoverability of debtors (specifically Burgerway Restaurants)
- Fraud – management override of controls/completeness of provisions
- Going concern (from potential breach of banking covenants or cash flow difficulties)

General Planning Matters
- Update on company performance for the year
- Going concern of the company and potential impact of economic environment
- Points forward from prior-year audit
- Consideration of relevant laws and regulations
- Consideration of fraud risk
- Materiality
- Timing and logistics of audit fieldwork and reporting
- Discussion of audit approach – tests of control and tests of detail
- Assignment of responsibilities, audit areas and review
- Discussion of budget/fees
- Ethical considerations – independence of team

Further Information Required
- Review details of secured/unsecured contracts for 2011
- Review budgets/projections for 2011

- Review management accounts
- Review copies of correspondence with legal advisers
- Perform preliminary analytical procedures
- Review board minutes
- Review of bank facilities
- Consideration of control environment
- Consideration of IT general controls
- Testing of application controls
- Changes in controls as a result of the fraud
- Management's assessment of going concern

QUESTION 3.2

Guidance Notes – RX Pharmaceuticals Limited (Planning Activities)

In this case there are three issues in relation to planning activities:
1. The risks relating to revenue for RX;
2. The audit tests in response to the risks identified – the appropriate tests of control and tests of detail to be performed and the basis of selection of the items to test in order to address the risks you have identified; and
3. Materiality – an appropriate materiality level to apply to the audit.

Risks Relating to Revenue

The question requires you to extract the risks relating to revenue, i.e. issues within the revenue processes which may lead to material misstatement. Specifically, areas where the auditor would need to focus the audit work to ensure that the risk is addressed.

In extracting the risks, it is extremely important to remember not to extract generic risks such as revenue recognition, or cut-off. Ensure that the risk is related to the question, e.g. revenue recognition of haulage costs, or cut-off of data capture and analysis services. Furthermore, you should not merely list the risks – give comprehensive explanations as to why you feel that particular risk exists. Finally, always remember that as an auditor you are only concerned with risks that are going to impact upon the financial statements, so always link the risk back to an assertion.

Addressing the Risks

This question requires you to develop audit tests to address the risks you have identified above. The tests should be explained in detail to show a strong understanding of what you are trying to achieve. As noted before, a good pointer to ensuring you have documented the audit tests adequately is to develop the audit tests as you would give them to an audit assistant and so that he would be able to carry out the test without any further assistance. This will ensure that you have included the necessary detail on the procedure for the examiner.

Furthermore, the requirement includes 'basis of selection' therefore, for each test, ensure you indicate what you are going to test, i.e. either the entire population or a selected sample.

Materiality

The question asks you to consider the selection of the materiality level and to comment on the appropriateness of using 5% of profit before tax. This question entails applying your professional judgement and knowledge as the auditing standards do not necessarily specifically answer this question for you. Remember, when selecting materiality, the key points to remember are:
- Most appropriate benchmark for the business, i.e. turnover, assets or profit;
- Prior year, i.e. is the benchmark significantly different from the prior year and, if so, is there an exceptional item in the current year that should be excluded from the materiality calculation for the current period? and
- Continual review, i.e. materiality should be reviewed throughout the audit.

Suggested Solution – RX Pharmaceuticals Limited (Planning Activities)

Based on the information provided, the risks relating to revenue are as follows:
- Data capture and analysis services revenue – the contracts appear to be long-term contracts whose complexities may lead to increased risk of revenue being recorded in the incorrect period, either through error or management manipulation. Cut-off of revenue is therefore a significant risk.
- Distribution revenue – the revenue is not recognised until the invoice is received from the haulier, however, it should be recognised when the service is provided. It would therefore appear that there is an increased risk of revenue not being recorded in the correct period resulting in cut-off of distribution revenue being a significant risk.
- Comparator products revenue – the company does not recognise the comparator products in stock as the sales invoice is raised as soon as the GRN is received. However, the cost is accrued once the goods are physically delivered, whereas the sales invoice is not raised until the sales department receives a copy of the GRN note. As a result, there is an increased risk of timing difference between cost incurred and revenue recognised, potentially resulting in an inaccurate gross margin. Furthermore, there is a significant increase in gross margin between 2008 and 2009 which may indicate the occurrence of error. Therefore, the completeness and existence of revenue and costs are significant risks that need to be addressed.

- Contract manufacture revenue – the revenue recognised for the manufacture of tablets, etc. is automatically calculated from the quantity on the despatch note and the contracted price entered onto the system. There is a risk that the contracted price may not be entered on the system correctly resulting in a higher risk of error relating to the valuation of revenue.
- Packaging revenue – reconciliation is performed between the total invoice value raised and the total packaging activities performed. If any variances arising from these reconciliations are not adequately followed up and resolved, there is a higher risk that revenue may not be complete.

The risks relating to revenue, as noted above, can be addressed as follows:

Risk	Audit Tests
Cut-off of data capture and analysis services revenue	<ul><li>Review all contracts in place during the year</li><li>Discuss with contracts manager milestones achieved compared with revenue recognised</li><li>Review invoices issued for revenue recognised once milestone achieved</li><li>Ensure long-term contract has been accounted for correctly, and revenue is recorded in the correct period</li></ul>
Cut-off of distribution revenue	<ul><li>Select a sample of haulier invoices during the year and for three months directly after the year-end</li><li>Review the timing of the service provided on the haulier invoice and trace to the related sales invoice</li><li>Ensure the revenue and the cost are recorded in the correct period</li></ul>
Completeness and existence of comparator products revenue and costs	<ul><li>Select a sample of customer orders of comparator products near the end of the year</li><li>Trace to the delivery note to customer; the GRN accrual and the related sales invoice</li><li>Ensure the cost and revenue are recorded in the same period</li></ul>
Valuation of contract manufacture revenue	<ul><li>Select a sample of contract revenue invoices during the period</li><li>Trace the quantities on the invoices to the despatch docket, and trace the contracted price to a customer contract</li></ul>

317

Risk	Audit Tests
Completeness of packaging revenue	• Select a sample of reconciliations of packaging activity during the year and invoices raised • Ensure that any reconciling items have been appropriately investigated and resolved • If the control test fails, consider additional substantive testing to ensure that packaging revenue is recorded in the correct period

When reviewing the materiality for RX Pharmaceuticals we first look at whether the correct benchmark is used. The entity is profit making and, therefore, best practice is to use profit before tax as the most suitable benchmark. Secondly, we look at whether the profit figure for the year is representative of the trading of the business, i.e. ensuring that there is not a once-off or exceptional item that may distort the basis on which materiality is calculated. It is evident that the profit for RX Pharmaceuticals is nearly 50% higher than in prior years, therefore, it would be a more accurate representation if the last three years' profit was used as an average for the materiality calculation. On further discussion with management, if there was an exceptional item resulting in the higher profit, this should be removed before calculating materiality. Taking 5% of the profit appears a reasonable calculation.

It is also important that materiality is reviewed throughout the audit and amended as appropriate should the profit figure change significantly as a result of audit adjustments.

QUESTION 3.3

Guidance Notes – Perchant Hotels Limited (Audit Risks)

There is one issue in relation to planning activities, namely identification of audit risks – the managing partner has requested that you advise him on the potential areas of audit risk arising from the information provided on Perchant group.

The question requires you to document the audit risks to which the firm should direct its attention. In extracting these risks, look for the issues within the information provided that might impact upon your audit. That is, issues that might impact upon the financial statements and therefore your audit tests must be developed to address these risks. However, please note that the question does not require any details on what audit testing would be required – it simply requires you to identify the risks. A point to note: when identifying the risks: always expand the point to provide information on why each issue is a business risk. Furthermore, a strong answer identifying the audit risks should link the risk to the financial statement balance or transactions, and the assertion it impacts upon. Remember, as auditors we are only concerned with risks if they impact financial statements and assertions. In the solution below, the financial statement impact and assertion have been highlighted.

Suggested Solution – Perchant Hotels Limited (Audit Risks)

The audit risks noted from the information provided in the question are dealt with below.

Incentivising Local Management

Hotel management is rewarded with bonuses based on profits in the individual hotels. Such reward systems always increase the risk of misstatement in the financial statements as there is a higher likelihood that management may manipulate the figures to receive bonuses.

Therefore, it is imperative that information on **revenue and costs** from each hotel is accurate information. The **completeness and cut-off** of costs and revenue may be impacted upon as a result of potential fraud at individual sites. Therefore, significant analytical review and cut-off testing should be carried out to ensure that the correct figures from individual hotels have been reported to head office.

Payroll Fraud

The lack of segregation of duties and the fact that many wages are paid in cash increases the risk of fraudulent activity in relation to payroll costs and, therefore, increases the risk of material misstatement. As a result, **cash** could be misappropriated and the **completeness and accuracy** of the **payroll** figure in the financial statements could be impacted upon.

Significant audit testing should be focused on the existence of employees, and completeness and accuracy of the payroll charge and relevant payments.

High Staff Turnover

The information notes the high staff turnover, which is not unusual in the industry. However, this may lead to weak internal controls as the staff has not been adequately trained. Furthermore, casual and part-time staff would increase the risk of misappropriation of assets due to fraud as they have more incentive than full-time employees to fraudulently misappropriate assets.

As a result, the audit team will need to assess the control environment prior to developing tests of control. Furthermore, increased testing should be carried out on the **existence of assets**, e.g. stock, cash and fixed assets.

Foreign Branch

The existence of the foreign branch may result in an increased risk of material misstatement regarding information originating from the branch. The auditor will need to understand the controls within the branch and may have to carry out some specific audit testing on the information.

Furthermore, the foreign branch will also result in foreign exchange transactions and, therefore, the auditor will need to ensure that the audit programme includes procedures to test the **accuracy** of foreign exchange transactions and year end balances.

Economic Environment

The uncertain economic environment, particularly in relation to the hotel industry, results in higher risk that the entity may have going concern issues. The audit team will need to focus their efforts on ensuring that the entity can continue as a going concern by reviewing budgets and projections of cashflows, bookings after the year end, financing and performance.

QUESTION 3.4

Guidance Notes – Pybex Limited (Audit Risks)

There was one issue relating to planning activities, namely the identification of audit risks – you are specifically asked to comment on the issues surrounding the joint venture in Spain and Portugal and any other issues that you regard as relevant.

Therefore, as an auditor, you must assess the information given to you and determine if there are significant issues that may potentially lead to the financial statements being misstated and, if so, how you would address these. Other issues that are noted in the information provided are the new operating location in Bulgaria and the changes in key personnel. Both of these are significant issues and, as auditors, we would want to address them so as to ensure that they do not result in misstatement, e.g. has the change in key personnel resulted in underlying issues we should be aware of – does it appear suspicious that the chief executive and auditors are changed in the same year? Furthermore, in relation to the joint ventures and expansion in Bulgaria, what additional procedures should we develop to ensure that these have been accounted for correctly? These are the questions that you should address in your answer.

Suggested Solution – Pybex Limited (Audit Risks)

The audit risks that can be extracted from the information are set out below.

Joint Venture

The investment is stated in the balance sheet at a value of €/£650,000 which, being 17% of net assets, would be regarded as material. The client has indicated that they want to exit the joint venture which, due to its complexity, may result in a higher risk of material misstatement. Therefore the audit team will need to focus their audit work to ensure accuracy and completeness in the accounting of the transaction. In order to ensure that the joint-venture investment and potential exit is accounted for correctly, the audit team will need to consider the following:

- Has the current joint venture been accounted for in line with IAS 31 Joint Ventures?
- Review contractual documentation in relation to original purchase of investment;
- Understand the significant transactions between the joint venture and the rest of the group, and ensure that they have been accounted for correctly, and disclosed adequately in the financial statements;
- Review the documentation surrounding a potential exit from the joint venture – are there any potential contingent liabilities that may be triggered?
- Consider the accounting treatment for an exit from the joint venture.

Foreign Subsidiaries

The group has subsidiaries in Italy, France and recently purchased one in Bulgaria. In relation to the new subsidiary, the audit team need to consider the reporting procedures into head office, and the controls surrounding the information provided. This is to assess the accuracy and completeness of the information feeding into the group financial statements.

Furthermore, as group auditors, we need to consider the implications of ISA 600 and the level of audit work that we may need to carry out in the components. This will involve assessing the size of the component, the competence of the local auditors and the level of group risks present in the components.

Recent Changes in Management and Auditors

Both the auditors and chief executive have resigned in the last three months, with little explanation from the current management team. Furthermore, if we were appointed, we would be the third audit firm in the last four years. Whilst there may be perfectly satisfactory reasons for these departures, we must remain sceptical as auditors and probe into the two departures.

In relation to the outgoing auditors, we should issue our usual professional clearance letter as well as doing some informal probing, e.g. other partners within the firm may have a relationship with the outgoing auditors, or indeed the company's legal advisors. Informal contact can also form part of the client acceptance procedures.

In relation to the exit of the chief executive, we need to ensure that the internal control environment is not negatively impacted upon by this change. Furthermore, the current chief executive appears to be quite a dominant character, e.g. he is already commenting on low fees. Therefore, in reviewing the internal controls, the audit team needs to assess if the board of directors can adequately act independently and sufficiently implement a stringent internal control environment. The result of these considerations will impact the level of audit testing that will be performed.

QUESTION 3.5

Guidance Notes – Daniels Stores (Business Risks)

There was one issue in relation to planning activities, namely identification of business risks. By referring to the notes provided, the audit partner has requested that you document the business risks for the audit file in order to help you understand the business.

The question requires you to document the business risks for the audit file to help understand the business. In extracting these risks, you are looking for the issues within the information provided that may impact upon your audit. That is, issues that may have an impact on the financial statements and therefore your audit testing should be addressing these risks. However, please note that the question does not require any details on what audit testing would be required, it is simply requiring you to identify the risks. A point to note: when identifying the risks, always expand the point providing information on why you think that the particular issue is a business risk and, where possible, link the risk to the financial statement balance/transaction and assertion.

Suggested Solution – Daniels Stores (Business Risks)

The business risks that can be identified in the information provided are set out below.

Recoverability of debtors

Credit has been offered to certain customers in an environment where unemployment has increased. Furthermore, debtors have increased from €/£11,000 in the prior year to €/£45,000 in the current year which may indicate a recoverability issue that needs to be provided for.

Valuation of stock

Grocery stock was over-ordered during the year. As these are perishable items, there may be stock which has not been sold at the year-end which is now obsolescent. Furthermore, stock has increased by 19% in the prior year, while sales have decreased. This increased stock figure, along with the issues experienced with stock-ordering during the year, may indicate that the stock figure is over-valued.

Going concern

There are numerous issues present that indicate there are uncertainties that need to be considered by the auditor when assessing the going concern assumption:
- margins have been eroded as they have not been able to pass on price increases to customers;
- the company are seeking investors to help financially;
- the company has breached its covenants with the bank (interest cover = profit before interest and tax/interest = €/£15,172/€/£10,618 = 1.43 which is below requirement of 2); and
- increased competition from petrol station due to post office.

Accuracy and completeness of information

The company introduced a new EPOS system during the year which resulted in some errors in information. This may indicate an increased risk of further issues with the accuracy and completeness of the information, resulting in material misstatement in the financial statements.

QUESTION 4.1

Guidance Notes – Progressive Construction Limited (Fraud)

There was one issue, namely the auditor's responsibility in relation to fraud – you are required to prepare a memo stating the auditor's responsibilities under auditing standards as well as the specific enquiries and procedures, which should have been performed in the 2009 audit, and which we should critically assess in preparation for the meeting with Corporate Solicitors.

As there is quite a lot of information required for this point, to help with the structure of the answer, it is advisable to split it down further into two requirements:
- Auditor's responsibilities under auditing standards, and
- Specific enquiries and procedures that should have been performed in the prior-year audit in relation to fraud.

The answer to this question can be extracted directly from the auditing standard, namely ISA 240 *The Auditor's Responsibilities Relating to Fraud in an Audit of Financial*

Statements, however, it is important that the answer is as specific to the question as possible. Marks will not be awarded for simply regurgitating the standard; it is important to document the relevant points and include references to the client in the question, i.e. relate the ISA requirements to the facts of the case.

The question requires consideration of the audit work that should have been carried out in the prior year that could have detected the failure to recognise the necessary provision for losses. As an auditor, it is accepted that we cannot detect fraud and indeed ISA 240 recognises that misstatements as a result of fraud are much more difficult for the auditor to detect as management may be intentionally concealing information. Therefore, as in this case, as auditors, we are concerned that whilst we may not have uncovered the potential fraud, we carried out the required robust audit procedures.

In approaching this question, whilst we have not been asked to develop audit procedures, our knowledge of the audit procedures surrounding fraud is vital. We are using the audit procedures to ask the questions if certain work was carried out.

Your solution should take the form of a memo to the audit partner.

Suggested Solution – Progressive Construction Limited (Fraud)

MEMORANDUM

From: Audit Manager
To: Audit Partner
Subject: Fraud Considerations for Auditors

Auditor's Responsibilities under Auditing Standards

In relation to Progressive Construction Limited, it should be noted that ISA 240 specifically states that the primary responsibility for the prevention and detection of fraud rests with both those charged with governance and management of the entity. It is important that management, with the oversight of those charged with governance, place a strong emphasis on fraud prevention, which may reduce opportunities for fraud to take place, and fraud deterrence, which could persuade individuals not to commit fraud because of the likelihood of detection and punishment. This involves a commitment to creating a culture of honesty and ethical behaviour which can be reinforced by active oversight by those charged with governance. Oversight by those charged with governance includes considering the potential for override of controls and other inappropriate influence over the financial reporting process, such as efforts by management to manage earnings in order to influence the perceptions of analysts as to the entity's performance and profitability.

The auditor's responsibility is to plan and perform an audit to gain reasonable assurance that the financial statements are free from material misstatement due to fraud and error. ISA 240 recognises the fact that misstatements as a result of fraud are more difficult to detect than misstatements due to error on the basis that there may be deliberate action to prevent detection of the fraud by the auditors through collusion, intentional misrepresentations and withholding of information. For example, it is unclear in the case of Progressive Construction as to whether the quantity surveyor and commercial director were colluding to suppress the information regarding the legal case, but the fact that both did suppress the information would make it much more difficult for the auditor to detect. Furthermore, the commercial director is in a position where he/she ought to have been acting as a control function over the quantity surveyors and hence management override of controls may also have played a part in concealing the fraud.

Nevertheless, as part of the audit of Progressive Construction, the auditor should carry out specific procedures in relation to potential fraud risk:

- Consider if there are fraud risk factors present, i.e. incentive, opportunity or rationalisation to carry out a fraudulent action. In relation to Progressive Construction, there is a bonus scheme linked to gross margin which may have played a part in suppression of information regarding the legal case.
- Inquire of management and others within the entity to obtain their views about the risks of fraud and how they are addressed – this will allow the auditor to assess the attitude towards fraud, i.e. if, in discussions, the auditors find that the entity has a very relaxed approach and very weak controls surrounding the detection and prevention of fraud, the auditor may focus more audit tests on fraud risks, e.g. in this case, by circularising third parties (e.g. solicitors), or reviewing third-party correspondence (from contract customer).
- Understand management's processes for identifying and responding to fraud within the entity and communication of this to employees. Again, this will allow the auditor to gain an understanding of the controls surrounding fraud prevention and detection which will impact upon the audit plan.
- Make enquiries of management and others of instances of actual or suspected fraud and how this is dealt with.
- Consider any unusual or unexpected relationships that have been identified in performing analytical procedures which may indicate potential fraud, e.g. revenue recognition.
- Consider information obtained from discussions among team members and other risk assessment procedures that may indicate a high risk of fraud.

This information should enhance the audit team's ability to identify areas (assertions, accounts, classes of transactions or disclosures) where fraud could occur and to develop an appropriate response. This identification process includes considering the type, significance, pervasiveness, and likelihood of the risk of fraud.

As a result of fraud risk-assessment, the audit plan will include tailored substantive tests of detail to address areas of fraud risk. Alternatively, the timing or scope of the audit may be adjusted to address any indications that an identified misstatement may be the result of suspicions of fraud.

Audit Procedures in Prior Year

Based on the information provided, there are a number of matters which we should have complied with in the prior-year audit of Progressive Construction such as:

- Discussion with management and the audit team at the planning stage regarding fraud risk in the entity. If fraud risk was considered high, were tests developed to address this, e.g. building unpredictability into audit testing?
- Consideration, in the planning section, whether the audit team had adequate skills and experience to carry out the audit.
- Circularisation of the company's legal advisors and follow up on replics received. Furthermore, review of correspondence with solicitors for any issues that may be relevant.
- Review of legal expenses to ensure that there were no other legal firms used during the year that we were not informed of.
- In relation to Castleford Shopping Centre project and work in progress balance:
  o Review of correspondence files;
  o Discussion of the contract with the commercial director or relevant individual in relation to the profit calculation;
  o Was there an external or certified valuation of the completion of the project undertaken by quantity surveyors? and
  o Were calculations checked and concluded on?
- Review of board minutes for discussion of any issues that may indicate the existence of the legal claim.
- Discussion with directors regarding any pending legal claims. Inclusion in the letter of representation of this confirmation by the directors.
- All issues raised during the audit should be adequately concluded on.
- Subsequent events review prior to signing the audit report to identify if any issues should be brought to our attention.

In the event that we carried out the above procedures satisfactorily we should be able to argue that we carried out all procedures which could be expected of us and that the omission of the provision resulted from collusive fraud between the quantity surveyor and the commercial director.

QUESTION 4.2

Guidance Notes – Castleford Credit Union (Anti-Money Laundering Regulations)

There was one issue, namely money laundering regulations – you are required to suggest any necessary improvements to their procedures.

The partner has asked you to read their anti-money laundering procedures and recommend any improvements to ensure they comply with the legislation. Therefore, a suitable format for the answer would be a memo to the partner. To answer this question, a good knowledge of *M40 (Revised) Anti-Money Laundering Guidance for the Accountancy Sector in the UK* (M40) or *M42 (Revised) Anti-Money Laundering Guidance – Republic of Ireland* (M42) is required.

Suggested Solution – Castleford Credit Union (Anti-Money Laundering Regulations)

MEMORANDUM

To: Kevin Maguire (audit engagement partner)
From: Anon (audit senior)
Subject: Improvements to Anti-Money Laundering Procedures

In reviewing the anti-money laundering procedures in place in Castleford Credit Union, the following are additional requirements for compliance with the legislation:

- Appointment of a money laundering reporting officer (MLRO) – a designated individual who is responsible for ensuring the credit union complies with the regulations, and to whom staff will report any suspicions of anti-money laundering activity. Furthermore, the MLRO is responsible for reporting any suspicious activity to the relevant regulatory bodies.
- Regular training of staff – the regulations require that all staff are aware of the legislation so that they have the ability to identify suspicious activity and perform the correct identification procedures on new customers.
- Monitoring of internal controls – the credit union must continually monitor its policies and procedures in relation to money laundering procedures to ensure that they are being complied with. This may take the form of review of new customer identification to ensure it is adequate, or a regular sample check on documentation received.
- The credit union must ensure all money laundering documentation is maintained for a period of five years (NI) or six years (ROI) from the date of the last transaction with the customer.

QUESTION 5.1

Guidance Notes – Comcomp Limited (Controls Testing and Identification of Weaknesses)

First, we determine what the question is asking, i.e. what the indicators are. Whilst reading the question, the indicators should become clear to you as:

1. Controls tests – you have been asked to document controls tests that you would carry out on the purchases and payable cycle; and
2. Management letter – you have been asked to identify and document the weaknesses in the purchases cycle, along with the related risk and recommendation for improvement.

In developing the controls tests, first identify a control and then design a procedure to test that control. For example, the purchase order approval levels are a control and therefore a procedure to test that control could be to extract a sample of purchase invoices and ensure that they have been approved by the appropriate level. Developing controls tests is not difficult, just remember that the procedure developed should be able to tell you whether the control is working or not. At this stage, you are not noting the weaknesses in the controls, you are merely testing them.

The question requires you to extract the weaknesses from the information provided on the purchases processes. For this, simply review the information and identify weaknesses that could result in material misstatement. Remember, as auditors, we are only concerned with weaknesses if there is a risk to the financial statements. As always, with management letter points, document the weakness, the implication or the risk, and your recommendation.

Suggested Solution – Comcomp Limited (Controls Testing and Identification of Weaknesses)

Controls Testing

The key specific controls tests that should be carried out in Comcomp are as follows:
1. Ensure that all purchase requisitions are properly authorised:
   - extract a sample of purchase requisitions,
   - check that the purchase has been approved by the appropriate level in line with the procedural manual,
   - ensure the purchase requisition/purchase order identifies the appropriate supplier from the preferred supplier list, and
   - ensure pre-determined re-order levels and preferred suppliers are reviewed periodically by the Purchasing Manager.
2. Test the purchasing process to ensure controls are operating effectively:
   - extract a sample of purchase requisitions in each month,

- trace to purchase orders, GRNs and invoices to ensure all relevant items correlate and no discrepancies arise, and
- if any discrepancies are identified, investigate how these matters were dealt with.
3. Test the reconciliation process:
   - compare a sample of the daily batch control sheets prepared by the purchases ledger clerk (detailing all invoices and the total amount payable) with the batch total produced daily from the purchases system,
   - in each instance, ensure that the relevant batch totals agree and/or are reconciled,
   - ensure that this reconciliation is signed-off as reconciled by both the input clerk and the purchasing supervisor, and
   - in any instance where the totals do not reconcile, investigate how this matter has been resolved.

Management Letter

The following are draft paragraphs for inclusion in the management letter:

Management Letter Point 1

Weakness Lack of segregation of duties – the role of the Purchasing Supervisor is overly dominant. This person is the first party who identifies when re-order levels are reached. At that point requisitions are printed by the Purchasing Supervisor and forwarded to the buying department. The Purchasing Supervisor does not require any further level of approval in respect of purchases up to €/£1,000. In such circumstances the Purchasing Supervisor can, almost always, ensure that requisitions are printed before the value of the new order exceeds €/£1,000 at which point further level of approval would be required.

The Purchasing Supervisor is also responsible for approval of the purchase invoice prior to it being posted to the purchases ledger.

Effect Arising from the involvement of the Purchasing Supervisor at the goods requisitions stage, the authorisation stage in respect of purchases up to €/£1,000, and the subsequent approval of such purchases, the risk of orders being placed with 'friendly' suppliers and/or orders being placed at inflated prices is significantly enhanced. This can result in the company paying significantly above the market price for necessary materials and/or purchasing items which the company does not require and which can be diverted to private/personal use.

Recommendation It is recommended that pre-determined re-order levels, purchases requisitions and purchases invoices should require a second level of approval by the Purchasing Manager.

It is further recommended that the Purchasing Manager should regularly review a sample of goods requisitions/purchases invoices approval initially carried out by the Purchasing Supervisor.

Management Letter Point 2

Weakness At stage 4 in the purchasing/payments system cheques are generated at the end of each month to clear the full balance outstanding on the purchases ledger. A reconciliation between supplier statements and the balance shown as outstanding to each such supplier on the purchases ledger is not undertaken on a monthly (or other regular) basis.

Effect This can result in payments being made to suppliers whose accounts on the purchases ledger system have not been reconciled with their statements. As a result invoices may be duplicated and paid in error; unrecorded invoices may not be identified (i.e. invoices received from suppliers which have been mislaid and/or are being held up within the system in Comcomp) or payment may have been made to suppliers which have not been accounted for by the supplier.

Recommendation It is recommended that the monthly cheque payment run should not be completed until all balances on individual purchases ledger accounts are reconciled with suppliers' statements. This reconciliation procedure should be carried out at the end of each month. Any outstanding items arising in respect of any reconciliation should be brought to the attention of the Purchasing Manager and approved by him before payment is made.

Management Letter Point 3

Weakness The goods inward clerk receives all goods into the goods inwards warehouse and ensures there are no discrepancies between the order and the goods received and signs the GRN. Furthermore, any discrepancies that do arise are physically marked on the GRN and the system is updated to record the actual quantities received. However, no goods GRN report is produced identifying where discrepancies have arisen; no system is in place to ensure any such discrepancies are subsequently satisfactorily resolved.

Effect Arising from the lack of the GRN report and/or formal controls, invoices may be approved for posting to the purchases ledger in circumstances where the related goods may have been 'short-delivered'. Furthermore, at the period end there is a risk that purchase invoices may be over accrued or that cut-off is not correctly accounted for, i.e. missing GRNs from a sequence may not be identified.

Recommendation We recommend that a monthly GRN report be prepared containing all GRNs in unbroken sequence with their related unique sequential invoice number. In each instance where any GRN shows any discrepancy in terms of quantity and/or quality with the related purchase invoice this should be highlighted. Arising from this report no invoice should be approved for payment until the Purchasing Manager has satisfied himself that all discrepancies have been properly identified and appropriate credit has been requested/obtained from the relevant supplier.

QUESTION 5.2

Guidance Notes – Coal Limited (Controls Testing and Identification of Weaknesses)

First, we determine what the question is asking, i.e. what the indicators are. Whilst reading the question, the indicators should become clear to you as:

1. Controls tests – you have been asked to document tests of control that the audit team intend to perform at year end to obtain sufficient audit assurance over the operation of the control activities identified.
2. Management letter – you have been asked to identify and document the weaknesses in the purchases cycle, along with the related risk and recommendation for improvement.

As noted in the solution to **Question 5.1**, in developing the controls tests, you first identify a control and then design a procedure to test that control. Creating controls tests is not difficult, just remember that the procedure developed should be able to tell you whether the control is working or not. At this stage, you are not noting the weaknesses in the controls, you are merely testing the actual controls in place.

As in the solution to **Question 5.1**, the question requires you to extract the weaknesses from the information provided on the cash and treasury cycle. For this, simply review the information and identify weaknesses that could result in material misstatement. Remember, as auditors we are only concerned with weaknesses if there is a risk to the financial statements. As always with management letter points, document the weakness, the implication or the risk, and your recommendation.

Suggested Solution – Coal Limited (Controls Testing and Identification of Weaknesses)

Controls Testing

The following controls tests should be performed:

1. Check daily reconciliation of deliveries:
   - extract a sample of deliveries during the year;
   - check that delivery books have been reconciled with cash receipts; and
   - identify how discrepancies are followed up and resolved.
2. Check purchases system:
   - extract a sample of purchases during the year;
   - trace each purchase in the sample to its related GRN;
   - trace each purchase through to the posting to the general ledger;

- check each invoice was approved by the relevant manager;
- trace each purchase to its corresponding payment; and
- if there were any discrepancies, identify them, and how they were resolved.

3. Select a sample of payment runs to ensure cheques are signed by two signatories as required.
4. Select a sample of monthly bank reconciliations to ensure they are prepared and reviewed.

Management Letter

The following are draft paragraphs for inclusion in the management letter:

Management Letter Point 1

Weakness No reconciliation is carried out between coal stocks given to the coal delivery men and sales/returns.

Effect As a result of the lack of such reconciliation unders/overs may occur which are not properly accounted for. This can result in fraud or error arising in relation to sales booked in the company's records or in relation to product delivered to the company's customers. In the former instance the company's books/records will be in error. In the latter instance the company's customers may be short-changed which will impact adversely on the company's goodwill and relationships with its customers.

Recommendation A daily reconciliation must be carried out of stock allocated to each coal delivery truck, sales booked by that delivery truck for the day and returns of coal to the coal depot at the end of the day.

Management Letter Point 2

Weakness Payment runs are made on a weekly basis. All payments are made by cheque. All cheques must be signed by at least two authorised signatories. However, no back-up is presented to the cheque signatories when the cheques are signed.

Effect In all circumstances when cheques are presented, two cheque signatories should sign the cheque. Each cheque must be accompanied by the original documentation (duly authorised) in respect of which payment is being sought. In the absence of such controls cheques could be issued in error, i.e. duplicated or fraudulently issued in respect of products which the company has not authorised for purchase and/or has not received.

Recommendation It is recommended that the financial controller should involve himself in the cheque-signing process. All requests for cheque payments to the cheque signatories should be matched to duly authorised Purchase Orders (POs) which are backed up by the appropriate invoice when presented.

Management Letter Point 3

Weakness The supervisor has an undue involvement/influence on the entire process. Arising from this there is an inadequate segregation of duties so far as the supervisor is concerned.

Effect In any circumstance where undue authority/control is vested in one individual this can result in human error which may not be picked up due to the lack of involvement of others or may, in certain circumstances, result in fraud. It is essential in all circumstances that the work of one individual is subject to review/supervision by another.

Recommendation It is recommended that the financial controller should examine the duties of the head office supervisor and seek to separate his/her duties so that at each stage in the process his/her work is subject to independent supervision and review. Such review process should involve the reporting of any exceptions arising directly to the financial controller.

QUESTION 6.1

Guidance Notes – Castleford Credit Union Solution (Loan Audit Programme and Collectability)

You are required to extract the issues in relation to substantive testing. There are two issues:
1. Loan audit work programme – it was agreed at the audit progress meeting that you, as audit senior, would pull together a work programme to address the collectability risks of the loans; and
2. An assessment of the impact upon the financial statements if we were unable to satisfy ourselves surrounding the collectability of the members' loans, and to consider the implications for the audit report.

The question requires you to develop an audit work programme for the collectability of loans, i.e. setting out the audit tests that you would carry out. When developing audit tests, always ensure they are detailed and comprehensive. For example, for a test do not just write 'Test cut-off' – instead, document exactly what is required from the test. A good reminder, when you are developing audit procedures, is to document the procedures so that you could hand the audit programme to an assistant and they could carry out the required procedure without any further assistance from you. This approach will ensure that you will document the procedure comprehensively.

Suggested Solution – Castleford Credit Union Solution (Loan Audit Programme and Collectability)

Loan Audit Work Programme

Prior to developing substantive tests, the audit team should review the control environment to ascertain the quality of the controls over members' loans. If the control environment is strong, they should consider testing the controls to reduce the substantive testing. The audit programme below sets out full substantive audit procedures on the collectability of the loans.

EXTRACT FROM AUDIT PROGRAMME

1. Test aging of loans:
   (a) Review the payment terms of aged loans;
   (b) Review date of last payment to the loan;
   (c) Consider recoverability of the loan; and
   (d) Consider if a provision is required.
2. Select a sample of loans from the credit union's records and perform the following:
   (a) Check to ensure that the loan was approved by the credit committee;
   (b) Ensure that the loan was made for a provident or productive purpose;
   (c) Check that the loan was made in accordance with the rules and lending guidelines of the credit union; and
   (d) Match the loan amount to the cheque payments book and bank statement.
3. Ensure that loan repayments are up to date:
   (a) Discuss late payments with management; and
   (b) Consider if these loans are recoverable.
4. Review the credit union's policies around provisions for loans in default and ensure that they have been applied appropriately.
5. Test the loan provision:
   (a) Discuss with management the basis of the provision;
   (b) Test a sample of the provision to ensure that it is calculated in line with your understanding and expectations;
   (c) Perform analytical review with the prior year and investigate any unexpected variances.
6. Review minutes of credit control committee, document their findings and identify any issues which may impact on the collectability of loans.
7. Review listing of rescheduled loans and loans in arrears (or loans referred to legal department for collection) and consider adequacy of provisioning in the context of the items on these schedules.

Inability to Gain Assurance over Collectability of Loans

The question requires us to note the impact on the audit report if we cannot satisfy ourselves over the collectability of the loans. It is really important in this scenario to read the question and understand what is being asked – the question does **not** state that we could not obtain sufficient audit evidence (which would result in a limitation of scope); it does state that we obtained sufficient audit evidence, but could not gain assurance over the collectability of the loans.

This makes sense if you put yourself into the circumstances of the example and imagine yourself reviewing loans in practice: we could never get 100% assurance that all loans are going to be paid within the required agreement. The reason for this might be the economic environment or the individuals' personal circumstances, neither of which can be predicted with reasonable certainty.

Therefore, we are into the space of fundamental uncertainty, i.e. there are uncertainties surrounding the repayment of the loans. In the case where there are uncertainties, we must ensure that management include a note in the financial statements regarding the uncertainties. Our audit report will then include an Emphasis of Matter paragraph drawing the users' attention to the note in the financial statements explaining the uncertainties, but not qualifying the audit report in this regard. It should be noted that, where uncertainties exist, it is not the auditor's responsibility to explain the uncertainties in the audit report, they are merely highlighting them, i.e. referring the user to the note.

If management refuse to include an explanatory note regarding the uncertainties, the financial statements will not have been prepared in line with accounting standards and therefore we would include a modified opinion on the basis of disagreement. As it is a disclosure issue, apply an 'except for' opinion.

QUESTION 6.2

Guidance Notes – RX Pharmaceuticals Limited Solution (Develop Audit Tests)

In the question there is a requirement to develop the appropriate tests of control and tests of details to be performed. There is also a requirement to state the basis of selection of the items to be tested and to address the identified risks.

This question requires you to develop audit tests to address the risks you have identified (the risks were identified in the solution to **Question 3.2**). The tests should be explained in detail so as to show a strong understanding of what you are trying to achieve. As noted before, a good pointer to ensuring you have documented the audit tests adequately is to develop the audit tests as you would if you were giving them to an audit assistant who would then be able to carry out the test without any further assistance. This will ensure that you have included the necessary detail on the procedure for the examiner.

Furthermore, the requirement includes 'basis of selection' therefore, for each test, ensure you indicate what you are going to test, i.e. the entire population or a selected sample.

Suggested Solution – RX Pharmaceuticals Limited (Develop Audit Tests)

The risks relating to revenue, as noted in the suggested solution to **Question 3.2**, can be addressed as follows:

Risk	Audit Tests
Cut-off of data capture and analysis services revenue	• Review all contracts in place during the year • Discuss with contracts manager the milestones achieved compared with the revenue recognised • Review the invoices issued for revenue recognised once a milestone has been achieved • Ensure each long-term contract has been accounted for correctly, and revenue is recorded in the correct period
Cut-off of distribution revenue	• Select a sample of haulier invoices during the year and for 3 months directly after the year • Review timing of service provided on haulier invoice and trace to related sales invoice • Ensure revenue and cost are recorded in the correct period
Completeness and existence of comparator products revenue and costs	• Select a sample of customer orders of comparator products before and after the year-end • Trace each order to a delivery note to a customer, GRN, and related sales invoice • Ensure the cost and revenue are recorded in the same period
Valuation of revenue from manufacturing contracts	• Select a sample of contract revenue invoices raised during the period • Trace the quantity on each invoice to the despatch docket, and trace the contracted price to a customer contract
Completeness of packaging revenue	• Select a sample of reconciliations, prepared during the year, of packaging activity and invoices raised • Ensure that any reconciling items have been appropriately investigated and resolved • If this control test fails, consider additional substantive testing to ensure that packaging revenue is recorded in the correct period

QUESTION 7.1

Guidance Notes – Executive Motors (Review of Workpaper)

You are required to extract the issues in relation to completion procedures. There was one requirement in relation to review of the workpaper – you, as audit senior, are asked to review the execution and documentation of the work performed by the audit junior.

In reviewing a workpaper remember to comment on the quality of the workpaper layout, e.g. are the test, procedure, results and conclusion clear on the workpaper; is it correctly dated and signed off? You should also review the quality of the audit work and, where relevant, note any further procedures required to gain assurance over the assertion the workpaper addresses, e.g has the mathematical accuracy of the source documentation been verified? Additionally, do not be afraid to comment on what was done well.

Suggested Solution – Executive Motors (Review of Workpaper)

The review points relevant to the Executive Motors workpaper are as follows:
1. The existence and quantities of stock were agreed and compared to Chevhall's records – this will allow us to appropriately report on the agreed-upon-procedures engagement;
2. The workpaper notes that one of the alternator fans was damaged – this needs to be included in the report. However, the workpaper should have noted this as an exception because it is outside our scope. (Alternatively, you could have chosen to scope out the damaged item as the condition of the items was not specifically requested in the agreed-upon procedures – equal credit would be given for either approach providing an appropriate explanation is given.)
3. The workpaper should be laid out with the following elements clearly presented: test, procedure, results, and conclusion. The workpaper does not detail the procedures performed.
4. The report does not state that we checked the mathematical accuracy of the client's stock report; it is important to ensure that we are testing complete and accurate information which feeds into our report.
5. The workpaper should note where we obtained the "minimum quantity per Chevhall" data. All workpapers should include references to where all the information came from and what work we did to verify it.
6. The workpaper should include the date that the work was performed – this is currently not clear.

Each of the items 1–6 above should be addressed and the workpaper updated prior to finalising the report.

QUESTION 7.2

Guidance Notes – RX Pharmaceuticals Limited (Management Letter Points)

You are required to extract the issues in relation to completion procedures. There was one requirement to prepare a management letter – you are required to draft management letter points arising from the documentation on the revenue streams, processes and controls during the interim audit.

The question requires you to extract the weaknesses from the information provided on the revenue streams and processes. For this, simply review the information and identify weaknesses that could result in material misstatements. Remember, auditors are only concerned with weaknesses if there is a risk to the financial statements. As always, with management letter points, document the weakness, the implication or the risk, and your recommendation.

Suggested Solution – RX Pharmaceuticals Limited (Management Letter Points)

Management Letter Point 1: Accounting for haulage services

Weakness Customers are billed for haulage services only when the corresponding invoice is received from the haulier.

Effect Revenue may be recognised in the wrong period: if a haulier invoice relating to one financial year is not received until the next financial year, both the revenue and the costs will be recognised in the wrong period. The profit for the year will be understated by the 5% mark-up. Alternatively, revenue may also be omitted entirely: if, for some reason, the haulier does not forward an invoice, then the revenue for the transaction will never be recognised in the company's accounts.

Recommendation We recommend that the company maintains its own records of haulage costs, recognising the revenue and accruing the costs when the haulage service is performed.

Management Letter Point 2(a): Procedures around data capture and analysis revenue

Weakness There does not appear to be an effective control to ensure that revenue from data capture and analysis projects is recognised on a timely basis. If the contracts manager is absent or omits to inform finance of a milestone then no invoice will be issued.

Effect Revenue may be recorded in the incorrect period or may not be recognised at all.

Recommendation We recommend that when contracts are signed a schedule of key milestones is supplied to the finance department and that this is reviewed and discussed with the contracts manager on a monthly basis to ensure that invoices are issued on a timely basis as each milestone is reached.

Management Letter Point 2(b): Procedures around data capture and analysis revenue

Weakness No verification of contract milestones takes place by anyone independent of the contracts manager.

Effect Revenue may be recorded in the incorrect period/too early.

Recommendation We recommend that when contracts are signed a schedule of key milestones is supplied to the finance department and that this is reviewed and discussed with the contracts manager on a monthly basis to ensure that invoices are issued only when appropriate milestones are reached.

Management Letter Point 3: Matching of comparator costs and revenues

Weakness There is no reconciliation between comparator products accrued for and those invoiced out to customers.

Effect A significant cut-off error may occur if costs are accrued but the GRN fails to reach the sales department and therefore no customer invoice is raised.

Recommendation Reconciliations should be performed on a regular basis to ensure that comparator costs and revenues are matched appropriately and both recorded in the same period.

QUESTION 7.3

Guidance Notes – Castleford Credit Union (Management Letter Points)

You are required to extract the issues in relation to completion procedures. There was one requirement to prepare a management letter for the audit partner.

The partner has asked you to note the management letter points which illustrate weaknesses you have identified in the information given to you in the question. When doing so, always remember to identify the weakness, the related risk and your recommendation.

When linking the weakness to the risk, the risk should always relate back to a potential misstatement in the financial statements. For example, one of the weaknesses is that bank reconciliations were not performed for two months; the risk associated with this weakness is that the bank balance in the financial statements may be incorrect, or undiscovered fraudulent activities as a result of lack of reconciliations may lead to misappropriation of assets. Therefore, the weakness impacts upon the financial statements.

Remember, an auditor's primary concern is whether or not the financial statements are materially misstated. The weaknesses should be issues that could result in misstatement of the financial statements. By applying this logic, you are more likely to identify strong, relevant management letter points.

Suggested Solution – Castleford Credit Union (Management Letter Points)

Based on the information provided, the management letter points can be extracted as follows:

Management Letter Point 1

Weakness Due to staff illness, bank reconciliations were not completed for the months of May and June 2009.

Effect Omitted, inaccurate or fraudulent accounting entries may not be identified and addressed timeously if bank reconciliations are not completed and reviewed on a timely basis.

Recommendation Bank reconciliations should be completed and reviewed monthly and contingency plans established to cover events such as staff illness.

Management Letter Point 2

Weakness A formula error was noted in the member dividend spreadsheet.

Effect Financial statement balances might be misstated if spreadsheet formulae are incorrect and there are inadequate review procedures in place to identify and correct such errors.

Recommendation Spreadsheets inherently attract a higher risk of error than integrated accounting systems. If calculations/transactions cannot be conducted within the system, adequate controls should be put in place to ensure the integrity of the spreadsheet input data and formulae and the results should be reviewed prior to posting to the financial statements.

Management Letter Point 3

Weakness Working papers supporting work performed by supervisors had not been retained.

Effect The board may find it difficult to monitor whether or not the supervisors are performing their duties adequately if working papers are not retained to support the conclusions they reach and to detail follow-up action resulting from any issues identified.

Recommendation We recommend that the supervisors document the work they perform, the results of their testing and the conclusions reached and that this documentation is retained for review by the board and auditors as required.

QUESTION 8.1

The solutions provided here are outlines only and represent a structured thought process to assist you in dealing with audit report issues as follows:
- What is the issue?
- What accounting standard or company law regulation is it in disagreement with, if applicable?
- Is it material? (If not, the issue has no impact on the audit report.)
- Will the directors make the adjustment? (If so, there is no impact on the audit report.)
- Is it 'disagreement' or 'except for'?
- Is it material or pervasive?

By documenting this thought process for audit report issues, you should easily find a solution and, even if your concluded qualification is incorrect, you should pick up some level of competency from noting your thought process as you will be highlighting why the issue results in qualification.

Suggested Solution – Crystal (Audit Report)

Finance Leases:
- Treated incorrectly – included in financial statements as operating leases when they should be treated as finance leases under IAS 17 *Leases*
- Immaterial income statement impact as operating lease rentals would broadly equate to depreciation charge plus finance lease interest
- Balance sheet impact is significant as omission of an asset and the related liability of €/£1.76 million
- Ask directors to adjust
- If they do not agree to adjust, the audit report should be qualified on the basis of disagreement with accounting standards

- As impact can be directed to two balances on the balance sheet, it would not be considered pervasive
- Qualification = Disagreement; 'except for'.

Going Concern:

- Significant concern in relation to the company's ability to continue as a going concern
  - Losses during the year of €/£1.56 million
  - Declining revenues
  - New rebate policy resulting in additional rebate costs
  - Significant development expenditure in relation to new Media Centre and PC
  - Substantial marketing spend on television and advertising for new product
  - Increase in rent on the company's prime high street rental outlet
  - Doubt surrounding renewal of bank facilities
- On the basis that the auditor has received projections and has obtained sufficient appropriate evidence that the company can continue as a going concern, the auditor will require the directors to refer to the uncertainties in the notes to the financial statements
- As required by ISA 570, where there is a material uncertainty, the directors should disclose:
  - That the financial statements are prepared on a going concern basis
  - A statement of the pertinent facts
  - Nature of the uncertainty
  - Assumptions adopted by the directors
  - Directors' plans for resolving the matter
  - Any relevant actions by the directors
- If disclosures are adequate
  - Auditor should include emphasis of matter paragraph referring to the uncertainty
- If disclosures are not adequate:
  - Request directors to make adequate disclosures
  - If they agree, the issue would be resolved and have no impact on the audit report
  - If they disagree, the audit report should be qualified on the basis of disagreement
  - As the disagreement is in relation to a disclosure and therefore does not impact upon numerous balances on the financial statements, the qualification would therefore be 'except for'
  - Qualification = disagreement; 'except for'

QUESTION 8.2

Suggested Solution – Build (Audit Report)

Recoverability of €3.5 million:

- Uncertainty surrounding the recoverability of additional costs which depends on the outcomes of assessments by experts employed by both the client and the customer.
- All available information has been received therefore there is no limitation of scope.
- Uncertainty surrounding the recoverability of the debt in that anything up to €3.5 million may have to be fully or partially provided for. €3.5 million represents 16% of net assets and is, therefore, material.
- In line with accounting standards and ISA 540 (UK and Ireland) *Auditing Accounting Estimates, Including Fair Value Accounting Estimates, and Related Disclosures* the directors should include disclosures relating to the uncertainties.
- If the disclosures are adequate, the auditor would include an emphasis of matter paragraph due to the materiality of the uncertainty and would refer, in the audit report, to the directors' disclosures.
- If disclosures are not adequate:
  - Request directors to make adequate disclosures.
    - If they agree there is no longer an issue and there is no impact on the audit report
    - If they disagree, the audit report should be qualified on the basis of disagreement
  - As the disagreement is in relation to a disclosure and therefore does not impact upon numerous balances on the financial statements, the qualification would be 'except for' (qualification = disagreement; 'except for').

Sale of Investment:

- Build is selling its investment in ABBA which is currently included in the financial statements at €/£3.575 million made up of shares of €/£1.575 million and loans of €/£2 million.
- Proceeds are dependent on profit for the last two years up to a ceiling of €/£2 million.
- Build has a balance due from ABBA of €/£2 million which will be paid from the proceeds of the contractual claim.
- Your audit work has concluded that ABBA will not receive the full €/£2 million claim and therefore will not be in a position to repay its debt to Build – you conclude that a provision of €/£1 million is required.
- Directors have indicated that they are not going to make any adjustments to the financial statements.
- The treatment is not in line with IAS 37 *Provisions, Contingent Liabilities and Contingent Assets.* Under this standard a provision should be posted as it meets the requirements:
  - Present obligation – contractual agreement to sell the company;

- o Resulting from past event – agreeing to sell the company in 2006; and
- o Transfer of economic benefits is probable – audit evidence has been received for €/£1 million.
- The misstatement is material as it is 5% of net assets.
  - o The auditor would qualify the audit report on the basis of disagreement with accounting standards. As the error does not impact upon numerous balances, and is 5% of net assets, it would not be regarded as pervasive, therefore the basis of the qualification would be 'except for' (qualification = disagreement; 'except for').

QUESTION 8.3

Suggested Solution – Tex (Audit Report)

Stock Issue:

A stock difference has arisen and no explanation can be obtained for this difference. The auditor cannot perform any further procedures to obtain information on the difference therefore, there is a limitation on audit evidence.

The difference is material as it represents 33% of profits (before the adjustment was made by the client). The audit report is qualified on the basis of limitation on scope. As the misstatement affects limited balances, the qualification would be 'except for' (qualification = limitation of scope; 'except for').

Tax Issue:

In line with IAS 37 *Provisions, Contingent Liabilities and Contingent Assets* consideration needs to be given as to whether the outcome should be provided for. It would appear that it should not be included as a provision as it does not meet all the criteria listed below:

- Present obligation arising from past event – yes, based on past intercompany transactions;
- Probable outcome of resources – uncertain based on outcome of the resolution of the matter with the revenue authorities; and
- Reliable estimate – yes, based on audit evidence the amount would be €/£360,000.

Therefore, the issue should be disclosed as a contingent liability.

If the directors disclose the contingent liability adequately, the auditor would include an emphasis of matter paragraph based on the materiality of the uncertainty – the contingent liability represents over 100% of current profit.

If the disclosures are not adequate, the directors must be requested to make adequate disclosures. If they agree, the issue would be resolved and there would be no impact on the audit report. If they disagree, the audit report should be qualified on the basis of disagreement. As the disagreement is in relation to a disclosure and therefore does not impact upon numerous balances on the financial statements, the qualification would be 'except for' (qualification = disagreement; 'except for').

Closure of Galway Store:

In line with IAS 37, consideration needs to be given as to whether the outcome should be provided for. It would appear it should be included as a provision as it meets the criteria listed below:

- Present obligation arising from past event – yes, an announcement has been made;
- Probable outcome of resources – yes, redundancy payments will be made; and
- Reliable estimate – yes, total costs can be quantified.

There is no further issue and therefore no impact upon the audit report.

QUESTION 9.1

Guidance Notes – Pybex Limited (ISA 600 Considerations)

The requirement is to extract the issues in relation to group audits. There was one requirement to consider the issues dealing with auditors in other jurisdictions. This is addressed below.

ISA 600 Considerations

Potentially we are going to be appointed group auditors of Pybex Limited. It is clear from the information given that there are group companies located in different jurisdictions for which the client does not intend to change the local auditors. Therefore, as group auditors we have considerations under ISA 600 in relation to the audits of the subsidiaries that we do not audit ourselves. The solution to this question can be extracted directly from **Chapter 9** of this textbook or ISA 600. However, the key to a high score in this question is the application of that technical knowledge to the question. Do not document a generic ISA 600 response, ensure that you have applied the ISA 600 requirements to the specific question.

Suggested Solution – Pybex Limited (ISA 600 Considerations)

ISA 600 dictates our responsibilities with regard to group audits. As the group has subsidiaries in Italy, France and Bulgaria where it appears the local auditors are going to remain, we need to consider what work is required in order for us to sign off on a group audit opinion.

The first consideration is whether or not the components are regarded as significant components as that will dictate our involvement. As the subsidiaries comprise 20–25% of net assets and one third of the group profits, it is assumed that the subsidiaries are regarded as significant. As a result, there are significant responsibilities in relation to the audit of the components. These can be summarised as follows:

Pre-audit Activities

Understand the component auditor and determine if they comply with ethical standards, are competent to carry out the work, and if they operate in a strong regulatory environment.

Risk Assessment

- Set the group audit strategy and audit plan for the overall group;
- Understand the group, its components and their environments, including the consolidation process and the fraud risk in all the components;
- Set materiality levels for the group and components as follows:
    - Materiality for the group as a whole,
    - Performance materiality for the group as a whole,
    - Component materiality which should be set at a level lower than group materiality to reduce the risk of aggregate uncorrected misstatements in the group financial statements,
    - Performance materiality for components, and
    - Clearly trivial amount for group financial statements;
- Consider if the components are likely to include significant risk of material misstatement of the group financial statements, e.g. the recently established Bulgarian subsidiary may have a higher risk of misstatement as the local accounting/auditing standards may not be in line with UK/Irish GAAP.

As a result of the above considerations, the group auditor needs to communicate with the component auditor at the planning stage to discuss risk assessment, to ensure that the component auditor will carry out an adequate level of audit work that will address group risks and agreed reporting requirements. This is largely done in writing by using group instructions.

Responses to Assessed Risks

The group auditor must assess the level of involvement in the fieldwork. This will depend on the competence of the component auditors as well as the size and significance of the component. The group auditor may decide to carry out a review of the component auditors' workpapers, or additional procedures which may not have been addressed by the component auditors.

Concluding Procedures

As the group auditor is forming an opinion on the group financial statements, they should maintain close involvement with the component auditor throughout the audit. As well as reviewing the component auditor's work to ensure that the component is free from material misstatement, the group auditor will require the component auditor to communicate concluding procedures such as material misstatements, significant matters, and overall findings.

QUESTION 10.1

Guidance Notes – Daniels Stores (Third Party Reporting)

The requirement is to prepare a third party report – the audit partner asks you to conclude if we can provide the independent accountant's report and to draft the example report, with details of the work required to address the requirements of the potential investors.

Two steps are required in this indicator:
1. Determine if the audit firm can carry out the work, and
2. Draft an example report with details of the work required.

The majority of the answer can be extracted from M39 *Reporting to Third Parties*. Therefore, the key to achieving a high competency in this question is to ensure the technical knowledge is applied to the client detailed in the question. Furthermore, the question specifically requests "details of the work required", therefore ensure it is understood what the investors are looking for in the report, and the required procedures to achieve this understanding are properly set out.

Suggested Solution – Daniels Stores (Third Party Reporting)

Before the agreed-upon-procedures engagement is accepted, ensure there is compliance with ethical principles. As Daniels Stores are not asking us to give an opinion, we are able to provide the report detailing factual findings, thus minimising the risk and therefore we are able to accept the assignment.

Secondly, we need to consider who is going to be relying on the report. At this stage, we know that the report is going to be issued to potential investors. Therefore, before we accept this engagement, we would need confirmation that we can obtain acknowledgement from the potential investors that we owe no duty of care to them. This is an extremely important issue as we do not want to be the scapegoat if the investor uses our report to make the investment decision and then the investment is not successful.

Finally, before acceptance of the engagement, we need to ensure that we have access to the information required to prepare the report – at this stage, this does not appear to be a problem as it is a factual report.

The report could be drafted as follows:

REPORT OF FACTUAL FINDINGS

To: (name potential investors who engaged us)

We have **performed the procedures agreed with you** and enumerated below with respect to the customer transactions of Daniels Stores Limited ('the company') for the year ended 31 December 2009. Our **engagement was undertaken in accordance with Miscellaneous Technical Statement *M39 Reporting to Third Parties*** issued by the Institute of Chartered Accountants in Ireland. The procedures were performed solely to assist you in evaluating the average revenue per customer transaction and are summarised as follows:

1. We checked the mathematical accuracy of the company's average revenue per customer transaction calculation ('the calculation') as attached at Schedule A.
2. We compared the total revenue figure used in the company's calculation to the company's trial balance to ensure that it had been accurately extracted.
3. We compared the total number of customer transactions used in the company's calculation to the company's electronic point-of-sale ('EPOS') system records.

We report our findings below:
(a) With respect to item 1 we found the calculation to be mathematically accurate.
(b) With respect to item 2 we found the amounts to be in agreement.
(c) With respect to item 3 we found the amounts to be in agreement.

Because the above procedures do not **constitute either an audit or a review made in accordance with International Standards on Auditing or International Standards on Review Engagements, we do not express any assurance** on the average revenue per customer transaction shown on Schedule A.

Had we performed additional procedures or had we performed an audit or review of the financial statements in accordance with International Standards on Auditing or International Standards on Review Engagements, other matters might have come to our attention that would have been reported to you.

Our **report is solely for the purpose set forth in the first paragraph of this report and for your information and is not to be used for any other purpose or to be distributed to any other parties.**

This report relates only to the items specified above and does not extend to any financial statements of Daniels Stores Limited, taken as a whole.

O'Sullivan & Co.

Chartered Accountants

February 2010

QUESTION 10.2

Guidance Notes – Executive Motors (Third Party Report)

You have been asked to prepare the report that is required by the franchise agreement.

The majority of this answer can be extracted from *M39 Reporting to Third Parties*. Therefore, the key to achieving a high competency in this question is to ensure the technical knowledge is applied to the client as detailed in the question. Furthermore, the question specifically gives information on the detail of the report required, therefore it must be ensured that, what the client is looking for in the report has been understood, and that the required procedures to achieve this are set out.

In the information provided it is noted that the independent accountant's report should detail whether the stock levels held by Executive Motors agree with the records maintained by Chevall **and** whether they comply with the minimum stockholding requirements. The report should be extracted from M39, and include the procedures required to be able to state whether or not the stock records agree and the minimum stockholding has been satisfied.

The key point to remember when developing agreed upon procedures reports like this is that the facts are being reported, no opinion is being expressed.

Suggested Solution – Executive Motors (Third Party Report)

The report can be drafted as follows:

REPORT OF FACTUAL FINDINGS

To: Chevhall Motor Company Limited

We have performed the procedures agreed with you and detailed below with respect to the consignment inventory, set forth in the accompanying schedules, held by Executive Motors Limited. Our engagement was undertaken in accordance with Miscellaneous Technical Statement *M39 Reporting to Third Parties* **or** the International Standard on Related Services applicable to agreed-upon-procedures engagements. The procedures were performed solely to assist you in evaluating the completeness and accuracy of the consignment inventory and are summarised as follows:

1. We obtained and checked the mathematical accuracy of the consignment inventory listing as at 31 December 2010 prepared by Executive Motors Limited, attached as Appendix A.
2. We confirmed the existence of each of the items listed on the consignment inventory listing and agreed the item code and description.
3. **We compared the quantity of each item on the consignment inventory listing at 1. above with the stock quantity on the Chevhall consignment inventory records supplied by you**, attached as Appendix B.

---

4. **We compared the quantity of each item on the consignment inventory listing at 1. above with the minimum holding quantity on the service level agreement supplied by you**, attached as Appendix C.

We report our findings below:

(a) With respect to item 1 we found the mathematical accuracy to be correct.

(b) With respect to item 2 we found all quantities counted agreed to quantities recorded and that the item codes and descriptions set out in Appendix A corresponded with our observations.

(c) **With respect to item 3 we found the amounts compared to be in agreement. (However one unit of item CM01-472 was found to be damaged –** *must be included where not scoped out with appropriate explanation in Indicator above)*

(d) **With respect to item 4 we found that the quantity of each item on the consignment inventory listing supplied by Executive Motors Limited was equal to, or greater than, the minimum holding quantity, with the exception of item code CM20-074 (fuel injection nozzles) which was found to be one unit short of the minimum holding quantity.**

Because the above procedures do not constitute either an audit or a review made in accordance with International Standards on Auditing or International Standards on Review Engagements, we do not express any assurance on the consignment inventory as of 31 December 2010.

Had we performed additional procedures or had we performed an audit or review of the financial statements in accordance with International Standards on Auditing or International Standards on Review Engagements, other matters might have come to our attention that would have been reported to you.

Our report is solely for the purpose set forth in the first paragraph of this report and for your information and is not to be used for any other purpose or to be distributed to any other parties. This report relates only to the items specified above and does not extend to any financial statements of Executive Motors Limited, taken as a whole.

Bentley Ferguson

Chartered Accountants

Date

Address

Index